THE WRITING ON THE WATER

Muhyiddin Shakoor received his Ph.D. in Counselling Psychology from Kent State University in 1973. Born in Cleveland, Ohio, he has held various academic posts and is currently Associate Professor of Counsellor Education at the State University of New York. A teacher–practitioner in individual and family therapy, he has written and lectured on mental health concerns in the United States and abroad. Active as a seeker, not only for the outer meaning of life but for the inner reality as well, he entered *Tariqa*, the Path of the Prophet, more than eleven years ago. He has travelled extensively in the East and made three visits to the Holy cities of Mecca and Medina, twice for the lesser pilgrimage, *Umrah*, and once for the greater journey, *Hajj*. Initiated into the Islamic Sufi Tariqa: *Al Hayyati, Ar-Rufai al Hussaini*, he presently lives near his Shaikh, devoting his energies to the cause of spiritual Islam.

The Writing on The Water

Chronicles of A Seeker on The Islamic Sufi Path

Muhyiddin Shakoor

ELEMENT BOOKS

First published in 1987 by
Element Books Limited, Longmead, Shaftesbury, Dorset

This book is published with the permission and approval of the
Shaikh of the Order

Printed and bound in Great Britain by
Billings, Hylton Road, Worcester

Designed by Max Fairbrother

Cover illustration: A Portrait by Abdul Raqib A. Salih

British Library Cataloguing in Publication Data
Shakoor, Muhyiddin
The writing on the water.
1. Sufism – Personal observations
I. Title
297'.4'0924

ISBN 1-85230-026-4

CONTENTS

ACKNOWLEDGEMENTS

Grateful acknowledgement and thanks are extended to the following authors, publishers and copyright holders for permission to use quotes, extracts and ideas from their works:

Bond Wheelwright Company: *Muhammad's People* © 1955 by Eric Schroeder.

Prophecy Pressworks: *The Whirling Ecstasy* © 1972 by Aflaki.

Shaikh Muhammad Ashraf publishers of Lahore, Pakistan, *The Alchemy of Happiness* by Al-Ghazzali translated by Claude Field © 1954.

Shambhala Publications: *The Conference of the Birds* by Farid ud-Din Attar. © 1954 by C. S. Nott. Reprinted by arrangement with Shambhala Publications, Inc., 300 Massachussets Ave., Boston, MA 02115.

Barrie and Rockliff: *The Sufi Message* © 1960 by Inayat Khan.

Samuel Weiser, Inc.: *Discourses of Rumi* © 1972 translated by R. A. Nicholson. *Rumi: Poet and Mystic* © 1974 translated by R. A. Nicholson. *The Book of Certainty* © 1974 by Abu Bakr Siraj Ed-Din. *The above mentioned editions by Samuel Weiser are out of print in the U.S.

Quotations on 'Separation and Suffering' from *Diwani-Shamsi Tabrizi* reprinted from *The Sufi Path of Love: The Spiritual Teachings of Rumi,* translated by William C. Chittick, SUNY series on Islamic Spirituality by permission of the State University of New York Press © 1983,

F. A. Davis Co.: *Sword and Masque* © 1967 by Julius Palffy-Alpar.

CTI Records: *'Window of a Child'* © 1977 lyrics by Seawind.

The Burger King Corporation: 'Sir Shake-a-Lot' Jingle.

Doubleday Inc.: *The Rubaiyat of Omar Khayyam* © 1952 translated by Edward Fitgerald.

Threshold Books: R. D. 3, Box 1350 Putney, Vermont 05346 U.S.A. for the poem 'The Question' in *Open Secret* © 1984 translated from the works of Rumi by John Moyne and Coleman Barks.

The University of Chicago Press: *Mystical Poems of Rumi* © 1968 translated by A. J. Arberry.

Special appreciation must be expressed to Mrs. Dorothy Reed who gave so much typing assistance and optimistic support during the manuscript's beginning, to Mrs. Debora Lang and Mrs. Loretta Lonnen who helped so patiently with word processing in the middle through to the end, to my wife Aliya, who spent many hours editing the manuscript through all its steps and stages. To my Shaikh whose vision sustained me when I had only a pad of scribbled notes and whose loving presence generated the contents of the book. To Jeremy Kay of Bartleby Press, an editor whose encouragement helped me to endure in the pursuit of getting published, perhaps more than he knows. To my mother for her love and belief in me. To Zahra Publications who introduced my work to Element Books. Finally, to my compassionate publisher and the staff of Element Books whose professional abilities and belief in the manuscript, by the grace of God, brought the book into the light of day.

It is a tale of a stranger and it requires a stranger to listen and to be able to hear the tale of a stranger.

MAWLANA RUMI

Know, O beloved, that man was not created in jest or at random, but marvellously made and for some great end, although he is not from everlasting, yet he lives for ever; and though his body is mean and earthly, yet his spirit is lofty and divine. When in the crucible of abstinence he is purged from carnal passions he attains to the highest, and in place of being a slave to lust and anger becomes endued with angelic qualities. Attaining that state, he finds his heaven in the contemplation of Eternal Beauty, and no longer in fleshly delights. The spiritual alchemy which operates this change in him, like that which transmutes base metals into gold, is not easily discovered, nor to be found in the house of every old woman.

. . . Now the treasures of God, in which this alchemy is to be sought, are the hearts of the prophets, and he who seeks it elsewhere will be disappointed and bankrupt on the day of judgement when he hears the word, 'We have lifted the veil from off thee, and thy sight today is keen.'

God has sent on earth a hundred and twenty-four thousand prophets to teach men the prescription of this alchemy, and how to purify their hearts from baser qualities in the crucible of abstinence. This alchemy may be briefly described as turning away from the world to God, and its constituents are four: (1) The knowledge of self, (2) The knowledge of God, (3) The knowledge of this world as it really is, and (4) The knowledge of the next world as it really is.

Al Ghazali

Writing which men carve in stone
to last for centuries,
is for Allah like
writing on the water.

A verse from my Shaikh

PROLOGUE

THE QUEST

Praise be to God, the First-Last Reality and Lord of the Worlds; the Friend of Seekers and Opener of Hearts. Praise be to Him Who befriended me and saved me from this *Dunya*: the space-age world of hypnotic-phenomenal distraction and technological bedazzlement. Praise be to Him Who brings the seeker to surrender: another name for self-confrontation . . . the name of the game which really is not a game. Surrender: a Seeker's first step in search of self: a giant-step, baby-step — neither yet both, and learning to walk is sometimes scary.

It was years ago, that yesterday when I moved towards my challenge. Inside a humble urban building converted to a mosque, it happened. I had come only to observe, at the invitation of friends. There were many empty seats: the teacher stood before a class of two. I quietly took a seat next to one of those already present, an old woman whom I later learned was Sister Majeed. I looked at the teacher, a bearded old man — a story unto himself, whom they called the *Imam* (religious leader). I surveyed the room: cracked ceilings, old fixtures, linoleum floors, home-made blackboards, and the wall behind the teacher — on which there was some writing. The writing was extraordinarily beautiful and very intricately painted. It fully dominated the wall and my attention as well. It resonated peace and was strangely familiar, yet I could not begin to decipher it. It held my interest for the entire length of the talk. Overcome by curiosity, I whispered a question to the old woman at my side:

'Ma'am, what is that?'

Turning a wisdom-worn face towards mine so full of youth, she looked at me with knowing eyes and said:

'It is the *outermost* out and the *innermost* in. Keep your eyes on that.'

In that moment, as her words fell on my ears, time seemed to stop. Deep within my being, something heard. Though I did not understand completely, I knew that what she spoke was truth. My knees grew weak and my heart beat fast. I wanted to trust both her and the moment, yet in my confusion, I did neither. As my mind acknowledged a situation obviously out of hand, my lips raced on with senseless questions:

'But what is it really . . . . What does it mean? How can I . . . ?

She stretched forth a hand more wrinkled than her face, yet equally as wise. Grasping my arm, she halted my stammer in mid-sentence. Smiling, she leaned close and spoke again:

'It is you. It is your very own self . . . . that is the what . . . . and as for the how, let's just say that you have to let go in order to go. *Assalaamu alaikum.*'

She translated before I could ask:

'Peace be on you, young man. It means the peace of God, Who is Peace Himself, be upon you.'

Gesturing for my assistance, she raised herself to her feet and nodded towards the wall:

'You'll see . . . . God willing you'll see. You'll find it all in that. It's called the *Kalima.*'

In those moments with Sister Majeed, there came a great initiation. My being itself witnessed the love-woven beauty of every woman I'd ever known as a teacher. I felt, I remembered, I realised the mercy of some unknown cherishing force reflected in my mother; grandmother; first-grade teacher; the lady across the street who gave me cookies for running errands; and the girl next door who struck me dumb with my first conscious feelings of love. All of them were there, clear in that moment, collected in the old woman's face. A great fragmentation began to unify and days from closed, senseless years of my past opened up to yield new meanings. Partly stunned, and deeply touched by the old woman's loving presence, I accepted her prescription without knowledge of its depth or its scope. I had come to find the strange inscription stretched across the wall, only to leave with its mystery slowly stretching across my mind: *La ilaha ill'Allah.* Such was the introduction of my search to me. The search for the meaning of this timeless phrase was in fact the beginning of my search for myself.

The weeks which followed my meeting with Sister Majeed often found me alone, deep in quiet interaction with myself. Still unable to make sense of the encounter, I had launched several fruitless attempts to deny it. Yet so strongly had my consciousness been gripped by the episode, I accepted at last that I had to know more. With unexpected suddenness, a major turning-point arrived in my life. I took a step forward on an unknown path. And so it was I returned to the Mosque, and grew to know Sister Majeed. Truly, as the saying goes: 'To know her was to love her.' So disarmingly beautiful was her wisdom-lit soul, one felt helpless to do otherwise. There was a kind of vibrant magnetism in her state of surrender, some effulgent tranquillity which tapped my own deep inward longing, and drew me closer to myself.

The bearded old man became my first formal teacher after Sister Majeed. He too had his beauty. His speech was alert and full of colourful analogy, with wit and humour and depth. His manner was absorbing. At first his words seemed like much of what I'd heard in the past: rituals, rites, and doctrinal laws. All the things I associated with organised religion which simply failed to touch me deep inside, much as I hoped that something would. None the less, I had to admit that there was something different here, something which I sensed might involve me perhaps, in an exciting new direction.

I came several times before the old man talked to me, save for a simple greeting. I would come with pad and pencil and I wrote everything. I collected painstakingly copious notes and studied the ideas. I overflowed with questions. After a time, I felt myself ready enough — nay, armed enough — to attempt to speak. To my surprise, the old man heard my questions. But more than this, he attempted to answer them, then challenged me and raised more questions. He sent me in search of answers and directed me to read, to think and understand. Never before in matters of religion and faith had I known a teacher such as this.

We spent long hours in that old building, the Imam and me. Often there were just the two of us. We would sit in the old kitchen in the back of the building, drinking coffee and talking about Islam. Other times we'd sit upstairs in the prayer room and talk about God, Whom he referred to as Allah. It was in that room that I began to understand, at the level of practice, what is meant by the act of surrender. I got down on my knees and laid my head on the floor before the Lord of the Universe. With tears flowing and my body shaking with a nervousness which rose up from some unknown inner place, I looked into oblivion. I muttered a phrase which was so foreign to me then, but which now feels just like home: *Subhana Rabbi al 'ala.* Glory to my Lord, Most High.

For the next several years I was a student in both my practical and spiritual life. During these years I was devoted to the Imam, and under his direction I grew clearer in my search. From him I learned the fundamentals: something of the Oneness of God most High, of the Unity of His Message in all the Revealed Books and the Brotherhood of Prophets, of Life after Death, and of Angels. Something I learned as well, of the nature of the human soul and the duties of a servant of God. I learned something of prayer (*salat*) and almsgiving (*zakat*), fasting (*saum*) and pilgrimage (*Hajj*). During these times came my first lessons of discipleship, by the guidance of God, manifested in the wise and loving care of Sister Majeed, the Imam, and the many others who touched my life. The years sped by, and there came the day when I knew I had to leave. The first stage of my practical education was completed now and it was time for me to move. It was a hard move to make. I had become very attached to the Mosque, to the Imam and to that particular community of Muslims.

I made the separation, and struck out on my own. Having been offered a job in another city, I made a move to get away and see the world. For three years life was wonderful. I had every kind of success, especially in terms of professional influence and recognition. Somehow though, I was not happy. I wanted a spiritual life but I did not see how I could have such a life without giving something up. Bored and scared, I made another move. Poorly considered, and poorly timed, my attempt to escape soon resulted in a catastrophic crash. After three months I was on the street with nothing. Beset by what seemed an endless series of problems, I was forced by my suffering to examine my life and turn my attention again back towards my Creator.

I eventually found another job, a modest, simple one, with none of the former frills. Just after I took the job I came across a Middle Eastern journal which was soliciting papers for a conference. I thought I had expertise in one of the areas for which abstracts were being considered, so I wrote. After quite some time I received a long-distance phone-call. In a businesslike tone the caller told me:

'Brother, I have been requested to inform you that your paper has been accepted. Can you prepare to present it in Saudi Arabia? Your tickets for air travel will be sent to you by mail and your visa will be taken care of by us.'

Astonished, I accepted and hung up the phone. Within a month I had received the visa and tickets and sat aboard the plane.

The conference was a source of many blessings. My paper was well-received and I gained a great deal of insight. I met many other beautiful God-conscious thinkers who taught me many things. A very important part of these learnings was how to move towards integrating all the aspects of my life: the practical, professional and spiritual. Indeed the counsel I received was more than welcomed. By that time I had grown very tired of attempting to live my life maintaining the straining separations. Among the varied experiences of the conference, I also learned about another quite personal and unseen attachment. It had to do with the Mosque of my home town and the old man, the Imam. Somehow I had always felt an allegiance to that particular group and city. During the conference I was speaking about my hopes and concerns to an older Muslim man I had met. He listened, then calmly looked at me and said: 'Don't you see, my brother? Allah has brought you here in order that you may realise that you are a citizen of the planet. Your family is everywhere.'

The words fell on my ears as if I were a deaf man restored to hearing. I had never considered my life so broadly before. With this answer another question came to clarity as well, concerning teachers and *Imams* (religious leaders). I had viewed the Imam as a kind of *Shaikh,* or master teacher. Somehow, I felt obliged not to seek another teacher because of my loyalty to him — yet much as I loved him, I knew that what I sought in my heart was not with him. The older seeker clarified the essential issue. He explained that a person can easily be someone's *Imam* — that is, one's leader in exoteric matters of religious practice — and not necessarily his *Shaikh,* or spiritual director and guide in more inwardly focused esoteric matters of spiritual purification and growth. I attributed too much to the Imam because he had been my first formal teacher after Sister Majeed. When I learned that I had done this, I was very much relieved. At the same time, I continued to hold a very special place in my heart for him. The Prophet Muhammad himself, peace be upon him, said: 'Be most humble and respectful to persons from whom you receive knowledge.' Also his companion, Ali, may God be pleased with him, said: 'I am a slave to the person who has taught me even a single word. He may sell me or set me free.' And so it was that during the conference many dark, unanswered questions had unexpectedly come to light. As I reflected on being there and all the many things I learned, I realised more and more about the mercy of God. I truly felt His unseen care. From one side of the world to the other, I looked backwards on my life. I saw that God had loved me even through my foolish days, and that He kept my heart alive. I had been lost it is true, but I never rejected Him, and the inward seeking was always there.

As I made my way about the conference I met another helper-guide whose name was Ibrahim. Somehow God caused us to be drawn together and we soon began to talk. Ibrahim knew many of the people at the conference, and he took it upon himself to take me around and introduce me to as many of those present as he could. The interesting people that I met through the efforts of this gregarious brother is a story in itself. Early in our rounds we came upon a man from Turkey:

'Here is someone whom you must speak to,' said Ibrahim smiling, 'but when I leave you, beware of this brother, for he may talk to you in *Sufi* talk. But Allah knows, you should have exposure to his views.'

Having made this baffling remark, Ibrahim departed. I stood there, momentarily absorbed in an attempt to decipher the meaning of what he had said. I had read the works of some of the great Sufis and had always been moved by their beauty and depth. I saw in them the most beautiful among Muslims and secretly I had always hoped that I might join their ranks. What was it in Ibrahim's statement which triggered such defensiveness in me? Suddenly the stranger's voice interrupted my thoughts and brought me back to the moment:

'*Assalaamu alaikum wa Rahmatullahi wa barakatu.* Peace be on you, the mercy of God and His blessings.'

The brother stranger was looking directly into my face. His own was a kind face and his eyes were moist and full of light. The simplicity of his dress and manner belied his inner depth. I extended my hand to shake his, but he took my hand and kissed it instead. Then, stepping closer, he touched my face and kissed my forehead. He continued speaking:

'Let us move to another place; I have much to tell you.'

We moved from the narrow corridor to a quiet, lighted area of the lobby where we stood together. Actually, there was no need to talk. Something in this person reached to my very depths. He touched upon my own deep longing for something which cannot be described by words. This man, a stranger whom I'd never met or seen before was a true spiritual friend. His presence was a great affirmation of hope. Speaking again he said:

'I have been sent to you by Grandshaikh Abdullah Daghistani the Shaikh of my spiritual Master, Shaikh Nun of Kibrus. As the Grandshaikh is now in the better world, when you wish to know more about him, I suggest you contact Shaikh Nun. The Grandshaikh has told me that you will find the Shaikh you long for, and many other things as well.'

I began to weep. The more he spoke, the more I wept. He told me many things. He spoke of God, of Prophet Muhammad and the brotherhood of Prophets (peace be upon them), of the way of Islam as surrender to God, and of the orientations of seekers, whom he divided into two classes: those who pursue only the external, largely through ritual and form, whom he termed the 'Outers', and those who go through the ritual and form in order to reach the oceans of meaning, whom he referred to as the 'Inners'. I continued weeping. What I heard and felt, moved me beyond words and touched some deep and unknown place in my heart. The love and truth which vibrated in the stranger were more than my mind could fathom, but somehow my heart understood.

During the Stranger's visit he presented me with a photograph of the noble Grandshaikh who had lived to be 120 years of age. I was very much struck by the lighted face of this man, who reached out to me from another world, and through the dervish, entered my life. I took the photo and put it away but having it was always a reminder that what my heart had known was real.

The Stranger stayed with me for the duration of the conference. We attended meetings together, and visited others who had presented papers. We left the conference together and travelled to the Holy City of Medina. There we visited the Prophet's Mosque, the gravesite of the Prophet, peace be upon him, and of his beloved companions Abu Bakr Siddiq and Umar Ibn Khattab, both buried beside him, may God be pleased with them.

This visit was of special meaning and importance, the realisation of which was to come much later. Here was established a city of surrender wherein was found the highest, most elevated community of servants of God ever to exist. There in the Mosque of Medina, I was privileged to pray in the *mihrab* (alcove) where the Prophet used to pray — a fitting place to remember my smallness and to pray to God that I might be among those who are truly with his Prophet. It was a fitting place indeed to reflect on the hope that my own being might in some way become as surrendered to God as were all of His Prophets, and that my own heart might become as full of love and light as had been *Medina al-*

Munawwara, the City of Illumination.

We continued to the Holy City of Mecca where God graced my eyes with the sight of His ancient house the *Ka'bah,* erected by Prophet Adam and later Prophet Abraham, peace be upon them. We performed the rites for the lesser pilgrimage (*Umra*) and bade each other farewell in Mecca. My Stranger friend was the personification of the vibrant spirit of brotherhood which I felt everywhere around us. Needless to say, when I left him, I was so full of joy that I could hardly contain myself. I felt extremely blessed to have had a guide and companion through the most holy cities on God's planet earth. As I boarded a bus in Mecca I reflected on my home. The world seemed smaller then.

During the return flight home, I became very sick. I lost all equilibrium and I could not eat or drink. I spent most of the journey back to the United States on my back, stretched across two seats of the jumbo plane. I arrived home still very sick and remained in bed for two weeks before I felt strong enough to return to work. During my illness I received several friendly and unsolicited diagnoses of jet lag. I resisted these to no end, but actually they were not far off. Now, looking back on the sickness I would myself diagnose what I had as a spiritual jet lag. My illness was alerting me to the big transition into which my life had come. The sickness also told me clearly where I'd be if I went back to where I had been in my past. In the weeks after my return from the journey, and after my recovery, a yearning took hold of me, the likes of which I had never felt before. Nothing seemed to satisfy. Suddenly it became very difficult to continue working. I reported each day with deep melancholy. I spoke very little and became very distant to everyone. Away from work, I went into seclusion. The yearning stayed and stayed. I relived the journey again and again. After several weeks in this state, I decided to visit my family: particularly my mother, whom I'd not seen for several months. Sitting with her in the kitchen I told the story of my restless inward search. Her only words were these:

'Trust God, He knows what you're to do.'

As the writing on the wall stretched across the years, the quiet yearning feeling which had welled up in my travels grew stronger still within. With a strengthened commitment to fulfilling this unknown inner longing, I worked to turn my life back to God.

During the time of my turning, the months passed by like an endless train. Each day was a slow-moving boxcar in which I paced back and forth, in search of a meaning for what I had lived.

Finding no answer, I bided my time and realised that I might search for years. One day, as I stood in the corridor of the building where I worked, a man walked by whom I did not know. I was introducing myself to someone else as he passed by, and he overheard me say my name. Hardly stopping, he commented in a matter-of-fact and casual voice, just loud enough for me to hear:

'Your name is not an American name.'

Partly surprised and partly amused, I regained my composure enough to address him. 'And what is your name?' I quizzically asked.

'Salah,' he replied with a smile.

Now understanding, I was almost in laughter, while together in near unison, we exchanged the greetings of peace (*salaams*).

It was through this man Salah that I was led to the Muslim community of my new city. Viewing my meeting with him in the context of my changing life, I felt compelled to take some initiative consistent with my renewed commitment. I had been in the city for nearly a year without having met a single Muslim. Following his lead, I came into a large but developing community of Muslims. There was much work to be done and sooner than I expected my small initiative caused my life to be filled with activity.

This period of my life was a time of much transition and personal learning. Many of the things I had learned in my early days at the Mosque resurfaced. Whenever possible, I shared them in the service of others. Throughout this time of activity, however, that yearning still remained. I stole away for silence whenever I could to reflect on my life and stay in touch with myself. I asked my Lord to forgive my past and I prayed for future guidance.

The new community of which I had become a part was very much in need of leadership. A few sincere workers bore the load of many. I learned, however, that a highly qualified and deeply religious man had recently entered the community. Among some there was already the expectant hope that he might become a new force in the strengthening of local Muslims. One of the more active and informed brothers of the community had given me this news. He had also shown me a simple business card on which was written the name of the man and the name of a particular place, a part of which included the word *Sufi.* Perhaps I was entering another cycle. I thought a thousand hopeful thoughts, then put them all aside. I thought it wiser to be patient and wait to see what might unfold.

Early one evening in *Ramadan*, the fasting month, just after the prayer at sunset, I received a phone-call. The brother who had told me about the new religious leader invited me to a meeting for an introduction. It was planned that we would come together about an hour before a larger gathering of the community for *Iftar*, the breaking of the fast. When I arrived at the meeting-place no one from the group was there. I searched for the brother who had called me but I did not find him either. When he finally did arrive, the time which we had planned for was lost, and others from the community had begun to arrive for the gathering. I accepted the events calmly, thinking, 'The Praise is to God, *alhamdulillah!*' I was so patient in the handling of this episode that I even surprised myself. As I stood there still concluding my thoughts on the unmet meeting, someone approached me and asked me to go outside and help to bring in the food.

As I turned to walk back to the building, I caught a glimpse of a man just stepping inside. Something struck me about him and gave me the sense that he was the person I was to have met. When I re-entered the room of the gathering, I found that several people had arrived and were moving about. In one area of the room I immediately noticed the man I had seen. He was dressed in simple white clothing, and he wore sandals and a strikingly plain, light-brown pointed hat. Over his shoulders was draped a long, black, cape-like garment. He sat with a small circle of people gathered around him who moved whenever he moved. I could easily see that they all were with him and not with the gathering at large. There was in the presence of this man, a kind of beauty, spiritual nobility and vibrating personal magnetism which I had not felt in anyone since the death of Sister Majeed. I sensed a great depth in him and great love. There was balance in his movement and a mystery in his manner which created in me a sense of harmony and discomfort, both at once. For those who were around him, he was obviously present, and yet he seemed inconspicuous for the larger group. When he looked at me, it was as if there was no one but us two. Something in his glance went straight to my heart and pulled me in his direction. I knew he was my Shaikh. He rose as I approached him with the greeting of peace and calmly he returned the greeting. As I stood before him nearly breathless, I introduced myself and extended my hand.

'I am Muhyiddin,' I said.

Not taking my hand, he put his to my beard, and grasping it, he said, 'I know who you are.' Then he gave me his name.

He looked into my eyes and in the moment a thousand days raced by. He kissed my face on either cheek and the voice of the Stranger I had met in my travels suddenly came up in my memory like a flashing light. With dramatic suddenness, this rare human being stepped into my life. Full and almost overwhelmed, I could hardly believe what was happening. Not really knowing what to do, I sat near him in silence like those in the circle, then I moved about the room.

Later that evening he spoke before the larger gathering on the meaning of *Ramadan* and fasting. His talk brought many teachings from the Qur'an and the traditions. It was eye-opening, to the point, and hard to ignore. Afterwards, the man who had called on the phone introduced us again and our meeting was rescheduled. Everything seemed to come together that night. This gathering only marked the beginning of many new things that were yet to come. In the years ahead I would come to know in my life, things which I had only read in books before. And so it was that almost nine years after I had stumbled into the mosque and looked into the wisdom-worn face of Sister Majeed, I peered into the knowing, loving face of my Shaikh. I saw reflected in him the light of Sister Majeed and every teacher I had known before.

That night before leaving, the Shaikh asked me if I could give him a ride on Sunday to come. We would go to the rescheduled meeting together. I agreed to do it even though I had no car, my own being in repair. It was easy enough to borrow a car, and to keep the appointment which I had hoped for so much, over the many endless months.

Having been brought to my Shaikh by the Grace of God, I acknowledged the great blessing of his coming as a guide. The true ones of God are rare as the phoenix, and the world is full of false teachers. Yet one must have help on the way to God, for without a guide the ego cannot be dissolved, nor will selfishness die. As I quietly reflected on the guidance of all my past years come to the present, the signs of the moment were clear. In my heart I knew that the Shaikh was true and I prayed that with him I would move closer to myself and my Lord.

CHAPTER 1

The Needle

The first time that I was ever alone with the Shaikh was on a Sunday afternoon. It was a bright and sunny autumn day in the fasting month of *Ramadan.* We had just met a few days before, and all the excitement and newness of my relationship with him had kept me flying high. He had instructed me to meet him by a certain clock in a small shopping plaza at noon. Having had several unexpected delays, I arrived a few minutes late. There was no one at or near the clock.

'Well, you blew it,' I thought to myself. 'You should have arrived here sooner — why didn't you take another route? Who are *you* to keep him waiting?' I was full of doubt and I didn't know what to do.

After waiting for about ten minutes, I decided that I would try to reach him by phone. I didn't have his number so I had to call someone else and ask. Somehow, much to my surprise, I got the number and placed the call. After several rings, he answered and in a very soft, calm voice he gave me the greetings of peace. He had hardly spoken when a man approached me at the phone-booth where I stood. He had come up suddenly. Startled, I looked into his face. I recognised him right away as being someone sent by the Shaikh. His face was familiar and later I remembered that this man had been with the Shaikh on the night when I met him.

The man wore the pointed woollen hat of a dervish. His face was deeply warm, yet serious and very kind. The moment was a strange one for I stood in it juxtaposed between the face of the dervish and the voice of the Shaikh — at my ear on the phone.

'I'm here to take you to the Shaikh,' said the dervish. 'We can walk from here.'

As I stood there returning the Shaikh's greeting in a phone-call I had made in much haste and doubting, I received my first teaching on the kind of interaction one has with a Shaikh. He was close when I thought that I was completely cut off. I later discovered that he could, in fact, see me quite easily when I arrived at the clock because the clock was in a clear line of vision from his apartment window.

As I turned to leave the phone-booth with the dervish, I noticed another man who was standing nearby collecting money for the needy. He had approached me earlier as I was rushing to the phone-booth. I knew that I could not ignore him as I left. I gave him some coins and said, 'God bless you.' The kindly dervish also searched his pockets and gave. The man smiled on us both and we walked away. I often wondered who that man could have been who stood asking for alms. Somehow he seemed a real part of the unfolding of events. Whenever I remember that day when I was first with the Shaikh, I remember the begging man. Even though he symbolised more than I possibly could have realised at the time, I later gained some insight on reading a tradition of the Prophet Muhammad, peace be on him, in which he is reported to have said: 'O God, grant me life as a poor man, cause me to die as a poor man, and resurrect me in the company of the poor.' The begging man was a clear sign for me, the seeker who almost passed him by. He was a symbol of a first step in search of the True and Ultimate Wealth which comes only to the poor.

> No one who recognizes poverty as better than money is a moneyed man, though he be a king; and a man who does not believe in poverty is a moneyed man however poor he is.
>
> *(from a Dervish autobiography)*

In a few minutes we arrived at the apartment of the Shaikh. I was quite surprised to find that it was not located at the top of a mountain, nor in the depth of some secluded cave. It was as simple and as practical as the home of any other person. There were windows, plants, a black and white televison, a simple carpet, a sofa, a refrigerator, and a fragrant atmosphere of simplicity, calmness, and warm refuge for the spirit. He greeted us with peace as we entered the room and took seats on the floor among a small circle of disciples who were there. He was just concluding a discourse and the disciples were pondering a question he had given them by way of metaphor, related to the Unity of the Creator and

His relationship with His creation. He propounded the question to me and I gave a simple answer which seemed to have been sitting on my heart for days before, waiting for the question.

'Alhamdulillah (Praise be to God)', he said. 'How is it that you have answered the question which none of my *murids* (disciples) could answer?'

I truly did not know. To me it only seemed that God was matching my inward longing with an outward experience which validated my hopes. In this instance He simply gave me the answer to draw me closer to His Path. He moved my limbs toward my Shaikh who was so near, and so conspicuous — yet I would never have found him, were it not for the guidance of God.

The discourse ended and I met the others who were present. We all left the apartment together. Outside the Shaikh gave farewell greetings of peace to the other disciples and he and I went to the car. We drove to the home of the Muslim man who was the host for a meeting which involved members of the community at large and the Shaikh in his capacity as *Imam,* or religious leader. Being with him that day showed me how he dealt with the more outer-directed activities of Islamic living and also with the mundane administration of activity in the world. He was gracious in his demeanour, strong in his emphasis of the Prophet's behaviour (*Sunnah*) and the pattern of God's law (*Shari'ah*). Moreover, he was brief, effective, and to the point. He did not ever waste time or words when dealing with the public. At the same time he was unfathomably patient and always willing to address concerns and questions. I also got my first lesson in how one serves him through the management of his minor concerns. During the meeting I kept the time for him and notified the host when it was time for him to leave.

That day I also enjoyed his personal company as we rode to and from the meeting. I asked him what we were to do together in life. I knew that I was destined to meet him and he knew that I was coming. He told me what I cannot say, but from the beginning I knew what I was to do as his disciple (*murid*). Still I must say that the knowing and doing and the knowing and *being* are often miles apart. Al Ghazali made the point quite clear by saying that information about the wine and having the taste of it are two entirely different experiences.

I drove the Shaikh back to his apartment and we sat for a moment in the car as he finished some thoughts. He took my beard in his hand and said a silent prayer. He got out of the car and bowed to look inside my window. He bid me farewell with the wish of God's peace, then turned to walk away. It seemed that it was a very long time before I saw him again. A few weeks seemed like months.

The days of Ramadan passed slowly and later I received news that the Shaikh had gone into *Itikaf*, a period of retreat for contemplation and prayer during the last ten days of fasting. During this time an incredible yearning overtook me and I really longed to see him. The longing was more than missing the Shaikh and the feeling itself was teaching me about the longing for my true Lord, God the Most Exalted.

It was during this time that I wrote a letter to the Shaikh in which I told him how I felt. Really, the letter was more for myself than for him, but writing it really helped me to crystallise where I was with myself as well as with my feelings. Early after I had met him, he had invited me to make a journey with him and some dervishes to another city. I wanted very much to go, but for whatever reasons there were, Allah caused my circumstances to be such that I could not go. Not being able to make this trip generated another collection of feelings which I muddled through during the time I was out of touch with him. Finally, towards the last few days of Ramadan, I received a postcard from him. He sent greetings for the *Eid-ul Fitr* holidays, which followed the month of fasting, in response to my letter. Shortly after that I saw him again on the day of *Eid* where he delivered a talk (*khutba*) before the community at large. It was truly good to see him. He was full of light and his talk was vibrant and intensely thought-provoking. He talked about the temporariness of life, and about the reality and imminence of the *Akhirat*, the life hereafter. His talks were always colourful, full of examples, stories, and metaphor. One of the stories that he told that day brought home to me, in a most dramatic way, the point of all he had said. It was the story of an arrogant emperor king who had much wealth and who raced his dashing steed recklessly through the streets. On one occasion an old dervish in a hooded garment approached the horse of the king as he made his way through the street. The king, in sudden impulsive arrogance, drew his sword, surprised that anyone would dare to cross his path.

'Who are you to approach me?' he shouted down to the dervish. The dervish slowly lifted his head and the king, with his sword still raised, looked into the face of death. It was in truth not a dervish but Azra'il, the Angel of Death, coming for the soul of the King.

'Let me have just a little more time, a few minutes more to conclude some affairs,' said the king, now recognising who had approached him.

The angel looked into his face not speaking a word and slowly shook his head. There was no time. The king would not touch the earth again with breath in his body.

We are like this king, many of us. Thinking ourselves to be the power, not recognising who truly is our Lord. Rushing recklessly through life attempting to have everything we want, and only working with the hope that each dollar earned will help us to have more. Forgetting the reality of our very own death and the truth of the life which comes after: *Akhirat*.

That day I approached the Shaikh to give him greetings of peace (*salaams*). He greeted me warmly but we did not converse. He directed me to his dervishes. After the holidays of *Eid-ul Fitr* there was another period when I was out of touch with him and all my contacts with him came through his dervishes. They were most kind and sympathetic and the more I spent time with them, the more attracted I became to them. Through these kindly souls I was led into the *Hadrah* gathering, the circle of disciples (*murids* and dervishes) and the company of the Shaikh. What it was like to be in that meeting is beyond words. The culmination of years of hoping brought me only to the doorstep of my beginning. More than this I cannot say as regards that meeting except that the Path of Seekers to God is true and that He is Merciful and He moves the limbs of His creatures towards Guidance.

After being with the Shaikh once or twice I longed to be with him always. But every disciple and those aspiring to be, felt exactly as I felt. This being the case, we were drawn together to share in our hopes because the Shaikh was a busy man. He travelled and moved in the most unpredictable patterns. During the time when I first met him he was often away on journeys.

On one such occasion when the Shaikh was away I made a trip to visit his disciples. There was only a small group of us and we whiled the day away, each harbouring the hope that he would come. He had given the disciples a task involving writing essays on *Hajj*, the greater Pilgrimage. This kept them busy for most of the day but left me with time on my hands. I was getting a very gentle introduction to the course of events around the Shaikh, but I did not realise it at the time. By late afternoon I was impatient, bored and ready to leave. I made my farewells and got into my car to go.

I had driven the car about two miles down the road when I heard a clear voice from within say, 'Turn the car around.'

I drove back to the house where the disciples were gathered. They welcomed me back as I told them about the voice. One of them smiled a knowing smile. That turning around was a major turning. I turned to face a series of teachings which were more intensely personal, involving, and spiritually growth-producing than any teaching I had ever known in all the previous years of my life.

That night on return from his journey, the Shaikh stopped at the house where we had gathered. Dressed in white, he came with the suddenness of an unexpected wind. He had brought with him a used stereo console which he asked us to bring into the house and into the room which served as a mosque. He cautioned us to carry it carefully, to sit it on the floor and plug it into the outlet. He then instructed us to start it and to play the record which was already inside it on the turntable. Two disciples were unsuccessful, the needle sliding across the record each time they attempted. He then asked me to try and somehow, much to my own surprise, I was able to make it play.

'*Alhamdulillah!* (Praise be to God!)' rang out the voice of the Shaikh as he quickly moved towards us three. He then spoke directly to me:

'You receive the *Baraka* — the blessings, let me kiss your hand. How did you make it work?' he asked.

'I simply turned the needle over,' I sheepishly replied.

'Many tried today,' he said, 'and none but you could make it work, *alhamdulillah!*' He then asked for another record, which we listened to as he spoke.

He asked for the reading of some of the essays which he had assigned. Three were read, while a fourth was not presented. Since I had not been given the task, I listened on. There were intermittent remarks about the stereo made occasionally during this time. One disciple was asked to make some minor repairs on it while the rest of the group made a decision about whether to let remain or remove a frame around the dials which had now come loose. We decided that the machine was just as attractive without it and that the frame was not necessary.

Later, before leaving the mosque room for dinner, he spoke to me again:

'Your task is to find the needle.'

Everyone present had suggested (and I had agreed) that a needle was indeed what was needed. I thought that it would be a simple enough task to accomplish. As I moved to remove the worn needle, he spoke again:

'I want you to find it without taking the old needle.'

At the record shop I found a baffling array of needles. For the particular type of stereo of the Shaikh, there were several types of needles which varied imperceptibly. I had eyed one needle but I did not choose it. When the shop assistant suggested that I could not choose the proper needle without the old one or its number, I found myself annoyed that I could not complete the simple task. I left the shop. Later, speaking to the Shaikh I told him that I had gone to the shop and found that there was a vast assortment of needles.

'Yes, I know,' he said in his characteristic manner. 'I wanted you to see that there are many needles, but only one is the right one.'

Upon hearing this I felt relieved and thought myself to have an insight and perhaps be nearing the completion of the task. I asked if I might come to get the old needle and he consented. After I removed the needle, he inspected it, smiled, spoke some words which I did not hear, and returned it to me. I placed the needle in my wallet for safekeeping and departed soon thereafter.

Upon my return to the record store, again standing before the cabinet of needles, I took out my wallet only to find that the needle was not in it.

'*Astaghfirullah* — may God forgive me.' I muttered. I searched my mind trying to think of where I could have lost it. I could only remember having removed my wallet the day before in a small shop. I phoned the shop: no answer. I eyed the needle I had originally seen but I did not choose it. I chose another, paid and left.

Walking along the street, I felt the doubt nagging ever so slightly but I took relief in having done something. At least I would not have to face the Shaikh empty-handed. As I was on my way I passed an old man whom I greeted and shortly thereafter a beautiful fragrance filled my nostrils. I felt the presence of the Shaikh. I smiled, praising God, and walked on.

Later, upon seeing him, I was immediately questioned: 'Where is my needle?'

I smiled and removed the needle I had chosen from my pocket. As I moved towards the record-player, he said, 'Unlucky for you if it is not the right one.' It was not. The Shaikh said many things to me about that needle. These I remember: 'The needle is your faith, you lost it.' 'You must fight the *nafs* (ego).' 'Your logic will not work.' 'It is not the record player, it is the record.' 'Confusion is the sister of mistrust.' Somehow that night, in the midst of my dilemma, he asked me if I wanted to take the Path and if I wanted to become a *murid* (disciple). I answered yes, *Insha'Allah* (God willing), to both questions, meaning it sincerely. He offered to relieve me of the needle task, but I asked that he allow me to complete it. He consented and said that my task was to find the needle, but now without the needle or its number and without taking the cartridge.

> Ye shall surely travel from stage to stage.
>
> *(Qur'an 84:19)*

The needle was on my mind night and day. It filled my thoughts. I could not forget it. I pondered it. I pondered more. I read. I tried to remember all of what the Shaikh said. I thought of how it would be for me if I could stay with God as much as my mind was staying with the thought of the needle. I reviewed the incident from start to the present: my feelings of annoyance, amusement, confusion, hope, mistrust, fear, inspiration. I had many bits and pieces but I felt no real sense of clarity approaching. Nothing fully crystallised.

On seeing the Shaikh again he questioned me as to my progress and I told him that I had little to report. I mentioned to him some of my personal reflections, but said that I had not yet arrived at an answer. Again he emphasised that the needle was my faith, my *Shari'ah.* He also mentioned that he had offered to relieve me of the duty in order to put me at my own initiative. He mentioned that I should especially know that the task was not for him, but without doubt there was purpose in the task and that I would come to see its deep spiritual meaning. I left him with much to ponder, and ponder I did. I reflected and pondered, and pondered still more. I could not stop.

> So wait with patience for the Command of thy Lord, and be not like the Companion of the Fish, when he cried out in agony.
>
> *(Qur'an 68:48)*

The following day the needle still lingered in my consciousness. As I went about my business, I continued to consider it. While driving along the street, headed to the hospital to a visit a friend, my eyes searched the buildings for an address I had in mind. Off in the distance, I noticed a very tall building. Something within said, 'That's the building. Go there.' Not listening, however, I went to the address I had in mind. Arriving there, the receptionist said, 'The person you want to see is in that tall building off in the distance.' As I drove there, realisation flooded me. Everything was clear. My task was to strengthen my faith.

The lesson of *Yaqin,* which is the attainment of certainty and confidence, is a most important lesson. By God's grace I came to understand. The Shaikh asked me to search for the needle without a needle in order that I might learn the necessity of faith and abandonment of forethought. These are most necessary for knowledge of God, for on the Path the disciple must move towards his object without doubt. Certainty such as this is what Al Ghazali alludes to when he speaks of the lesson of faith being like shooting the arrow at a target in the dark.

The *nafs,* or the ego to be fought, was reflected in my annoyance at the counter before the needles. The Prophet Muhammad, Peace and Blessings of God be upon him, spoke of *Jihad al Akbar* and when asked what is was, he said that it was the war on the *nafs*: the struggle with one's very own self. The way of the Path is a way of selflessness, and agitation has no place, puts one out of rhythm and blocks one's progress. There is a saying of the Sufis that if the attitude is right, all will come right. I came to see that my own annoyance and doubt actually blocked my success.

My confusion was a sign of my mistrust in the sense that I doubted myself. I had also not fully realised that the task I was performing was for the pleasure of God through my service of the Shaikh — but not for the pleasure of the Shaikh. This was a teaching of subtle distinctions: pleasing God, pleasing self, and pleasing others. There is a saying of the Dervishes that 'a right step is a step taken in true self-forgetfulness, and neither capriciously, nor correctly.' The lesson is to learn to remember Allah through all; to become passive to both divine command and divine prohibition. When the disciple comes to love God Most High, he rushes to fulfil His commands, and runs from that which He, the Exalted, forbids. One learns to live in the present moment, without a future. One's spirit then comes to reflect the peace of knowledge of God Almighty.

The Shaikh had said to me: 'It's not the machine, it's the record.' The teaching is now apparent: Faith is the needle and the record is the Way. If one does not have a good faith, a strong faith — one will slide from the Way as the worn needle slides from the record.

He had so often questioned his disciples: 'Why don't you start living?' And in this question is a teaching, for one who has not reached the realm of faith in actuality is *not* alive.

The word of the Shaikh is to be heard — but more. It should then fall to the disposition of the disciple, not to his mind, or will. The word is to be applied in earnest to the life of the disciple. Strength of faith, this is what is needed on the Path. Straight ahead. *Hasbi Allah.* God is sufficient.

> Verily in this is the very truth and certainty.
>
> *(Qur'an 56:95)*

And so it was that I returned to the display of needles for a third time. I asked for the needle I had seen when first entering the shop two visits earlier. The assistant said to me, 'Are you sure this is the one?'

Again doubt raised its head ever so slightly, but now my sure foot crushed it low. I answered, 'Yes, it is the one, *Insha'Allah* (God willing).'

Exchanging the needle I had purchased before, I took the new needle and left.

I called the Shaikh to tell him I had solved the task. He invited me to him and I rushed, arriving full and overflowing with joy. I brought with me this very story which was still unfolding as I entered his presence. He greeted me quietly with the blessings of God and touched my face with care and love and prayer. The fragrance which filled my nostrils days before was with his hand as it moved away. Having arrived without dinner, I was graciously fed. We spoke as I sat to eat already full with feelings and realisation still dawning. He listened to me and enquired about the meal. As I finished, he left the room and returned with a record which he carefully placed on top of the stereo. He took a seat across the room.

'Now come and read your story,' he said.

As I sat before him reading aloud, the feelings continued to swell in me. Somehow I sensed myself suddenly more at the beginning than at the end. The moment drew near as he calmly spoke:

'Where is your needle? Let us see how it works.'

Silently I replied by putting my hand over my heart, at the same time feeling the needle in the pocket of my shirt. As I moved toward the stereo, the Shaikh remained seated chanting. And what did he chant? It was a *qasida*: a mystical song in praise of

God. I hardly heard. His voice was steady but far away — I was struggling between fear and hope.

And so the moment came. I uttered *Bismillah* (in the name of God) and began. I shifted the needle around in the small space of the cartridge. It stuck awkwardly for only an instant, then suddenly clicked into place with a loud snap. I will never forget that sound, for with it my faith was purified. My soul entered a new sphere, and my mind rose to the heavens.

The record began with praises to God, the wish of blessings on His Prophet, and then *Al Asma Husna*: the recitation of Divine Names. Sitting with the Shaikh my heart swelled larger than the room. I felt the mercy of God and His favour on me. The sounds from the record were the music of my very own heart. Melodic sounds of indescribable sweetness and simplicity. Sounds far more beautiful than stereo or quadraphonic. My heartbeat vibrated in the universe in those moments. There were no words.

That night the needle travelled in its groove. I came into harmony with my self and was led by my Shaikh through a door, on the other side of which I fell into the Ocean: an ocean of many notes but only one sweet reverberating sound. I cannot say more, except all of the Praise belongs to Him: *Alhamdulillah. Alhamdulillah. Alhamdulillah!*

So celebrate with praises the name of thy Lord the Supreme.

(Qur'an 56:96)

CHAPTER 2

THE DRAINS

After coming onto the Path, the affairs of life seemed to go well. The Shaikh had given me the task of finding a certain needle, and having successfully found it, I soared off into a period of feeling good. The solving of the task brought me into greater contact with the Shaikh, who was truly a blessing. It was a great comfort to have him in my life to provide me with sound spiritual direction and assist me in resolving my inner doubts. For this the praise is due to God alone, Who in His Graciousness and Mercy brought me, His seeking servant through a Secret Door and onto the Way of Love and Guidance.

My 'feeling good' time was very sweet, and very brief. When I felt this absorbing comfort at its highest peak, something happened. With awesome suddenness everything became difficult, in both my practical and spiritual life. That difficulty hovered over me like a puff of fuming black smoke which filled my consciousness and choked my spirits.

Standing at my kitchen window I looked at the sky and reflected on this change so unexpectedly present. An inexplicable sadness and melancholy took me in its grasp. A lump grew in my throat as one of Shakespeare's sonnets floated through my thoughts:

When in disgrace with Fortune and men's eyes,
I all alone beweep my outcast state,
And trouble deaf heaven with my bootless cries,
And look upon myself, and curse my fate,
Wishing me like to one more rich in hope,
Featured like him, like him with friends possessed,

Desiring this man's art and that man's scope,
With what I most enjoy contented least;
Yet in these thoughts myself almost despising,
Haply I think on thee, and then my state,
Like to the lark at break of day arising
From sullen earth, sings hymns at heaven's gate;
For thy sweet love remember'd such wealth brings
That then I scorn to change my state with kings.

But my heart knew that God truly is not deaf — He Who hears the footsteps of ants surely hears my breaking heart. What did I have to be sad about? Had He not brought me onto this Path? And is that not itself a mystery, which baffles reason and description?

Tears welled up from deep within me. My eyes clouded. I looked away from the sky to the sink before me. It was stopped up. Almost as suddenly as everything else seemed to have stopped; as suddenly as things seemed not to flow in my life, so it was that the drains too seemed to clog. They had just been unclogged a few weeks before. I reported them to the landlord and he had, in his usual responsiveness, come quickly. He unblocked the drains and they flowed well for a while — better in fact, than they ever had since I had lived in the apartment. But suddenly they were blocked again. A simple bath became a major undertaking. The clogging and closing was so definite, it rippled through my very being. I did not understand. Staring into the flooded kitchen sink, I reviewed the events of my recent past.

> So We opened the gates of heaven, with water Pouring forth. And We caused the earth to gush forth with springs. So the waters met (and rose) to the extent decreed.
>
> *(Qur'an 54:12)*

My relatively dependable and serviceable car had also suddenly gone out of service. Everything on it seemed to be breaking, from the windscreen wipers to the brakes, to the engine itself — the very heart of the car. Twice in three months the car was at the dealer's for major repairs. Each repair tied the car up for at least one month. During this time, all sorts of unexpected delays and difficulties emerged, causing one postponement after another. Soon after getting the car back the first time, having been without it for six weeks, I asked the Shaikh if he knew about it. As we stood at the door of the car, he replied with a story. It was about a great

Shaikh who rose up from the dead to remind the living not to quibble about the unimportant.

> *Or do ye think that ye shall enter the*
> *Garden of [Bliss]*
> *Without such [trials] as came to those who*
> *passed away before you?*
>
> *(Qur'an 2:214)*

Not long after getting my car back, I was supposed to make a journey. Speaking to the Shaikh about it, he cautioned me to be watchful on my return. The trip went well. As I sped along towards home looking for a lesson reviewing the trip, yellow lights suddenly flashed on the dash. Then came red lights. A moaning whine came from the engine and the car rolled to a confirmed stop on the shoulder of the highway. It was towed back to a nearby town, where it spent the weekend in a garage, and I spent the weekend with a friend and his family. I was without my car for another month, but this time, God, in His mercy caused the dealer to give me a car on loan.

During the weeks which followed, my workload grew as heavy as the rush-hour traffic in which I drove. I counted remembrances of God (*zikr*) on cars lined up ahead of me on the street. There were more demands on my time by wordly affairs in these weeks. I often found the temperament of my colleagues and others unusually impatient and overbearing. But beyond these things what made everything so much harder to bear was being out of touch with the Shaikh. He continued to do his usual work, but also giving a series of weekly lectures. As was then my plight, these were not available to me. They came on a night when I could not attend. Each time the Shaikh came to *Jumah,* the Friday community prayer meeting, he would invite me to the lectures. I was never able to come. It was on such a *Jumah* afternoon that I noticed the clogged drains for the first time after the landlord's repair. When I attempted to use the sink and found it clogged, my heart sank to my feet. In that moment everything seemed closed to me — my car, the lectures, the Shaikh — all of these seemed to be out of reach. It was a hard time.

During this period, I saw the Shaikh only once. On that occasion, he was very quiet and seemed very tired. I knew through reports from others that he had been very busy, in fact even more busy than usual. That day we sat together in the lobby of his apartment. We did not speak much. As we sat there, he was drawing on a small notepad which I had given him. Looking at him that day, I loved him very much. It was the time I felt his humanity more than ever before. No doubt he is a man of God, but on that day I realised, more clearly than ever before, this simple fact: Shaikhs too have their trials.

> They encountered suffering and adversity, and were so shaken in spirit that even the Apostle and those of faith who were with him cried: 'When [will come] the help of God?' Ah! Verily the help of God is always near.
>
> *(Qur'an 2:214)*

On the pad was drawn a map of the way to a disciple's house to whom we were to deliver a cassette tape. There were also listed five things I was to remember: (1) self-restraint, (2) alertness, (3) hope, (4) trust, and (5) *'amal*, which the Shaikh translated as hard work. We rode in the car that day for a long time. Missing a turn and thus not reaching the disciple's house, he told me that we should turn around.

'It is Allah's *Hikmat*, the Wisdom of God that we do it,' he said.

It was wise, no doubt, for we were nearly out of petrol and far from a petrol station. What is more, we had gone far past the road on which the disciple lived.

> The Truth [comes] from God alone; so be not of those who doubt.
>
> *(Qur'an 3:60)*

Many things happened on that day as we drove. It was a remarkably beautiful day: the loveliest day of the autumn. It seemed to roll by us like a film in technicolour. The Shaikh and I laughed together that day, our smiles a toast to the true illusoriness of life. Aside from this there was little talk, but much meaningful silence. As we neared his apartment he asked if the ride had been a waste.

'No, of course not,' I answered.

'*Alhamdulillah* (Praise be to God), for me too it has been very beneficial,' he said.

The Shaikh taught me so much that day in silence. I came to know in my heart something which only my mind had known before and only through books. It has to do with the establishment of sympathy between the Shaikh and the disciple (*murid*).

Prerequisites for this link are *Iman* and *Yaqin*. *Iman* is faith, and *Yaqin* is the disciple's inner certainty and confidence in the Shaikh. The Shaikh's spirit is reflected in his pupil, the *murid*, as is light reflected in the eye, which responds accordingly. The *murid* begins to show forth the teacher, his *Shaikh*, in all he thinks, says or does. The teaching which that day came so clearly, was not a teaching given in words. Inayat Khan has said it well: 'One can only learn this lesson by reaching, grasping, and feeling what the teacher has to convey.' And now I realise still another teaching as the words of my own teacher unfold in my thoughts. He has often said: 'Keep all doors open.'

> Some people before you did ask such questions and on that account lost their faith.
>
> *(Qur'an 5:105)*

Back at the Shaikh's apartment, we sat in silence for a while. We listened to the cassette of his own Qur'anic recitation. Soon thereafter, I left. As usual, I was sent away with prayers. It was especially hard for us to part that day. The Shaikh knew what was in my heart. After I had closed the door, he opened it and came out. We looked at each other. His hand placed over his heart, he paused and bowed, then slowly re-entered his apartment.

I heard the door close as I walked away. Down the hall I stopped to look at it. I wanted to go back, but I could not. Already the list I held in my hand was teaching me. The first thing listed was self-restraint. As I continued on to leave, a familiar fragrance wafted past my nostrils. I knew it signalled another important cycle ending and beginning anew.

Again, Inayat Khan once said: 'The friendship formed in Allah and in truth between the teacher and disciple is for always, and nothing in the world can break it.' I began to know the meaning of these words that day. God willing, I will know more. As I left the Shaikh, I reflected on some of what he had said. I knew that the testing time would come for me. In fact, it had already begun. After the development of sympathy, which grows out of confidence in God, in the teacher and in oneself, the test comes. This test, called by Sufi Masters the Ideal on the Path to God, is sacrifice. When one agrees to take the Path, nothing is too valuable, and no possession is too great to sacrifice — not even one's life.

> Behold! Verily on the friends of God, there is no fear, Nor shall they grieve.
>
> *(Qur'an 10:62)*

A long time passed before I saw the Shaikh again. My calls to him were fruitless. I could not reach him at any hour. Actually, I knew that I could not reach him. Inside myself I can always sense when he can be reached. In these cases, however, I did not attend. Already forgetting the next item on the list — alertness — I fell into my unenlightened compulsive human habits. It is the fight with *nafs lawamma,* the ego in reproach of itself. Nothing seemed to be working in the practical sphere. My car was still in repair, I was still busy in my worldly work, I was still missing the lectures, and keeping my prayers was becoming a struggle. Now, on top of all this, the drains were clogged in both sinks and the bathtub. As I stood looking at the water backed up into my kitchen sink, I realised how very long the drains had been clogged.

During this time I finally reached the Shaikh by telephone only to be told that he could not speak. Having been commanded into silence by his Shaikh he referred me to another disciple. He requested prayers and hung up with words of peace. Such was the state of my plumbing in those days. Though I did not fully realise it then, later I knew this: there is a certain kind of clogging of the drains for which patience is the only plumber.

'What is taking the landlord so long?' I wondered as I stood there in the kitchen bemoaning my circumstance. I searched my mind for a problem: 'He is usually so quick to respond. Why this unresponsiveness? Could it be something I've said? Something I've done? Late perhaps with the rent? Some unexpected expense I might be causing him?'

Thousands of things crossed my mind. Unable to realise what I might have done, I went to him concerned. Respectfully, but flatly, I asked about the drains and the waiting, and whether there was any problem I might be causing. Being the kind man that he was, he leaned close and gently spoke these words: 'There is nothing between us. Actually I have had you in mind, but I have been very busy.'

I walked away overcome with guilt and sadness. The sacrifice I had to make in being without the sink was such a small inconvenience. Reflecting on my relationship with the landlord, I realised how senseless my complaint and concern was. With God My Lord Supreme, it is the same. What have I to complain about?

His bounty, and majesty, and generosity are manifested everywhere. The Shaikh had once told me one of the most important things that anyone can come to know. It was this: 'There is nothing between you and God.' Nothing veils us really, except our own false selves. And so it was that I learned from my landlord — though quite unbeknown to him. God used him, and by his one simple statement he opened so much to me. Though the drains remained clogged for a while, something opened for me. Moreover, I was, through the Grace of my Lord, engaged in a process which taught me the universal actuality of learning. One can come into greater knowledge of oneself, or knowledge of God practically anywhere — even standing at the kitchen sink.

> Fighting is prescribed for you, and ye dislike it. But it is possible that ye dislike a thing which is good for you, and that you love a thing which is bad for you. But God knoweth, and ye know not.
>
> *(Qur'an 2:216)*

The time was approaching for another lecture by the Shaikh. I knew that I had to get there. As I rushed to the meeting place, I considered that I might miss the lecture. It was late, but I was not rushing for the lecture. Yes, that too, if God willed — but it was a glance at my Shaikh for which I rushed. I arrived running. There, outside the door, stood the Shaikh speaking to a man. I immediately noticed two things as I looked at them. The first was that the man was standing very close to the Shaikh and though he spoke into his very ear, he was yet far from the Shaikh. This I knew. The second was the way the Shaikh was dressed. It was unusual for him. He wore a suit coat of the West and an *Ahmediyya,* a type of turbaned fez of the East. It seemed at that time a bold statement of a man between two worlds and, as the saying goes, 'in the world but not of it'.

I approached the Shaikh but stopped until he motioned for me to come closer. Before him, I looked into his face. It was a face so abundantly kind, but tired and pained. He touched my face, grasping my beard, praying as he does. I stood there, my head bowed, holding his arm. In a brief instant, I looked at the other man whom I'd interrupted. Something happened to him in that silent interaction. Glancing into his eyes, I could see that he was moved by the hand which touched me. Though the hand did not touch him, I knew he was touched. The voice of the Shaikh shifted us to another place.

'Go inside,' he said, 'Go downstairs to the rest of them.'

As I entered the building, I heard the Shaikh ask the man to take him home. Inside I watched them walk away, then moved quickly to carry out my instructions.

At the elevator I waited a long time. I could hear voices below, but the elevator was not moving. It came after a while, and the door opened. There inside it was an oriental family — people not from among us. For a moment I was surprised. They were completely surrounded with stuff. Heavy trunk-like boxes and packages filled the elevator. One of the family was a small child who walked out of the elevator and stumbled around. The mother soon took hold of the child as an older son and the father attempted to unload their things. Wondering who they were, I turned away to take the stairs.

At the stairs I was greeted by a friend whom I had sent to hear the Shaikh speak. I was told that the Shaikh had made a very strained delivery and that he had focused on *'Ashq*, which is love, and on pain. He had also told the story of one who travelled miles through hardship and storm to see the beloved, only to arrive and be turned away. Though I was not in the meeting, I understood the meaning of the story. It was a teaching of faith, but more: the teaching of love and pain.

The lover does anything for the beloved. Anything in the way of service, kindness, help or sacrifice. The lover understands the beloved's many moods, and bears them with quiet resignation. The virtues of tolerance, forgiveness, mercy and compassion so often spoken of by the Shaikh can only arise in a heart which is awakened to love.

Again, the Sufi thinker Inayat Khan has said: 'Man has learned from the moment he is born on earth the words "I am" and it is love alone that teaches him to say "Thou art, not I"; for no soul can love and yet affirm its own existence.' This affirmation is epitomised in the first part of the *Kalima* which itself has two parts. The first of these is *La ilaha,* the absolute denial of all other gods. The second is *Ill'Allah,* the absolute affirmation of God, Who is the Source of Love and Love Itself. There is a saying, 'Only the lover knows.' It is hard to accept perhaps, but true: one who has not loved, really knows nothing. It is only love, pure love free of jealousy, prejudice and hatred — this alone raises man to immortality.

Love has another aspect. It is pain. 'Many speak of love, says Inayat Khan again, 'but those who stand the test and bear the pain are few.' There is again, another saying that 'the love that has no pain is no love.' This is also true, for the human heart does not live until it knows pain. It is for this reason that until one has fully lived life, investing with mind, body, and heart, one really has not lived.

Soon the group of disciples appeared, coming up the stairs. Some of them seemed pained and perplexed. They each greeted me as I stood smiling on them. One of them looked into my eyes and said: 'We cannot explain.' They quickly departed, leaving me with two friends who were now standing near. I saw each friend off then walked to my car.

> Muhammad is the Apostle of God; and those who are with him are strong against the Unbelievers [but] compassionate amongst each other.
>
> *(Qur'an 48:29)*

Driving home in the night, a wave of inspiration came. I remembered the family in the elevator. I realised who they were. They were us! Like the drains, the elevator was clogged with stuff which bogged them down. They were from a foreign land, as the Way of God is foreign to a heart without love. Again, like us, they were carrying most what is needed least, and carrying least what is needed most: *Iman* or faith and love. They were the embodiment of the Shaikh's talk to those who had gathered that night. The child represented those of us who are stumbling along, but who have the capacity to love and be receptive. The mother was the representation of the Shaikh responding to the Divine Father and guiding us, the children, taking us by the hand. Now it was all so very clear. I arrived home full of hope. Something else was opened from the list. I sat to write and the story began to flow.

A week later, on the Friday before the holidays of *Eid al Adha*, the landlord unclogged the drains. Looking into the sink, I thought of the Shaikh. He had not been at Friday Prayer (*Jumah*). I thought of him throughout the day. In my heart I felt him on the dawn of a new ascent. I knew the Shaikh was well. The praise is due only to his Lord, your Lord and my Lord. *Alhamdulillah!*

> Follow the inspiration sent unto thee, and be patient and constant till God doth decide: for He is the Best to decide.
>
> *(Qur'an 10:109)*

Two days later I learned from another disciple that the Shaikh had left town on the evening of Friday past. He had taken with him two disciples. They were instructed to visit an art gallery where there is housed a striking painting of the sacrifice of Prophet Abraham, peace be upon him. Secretly I felt a little disappointed that I was not sent with them. Alone in my car I faced this tiny desire. I struggled with myself in the early evening quiet, on the road to home.

> But indeed if any show patience and forgive that would truly be an exercise of will and resolution in the conduct of affairs.
>
> *(Qur'an 42:43)*

That night the telephone rang. To my surprise it was the two disciples, returning from their journey to the art gallery. They were safe, but they were exhausted and needed a place to rest. Their return drive had brought them near my home. They had been so much in my thoughts, it seemed a blessing that Allah would direct them to me. They soon arrived and I welcomed them at the door with *salaams,* the greetings of peace. It was the first time they had come to my home. I was pleased and wanted them to be comfortable in it. I offered them what there was at hand to eat or drink. One disciple accepted only a glass of water, the other had nothing. There is a saying that 'Two Sovereigns cannot live together in the same country, but forty Dervishes can live together in one room.' The thought of this saying was in my mind as I served them. I knew that they did not require much, but on this Path the Resident and the Traveller each has duties, among which are mutual care and consideration.

In the late night hours, the telephone rang. I looked at it with one eye, thinking of whether or not I should pick it up. Answering with *salaams,* I heard them returned in the voice of the wife of one of my guests. Being a disciple, she gave a brief explanation, although she knew it was not needed. The Shaikh had arrived and was with her and some other disciples. Both the travelling disciples spoke on the phone. I heard them describe the painting they had seen. They were speaking to the Shaikh.

Wide awake now, we all sat in the kitchen. The call brought us together in a way that had not happened before. The Shaikh had extended himself into our sleep and brought us to wakefulness. I shared some of my thoughts and feelings with the travellers. I told them how it seemed I was on the periphery of things as I heard about their trip. It was in that late-night conversation that one of them said:

'It sometimes seems that there is the inner and the outer, but on the Path, we know that the Truth is One. So, really, in or out matters little.'

The words were spoken kindly and they were true. Again God should be praised. He, glory be to Him, used my brother disciple to help me see more clearly that *we are one* on the Path, no matter what the seeming differences. Each disciple has his or her own particular work. Each occupies his or her own particular place on the Path. Allah is ever present. The Shaikh knows what is needed. He knows the heart of each of his *murids.* The list was still teaching. It was now the lesson of trust.

> Those who believe, and whose hearts find satisfaction in the remembrance of Allah: For without doubt, in the rememberance of God do hearts find satisfaction.
>
> *(Qur'an 13:28)*

That morning I performed the call to prayer (*azan*). We said the morning prayer and exchanged *Eid* holiday greetings in the wake of dawn. We sat for a while and heard some Qur'an, and then two of us ate a bit of bread. We collected our things after a while and departed for the *Eid* gathering-place. We entered the gathering and gave our *salaams.* We were at once faced with a barrage of questions as to the whereabouts of the Shaikh. One of the two disciples answered these questions. Then we sat to await his arrival.

After some time, the Shaikh arrived with another one of his disciples. He wore a *Sikke,* the tall woollen hat of Dervishes and a long black Dervish robe. He moved with gentle authority and humility. He gave his greetings, acknowledging some by name whom he recognised among those gathered.

The Shaikh opened with a short prayer (*du'a*), recited Qur'an and in the course of the morning gave three talks. The first was a Dervish talk to the *Eid* gathering. It was a powerful talk on love of God and the necessity for cultivating the heart qualities in Muslim life. The second was a special talk (*khutba*) which followed the *Eid* prayer. It dealt with what *Eid* is, as well as the faith and obedience of Prophet Abraham, peace be on him. There was in that talk a powerful warning on the necessity of remaining mindful of permissible *halal* deeds and the day when life will end. Later, after exchanging greetings with those who were present, the Shaikh sat with a small circle of disciples in a corner of the mosque. For all of the talks, the common threads were faith (*Iman*), love, sacrifice, and pain.

In the third talk, the Shaikh continued to speak of the faith of Abraham and his high place among the prophets. He also acknowledged the faith and love of Prophet Abraham's son. He shed tears as he called to mind the event. He spoke the son's words to his father, saying 'tie me carefully' in order that he not accidentally strike him in his agony. Again, the Shaikh brought up the story of the lover travelling through the storm to see the beloved who turned him away. He questioned us again and again, asking what we would do. In fact, he told us to meditate on this question and be ready to speak our answers that night when we'd meet at the Tekiya for the *Eid* holiday dinner.

'Iman (faith), love, sacrifice and pain. It is better to love *haram*, the forbidden and immoral things, than to have absolutely no love in one's heart . . . the wisdom which God did not give us is the knowledge of pain without suffering . . . *'Ashq* (love), where is your *'Ashq!* Keep all doors open . . . The weight of the heavens and earth and all in between is lighter than love . . . Remember the sacrifice of the heart . . . What will you do when the Angel of Death reads your name? . . . When will you start living? Enjoy . . .' So much was said by the Shaikh. Of what was said of love and the lover; of love and pain . . . above all else, Love was the point. In the final analysis, Love is all there is.

Lovers have heartaches which no cure can mend;
Neither sleeping nor faring abroad nor eating,
Only the sight of the beloved.
'Meet the friend and your sickness will end'

MAWLANA RUMI

God has not made for any man two hearts in his one body.

(Qur'an 33:34)

That afternoon, while the Shaikh was not present, three goats were sacrificed in commemoration of Prophet Abraham, Peace be upon him. Standing there I realised what made him so loved by God. Above all else, the extent of his willingness and submission to his Lord were now clearer in my heart. Once one understands how precious life is, it is difficult to take any life. Yet Prophet

Abraham, peace be upon him, was willing to surrender the life of his very own son.

In that sacrifice I realised how we sacrifice the lower for the higher, by the will and command of God. There were so many parallels to life. Each goat was beautiful and each was different. Each was sacrificed none the less. It was another teaching on the illusion of life. It did not matter if they were male or female, nor how different or beautiful. Like each of us will — goats that we are, they each lay there still and quiet. They each met the moment decreed. The words of the Shaikh's talk passed through my mind: 'There will be no distinction in the *qabur*, the grave. The rich, the poor; the Capitalist, the Communist; the Believer, the Unbeliever will all be Muslim: they will all be submitted to God.'

More wonders unfolded as the animals were skinned and prepared for use and charity. Viewing another aspect of God's creation, I felt His true generosity. Even at the time of sacrifice, God stopped the rain and all was quiet. As we were finishing, I stooped near a tree to assist a disciple. A fragrance floated past my nostrils. It was again, the sign of another cycle completed. In my heart I knew that my Shaikh had been there.

Later, when the Shaikh arrived, we sat for dinner. He said that he knew that God had accepted our sacrifice. My mind went back to the fragrance. We ate that day in quiet good cheer. It was a blessed meal. I ate each bite with humility and respect. Again, all the praise is due to God, the Lord and Sustainer of all the Worlds.

> Surely We have given then the fountain of abundance. Therefore turn to thy Lord in Prayer and Sacrifice. Surely those who are not with you are outcast.
>
> *(Qur'an 108:1-3)*

After dinner we gathered together in the Mosque of the Tekiya. True to his word, the Shaikh questioned us about the story of the lover, on which we were to have meditated. Whether to stay or to go, that was the question. There were some who said stay and some who said go. My own answer was the same as what I felt in my heart, when I stood at the top of the stairs nearly two weeks before. The Shaikh made the question more and more involved, more and more complicated. Some wavered. Then came another question in the midst of the dialogue:

'Who is willing to sacrifice their life for God?'

Many hands raised. As I looked around the room, another verse of Mawlana Rumi floated through my mind: 'Few in the numbering, many in the charge.' We know that those who stand the test on this Way are few. We pray that God will have mercy on those of us seeking to know Him. May we be numbered among those who see His Beloved Face.

Very late, towards the end, the Shaikh began to read *Farid ud-Din Attar's* story of Shaikh San'an. Within this story is a precious gem. However, it was not found by many that night. The Shaikh did not complete his reading. He stopped and told us to be tolerant of each other. For me it seemed that he was giving the same teaching another way. Many disciples do not see the wealth of learning to be obtained by observing their relationship with others (particularly other murids). It is another place for learning the lessons of love and tolerance, sacrifice, growth, and realisation. We often focus so strongly on the Shaikh that we do not see him. We listen so closely we miss his point. For me, the point is Love. And as a novice on this way, it seems that what I am learning most is how to love truly.

That night I drove the Shaikh home. We dropped a disciple off along the way and continued on. There was little talk. We travelled some of the same roads we had travelled when we last rode together. I delivered him to his apartment. As he walked to the door, I watched him. I quietly reviewed my life since knowing him. My heart repeated the words he had spoken on nearing the end of our previous car journey: 'It has been very beneficial.' On reaching the door, he unlocked it, bowed towards my car, then stepped out of view.

Thus goes the story of the Drains. The Drains of the Path along which there are cycles of flowing and clogging. The faucet symbolises the Fountainhead, Allah Himself. From the Fountainhead comes water: the Love and Forgiveness of God. The drains finally empty at the Ocean which is the Source. At the Source, the Ocean and drop are One. The flowing represents the Mercy of God. The clogging: *Fitna,* the trials and tests of life. Both of them are from Allah. In order to travel the Drains, one needs these things: *Iman* (faith), *Yaqin,* (certainty), self-restraint, alertness, hope, trust, and continuing hard work — *'Amal.* Especially one needs love. One must also remember that there is a certain type of clogging of the Drains — as we earlier mentioned, for which Patience (*Sabr*) is the only plumber. May God have mercy on us.

THE WRITING ON THE WATER

O thou Man! Verily thou art ever toiling on towards thy Lord — painfully toiling but thou shalt meet Him.

(Qur'an 84:6)

CHAPTER 3

BEYOND THE DRAINS

When I had last seen the Shaikh, on the night of the *Eid-ul Adha* feast, I mentioned to him that the story of 'The Drains' was in progress. His suggestion that I complete it launched me into a period of writing night and day. When I had finally finished the story I wanted to get it into his hands at once. I decided to call him. He answered the phone quickly and gave me the greeting, '*Assalaamu alaikum* (Peace be upon you).'

'*Wa alaikum salaam* (And upon you be peace),' I replied.

'I must tell you', he said gently but directly, 'that I cannot speak to you except on Thursdays — you do understand?'

'Yes I do,' I said. I understood that he was genuinely busy. He worked in the world as I did, but in a job which made greater demands on his time than my own did on me. I didn't want to intrude on him, but at the very same time I did want to see him and I didn't want to wait. He ended without speaking further. The next second I stood listening to the dial tone, attempting to digest his message, to accept it and be patient. Thursday was only a few days away.

On Thursday morning I telephoned him again. He answered and we exchanged greetings. He asked me how I was spending my time alone, and I told him about my job, my writings and the trivia of my daily affairs.

'What is it that you *truly* look forward to in life?' he calmly asked.

'*Fana' billah,* to be fully absorbed in God,' I replied, taking his question to the absolute.

'Actually', he said, 'it is too much to expect today.'

We went on in that conversation to discuss several things related to my life at the time and my general spiritual growth. Finally, I was able to mention that I had completed the story of 'The Drains' and that I would like to see him.

'It is not possible this morning,' he said, 'but perhaps tonight, God willing.'

It just so happened that my Thursday evenings were regularly committed and had been for quite some time. He told me that he might see me after my commitment but that I should call before coming. That night my scheduled meeting ended earlier than I had expected so I rushed to call the Shaikh. One of his disciples answered the phone and instructed me to give my completed story to another disciple who would deliver it to the Shaikh. Nothing more was said beyond the *salaams,* and again I found myself standing speechless, mortally wounded, and listening to the dial-tone.

Oh fool! Is the door shut?

(Hazreti Rabia)

The Story of the Bird

I was on my way to *Jumah,* the Friday prayer. Driving along reviewing the events of the week, I turned my car onto a narrow little street which I usually took for a short-cut. There was a car ahead of me speeding along and I noticed that the driver had struck a bird which had flown near its wheels. I was far enough behind to notice the bird fluttering in the road after the car had passed. It was nearly time for *Jumah* to begin and I was undecided about stopping. Not listening to myself, I drove on, passing the bird which lay there fluttering. As soon as I passed it, I knew that I had to go back. I turned around and drove up the hill to the top of the narrow little street. The bird was still there. I parked the car and began to walk towards it. I noticed that another bird had come to stand by its ailing friend and as I came closer it flew to a nearby tree. Perplexed by the strangeness of the events of the day, I stood before the bird attempting to understand the meaning of all that seemed to be happening in the moment. There was complete silence in those seconds, save for a quiet whisper of the wind and an onlooking dog who began to bark. The bird which had flown to the tree also continued to watch. The barking grew louder and the dog seemed to say:

'What are you standing there for? Take the bird out of the road and be done with it!'

I picked up the wounded bird and put it at the base of the tree on a pile of soft leaves. I felt a great deal better for having gone back but my quandary persisted none the less.

The talk (*khutba*) was just ending as I entered the gathering. I wondered if my own was to be taken from the incident with the bird. Was there a connection? Somehow, for me, everything seemed to be interrelated. I turned all the bits and pieces around in my mind. I reflected back on my attempts to see the Shaikh, the telephone conversations, the feelings which came up inside when I was not able to see him, and especially the bird.

> Has there not been over man a long period of time when he was nothing [not even] mentioned?
>
> *(Qur'an 76:1)*

On Saturday I happened to see my landlord. He matter-of-factly queried, almost immediately on my approach:

'How are your drains?'

His simple question shocked me into a stunning awareness. Perhaps it was that the drains were clogging again. Could it be that I might have to call on the plumber again? I knew that while I waited there was much work which I needed to do and something apparently different could be felt in the air.

Just a few days after I had last seen my landlord, the incident with the bird had begun to come clear. I picked up Fariduddin Attar's book, *The Conference of the Birds*, which the Shaikh had suggested that all disciples should read. I came upon the story of the speech of the second bird who was complaining of the difficulty of the road and the journey to the Simurgh. Of the many things he was told as he stood with 'doleful countenance', and feeling 'oppressed at heart', the following statement of the Hoopooe guide bird struck a note in my own heart: 'It is better to lose your life in the quest than to languish miserably.' The ailing bird in the road was actually me. Part of the teaching was simply this: It is better to die on the road of spiritual quest than on the road of pursuit of the world. Part of the journey may even bring us to a kind of death which was also part of the statement to the bird in the story of Shaikh Attar:

'So long as we do not die to ourselves, and so long as we are identified with someone or something, we shall never be free. The spiritual way is not for those wrapped up in exterior life.'

> Until you seek you cannot find — that's true save of the Lover: You cannot seek Him being blind, until you shall discover.
>
> *(Mawlana Rumi)*

When I had finished recording my experiences with 'The Drains', I thought I had also completed the learning of its teaching. The fact was, however, that the teaching had only begun. The general difficulties that I had in seeing the Shaikh brought up all of the old feelings which I thought I had resolved when I had been out of contact before. When the next Thursday came I tried to reach him again but his line was busy. I tried several times but I never got through. Each time that I was obliged to listen to a dialling tone or engaged tone brought with it a tremendous teaching. Left alone with whatever feelings came up in these moments, I came face to face with myself. Every time I tried to reach the Shaikh I found that I received a teaching whether I was able to reach him or not.

One day during this period of struggle, I was driving to work. It was a very cold day and the snow was just beginning to fall. I had driven half-way to my destination, which was several miles. I turned on my left indicator as I approached an intersection on the way. I noticed that the snowfall was getting quite heavy so I turned on my windscreen wipers. The wiper on my side of the car failed to work, but I continued on into the intersection in order to complete the turn. Half-way into the turn I came onto a very large and slippery spot where the car went out of my control and spun completely around. When it came out of the spin, it was pointed in the direction opposite to which I had been travelling. Partly stunned and partly surprised, I sat watching the traffic moving directly towards me. By God's grace the cars passed me on either side and I escaped without harm. I drove into a nearby service station to repair the disabled wiper. Not even looking at it, the man told me that it could not be done. I tried another station and received the same treatment and diagnosis. Finally, I let the message in:

'You are safe now. Turn around and go home.'

Immediately, I drove home and by the time I arrived, the first light snowfall had become a full-fledged storm. Safe at home I thanked God as I casually sat down on the radiator to warm myself and review the events of the day. The very fact that the storm had now arrived was very thought-provoking. The Shaikh had told stories with teachings involved with storms in each of the last two or three discourses I had heard. There was another snow-storm forecast by the weather bureau which was supposed to arrive on Thursday of the week to come. I meditated on the story of the lover who travelled in a storm warmed only by the hope of seeing his beloved. Somehow in the process of my continued contemplation, the incident with the injured bird evolved into a bigger and still bigger teaching. When I looked at the *Conference of the Birds* in the broader perspective, I realised that it was the story of the pilgrimage of several birds who faced one hardship after another on the way to the Simurgh, their Glorious King. If there was any lesson at all in this story which was relevant for my own life, it was this: I could prepare myself for many stormy days ahead, as I made my Journey to God Most High.

Thursday came again and once more in half desperation, I tried to reach the Shaikh. The telephone line was busy and it stayed busy. I could not reach him. Another Thursday passed with no word from him nor of the storm which had been predicted for that day. In fact this day for which the entire city had anticipated having a storm, turned out to be the day of the great 'non-blizzard' which was actually the calm before the storm. The Shaikh was not at Friday prayer the following day. I gave the *khutba* (talk) in his absence and returned to my apartment. Standing at the window I looked into the snowy street and realised that my drains were clogged again. The drains leading from my kitchen sink were working fine but the drains of the Path were clogged. I finally accepted that I would be out of touch with the Shaikh for a while. I truly let the message in and readied my heart for the next stage of struggle.

On the Thursday after the non-blizzard I spoke to the Shaikh. Interestingly enough, the subject of storms came up in our conversation, whereupon he said: 'The storm is for us the safest place to be. Only the cowards are afraid, for the only peace is in the storm. It is those sitting before their televisions in the warmth of their homes who truly are in danger. The peace of home is the illusion of Satan — homes where we are never really at home.'

After we had spoken briefly, he left me to ponder his statement, and ponder it I did. The storm began that night and it continued through the next several days. On Friday of the storm week I received a phone-call from one of the dervishes and his wife who invited my wife and me to their home for dinner. The Shaikh would be there. The storm was at its height but of course, we accepted the invitation and quickly made preparations to go. As we started out, the winds were generally calm, but as we drove further along they grew increasingly turbulent. The radio had said that the roads we were using were closed but when we set out that evening they were the clearest ones. Suddenly, however, we found ourselves in the very heart of the storm. Visibility was practically zero. I asked my wife to look out of her window to guide me away from the edge of the shoulder of the road. She could hardly see as gusts of wind and snow were blowing through the window into her face. We crept along hoping to make it to the main road about a quarter of a mile ahead. Nearly there the visibility grew worse and we slowed to a stop to wait. Faintly, I heard a voice:

'Help! Help! I'm here, help!'

I rolled down my window and looked out. The voice came again:

'I'm here — over here! Can you give me a hand? My car's completely stuck!'

As I looked more closely the figure of a snow-covered car came dimly into view. Its engine was running and its driver spoke to me through a slightly open window. I got out of my car and made my way to him in the darkness and driving wind. I attempted to push his car but had no success. I asked my wife to sit at the wheel while the stranger and I pushed together, but we were still unable to move his car. The storm continued to rage and we soon became so cold that we could not stand outside any longer. We suggested that he leave his car and come with us. Inside our car he told us how he had given up the thought of anyone arriving in the storm to give him help. He had wrapped himself in a blanket and settled down to wait for the storm to subside. He talked about his family and particularly about his young daughter who was to have an operation the following day. On the way I passed another motorist in distress, an elderly lady whose car had stalled. I told her that I'd return to assist her. I delivered the stranger and my wife to the home of the dervish and returned to help the stranded lady. I was able to get her car started without great difficulty and soon I was back at the home of my friend.

I entered the living room, where I found the Shaikh with the dervish, the stranger, and several disciples gathered about him in a circle. He wore a hooded robe and Dervish hat and sat in dignified simplicity. It was good to see him. I gave my *salaams*, whereupon he returned them and motioned that I come before him. Speaking what seemed an inaudible prayer, he touched my beard with his usual warmth and kindness. I took a seat with the others and settled into the atmosphere. It was only a moment later it seems when the call came for dinner and everyone moved into the next room. We took seats on the floor on cushions and a simple meal of rice pilaf and lamb was served. Everyone seemed content except for the stranger, whose name we learned was Richard, who now sat quietly on a couple of cushions. Even though there was nothing negative in the feeling of the room, and certainly no strange and secret practices, Richard seemed to wonder about us. The Shaikh sensed his feeling and lightheartedly asked if he was comfortable.

'It's better than sitting on top of a snowbank,' he seriously replied, causing the Shaikh to smile and laugh a warm and hearty laugh. It caused the others of us to laugh with him and in that moment we were all together. Richard feeling a little more at ease later asked his only question:

'What kind of group is this?'

'We are just friends,' replied the Shaikh.

The Shaikh had a very disarming way of interacting with those whom he met. He was very natural and warm with a surprisingly good sense of humour. He and Richard chatted. As they did, I found myself amused at how Richard had unknowingly found his way into our circle. Many search and never find, yet what is sought is close and in reach. Richard made some phone-calls, arranged for a breakdown van and was delivered back to his car by the dervish who hosted us. While they were out, we reconvened in the room where everyone had been together when I had entered. The Shaikh addressed me enthusiastically, as we settled down into the circle:

'I have read your tractate. It is a miracle that you have chosen that sonnet of Shakespeare. Can you tell us that sonnet?'

Nodding, I began to recite:

When in disgrace with Fortune and men's eyes,
I all alone beweep my outcast state and . . .

I continued with the poem, alternately reciting lines with the Shaikh. Near the end of the sonnet, I forgot three of the most important lines. They were:

Haply I think on thee, and then my state,
Like to the lark at the break of day arising
From sullen earth, sings hymns at heaven's gate.

Somewhere in this process the Shaikh asked the dervish if he had a book in which the sonnet might be found. Whatever book was brought did not satisfy the particular request. He then asked if I had a copy of 'The Drains' with me. I said that I did and he asked me to read the story to those present. When early in the reading I came to the place where I had included a few lines of sonnet, the Shaikh asked that I read it twice. He told me that this sonnet was one of his favourites and that when he read it in the story, it had come at a very important moment for him. He then recited slowly and with great feeling the concluding lines which touched him most and which for us contained the teaching:

. . . and then my state
Like to the lark at the break of day arising
From sullen earth, sings hymns at heaven's gate;
For thy sweet love remember'd such wealth brings
That then I scorn to change my state with kings.

Pausing for a moment, he sat with eyes closed, then said to us that Shakespeare was very important. He then said to me:

'There is a little green book; its title is *Thy Sweet Love Remembered.* Find that book.'

He then asked me to continue reading. I read the story in its entirety. I am sure that I have not fully realised what I was to learn by this direction. When I had completed the earlier story of 'The Needle', he had sent me to several of his disciples to present myself and read it aloud. I am sure now that there was meaning in every direction which he has ever given me. At those times when my writing was involved, there were things I had touched which he knew were meaningful to others, but of which I myself was unaware. What became increasingly clear, however, was that I would be doing more and more writing and presenting it to others.

That evening after my reading, the Shaikh talked. Of the many things he told us, I remember that he gave a brief discourse on Nimrod and the Prophet Abraham, peace be upon him. Nimrod was the personification of the enemy of God. In his ignorance and his arrogance, he persecuted Hazreti Abraham, peace be upon him, who was referred to by God Himself as Khalilullah, the

Friend of God. It was Nimrod who commanded that Prophet Abraham be thrown into the fire, which by God's command became cool for him. It was Nimrod who raised the tower of Babel and who also failed in this attempt for direct confrontation with God Almighty. Again, it was he who finally waged war against Prophet Abraham, peace be upon him, and he whose army failed, being divided by God and overwhelmed by swarms of gnats. It was only a single one of these gnats which entered Nimrod's nostril, eventually causing him to die.

This discourse was tied to a practical story of a woman gone astray from God. The story of Nimrod and the context in which it was told actually being a direction to see that whether in the past or present, God, may he be exalted, is capable of teaching the greatest lessons, even by one of His smallest creatures. The story showed, moreover, that God Almighty, glory be to him, is in truth the Lord over those who in their arrogance, attempt with futility to be the lords of all. It was a discourse which taught enduring trust and reliance on God when thrown into life's fire. It was a teaching on how to survive.

I drove the Shaikh to his apartment that night. We talked only briefly and then he went off into meditation. I delivered him to his doorstep, whereupon he looked at me and said: 'Keep all things in the balance.' He gave me his *salaams* and in a moment, he was gone. Something in that evening had been very beautiful and each one of us who were there shared in this unspoken feeling. Much later, nearly two years after we had been there, the Shaikh referred to that night and how the time had been for him:

'It was for me', he said, 'like a star in the night.' This night was for me a slight preview of the feeling of love and sharing which exists in the family of *fuqara*, those who are poor, but rich in God.

It was a very long time before I was alone with the Shaikh again. Suddenly thrust into a period of weeks where it seemed that I was entirely cut off, I neither saw him, nor received any phone-calls or instructions. Everything fell into silence as I waited out the days and reflected on my state.

> By the glorious morning light and by the night when it is still, thy Lord hath not forsaken thee nor is He displeased.
>
> *(Qur'an 95:1)*

In the early times of my interaction with the Shaikh, I found that most often when I was out of touch with him I was left with some task to perform. During this particular time, one of the things I worked on was finding the little green book. My first effort took me to the city library. I searched the card catalogue and checked the guide to books in print only to find the book unlisted and unknown. Speaking to the librarian, I asked if he knew of the book. I told him that a friend had suggested the book and encouraged me to find it. The librarian looked at me with a smile, repeating my words as though he were Sherlock Holmes:

'You were asked by a friend? Hmmm, perhaps if he were to call, we could solve this mystery.'

'Indeed we could,' I thought, as I thanked the man and turned to walk away. Suddenly I realised that I was not as cut off as it seemed. Across the seeming silence the Shaikh was in quiet, uncalculated brilliance generating activity inside of me in a way that only a Shaikh can do.

My next attempt to find the book took me to a local bookshop where I enquired about it. The assistant who was a pleasant young lady, did not know the book either but suggested I try the books in print catalogue listed by authors. Checking the works of Shakespeare, I found that his writings were voluminous. It was a *déjà vu* experience, something akin to what I had felt in standing before the case of needles in the record store, searching for a needle without any clue. Flipping through literally page after page of Shakespeare's literary achievements, yet not finding the book, I smiled at this process of the developing disciple which I was apparently caught up in. The voice of the assistant interrupted my musing:

'I have an idea,' she said. 'We can run a search for the book through a service we have. If we can locate a private owner who is willing to sell the book, we may obtain it that way and soon you'll have it in your hands.' I agreed, and after setting the locator service into action with the assistant's help, I quietly left the store.

The next several days found me living in a cloud of smoke. Everything seemed dull and routine. Going to work was a bore, the sky was grey and the sameness of the days sent me reeling into near-depression. I awakened one morning for *Salatul Fajr*, the morning prayer, to find my television fiercely glaring in my face. Strangely in this pre-dawn hour there was a children's television show being broadcast. In this particular programme, there was a young boy dressed as a tin man repetitively singing the following song:

I'm a mechanical boy,
like a mechanical toy.
I do what I'm ordered and never ask why,
I never have lived so I never can die . . .

Indeed this broadcast was an existential statement of the moment. It was so timely that it pierced through my sombre sleepiness. I walked to the bathroom amused as I pondered this strange opening of the day. The lines: 'I never have lived so I never can die' stayed with me. It seems, however, that what is truer for those on the Path of God, is to realise and acknowledge one's utter mechanicalness and die in order to live. This is the death before death, to stuff and to the senses, in order to come alive in God.

I passed several more days in my state of in-betweens and waiting, then early one Saturday morning my telephone rang. I answered to hear the enthusiastic and encouraging voice of the Shaikh:

'Salaamu alaikum.'

'Wa alaikum salaam,' I answered, half surprised that he was calling me. 'How are you?'

'Alhamdulillah (the Praise belongs to God) he replied, quickly going on. 'Brother, your time has come. You have passed the test of patience. You did very well and my own Shaikh and I am pleased. When can I see you?'

The following morning I went to the Shaikh's apartment. As I drove along, I surveyed my inner state for by now I had come to see that there was an interesting and seemingly obtuse relationship between my own inward condition and the difficulty or ease I had when coming into the presence of the Shaikh. He lived in an apartment with a buzz-in entrance. Occasionally the outside door was open and the inner door was closed. Waiting at the door of the Shaikh was a basic teaching which clearly showed me my own culturally shaped and absurd expectation that any door I approached will open, regardless of how unconscious I am when I knock. God knows that the Shaikh had no need of any special acknowledgement or regard. It was not that he expected this, rather it was something personal for me: the simple act of just standing at his door waiting for it to open taught me much about myself.

He opened the door quickly that day and welcomed me with his usual warmth and blessings. He offered me a cushion as I took a seat before him where he sat on the floor. He began to tell me the story of an old woman who was very ill and poor who had befriended him in kindness, sharing with him her few possessions. Of this story which he shared with me with great depth of feeling, I remember most his concluding words: 'She gave all she had and I gave all too.' The Shaikh sensed my inward doubt and spoke to me with surprising directness: 'You are on the Path but you are only at the beginning.' Then expressing my lack of certainty, I told him how little I thought I deserved what came to me and he said in calm matter-of-factness: 'No one can really deserve the *baraka* (blessing) of God.'

That day I was led through another door. About this door, I can only say that Allah is the Best of Knowers and all praise and appreciation belongs to Him. The story of the old woman is, however, a direction for the seeker: Give all to the seeking if you would be sought.

> Your eyes will not always be shut; seek the door.
>
> *Shaikh Attar*

Later that morning I drove the Shaikh to the home of a dervish. It was a crisp and quiet day on the very edge of the transition between the fading winter and anticipated spring. As the car sped along through the countryside, the Shaikh spoke to me with a brotherly warmth and loving kindness which struck at the very depths of my heart.

'You can tell me whatever troubles you, and you will always have a place with me. If you came to me with bloody hands, I would take you in and give you shelter.'

After a brief period of silence, he turned his attention to some thoughts which he had about the story of The Drains:

'Your story was about the test of patience and you must remember now the seriousness of clogging. Know, however, that there is the type of clogging which can be fatal. Once the dirty pipes have been cleaned and you see the pipes begin to clog again, you must be very careful. Watch the grease and hair which may get into the drain . . . there is a point beyond which there is no return, like the season of the Fall and the point beyond which there is certainty of winter. It is a clogging much like the point in the rapids rushing towards the falls beyond which the person can swim neither right nor left.'

During this talk, the Shaikh told the story of a young woman caught in the clogging of desires to the point of no return.

Hers is the story of those who know of the dangers of the clogging, but who are careless none the less. Like one who lets the drains fill up with grease and hair — they continue getting all they can of both their desires and the world (*dunya*) with no consideration of the risk.

This story was clearly a story of warning, for the Shaikh had said often that 'What one wants, one gets. One can in fact do whatever one wants, but not for as long as one wants.'

It is a warning against the entrapments of the pursuit of possessions and personal desires beyond bounds. There is a point in life beyond which one experiences no restraint and where one may feel free to pursue one's desires, even beyond bounds. The Seeker's reality, however, extends from this life, which is *dunya*, to what comes after: the *akhirat*. Beyond this life there is no return and yet whatever went into the drains will affect one's final state of clogging on the other side of life or one's final state of flowing and joy.

In the very practical sense, the Shaikh seemed to be pointing to a special balance between when to be patient and when to act. Even though I had experienced a teaching of patience, he showed me that there is a point where patience and waiting is not the only teaching. Rather, the Seeker's work is to be conscious in approaching every circumstance of life. After leaving the Shaikh that day, nearly six weeks passed before I was alone with him again. Life continued to bring its mundane trials and all of my early learnings were put to the test. There were long series of days where everything was difficult. During this time I awakened one morning with the vision of a smooth sailing ship imprinted on my consciousness. I stumbled to the bathroom sink to perform my morning ablutions and, for no reason, I flipped on the radio which sat on the nearby window-sill. A song was playing and its lyrics were as follows:

There's a land so far away
Where ageless children play
And everything is real
In this land of make believe
You can hear a song on high
Or watch the wind dance cross the sky
As the ship begins to sail away across
The Magic Sea
The journey is taking place – today.

Oh Captain, my captain
There's so much to be known
But I have this feeling deep inside
That I'm on my way home.

The song was for me, broadcast in that moment in space and time as a message of encouragement and hope. The journey is always taking place now. Today. The journey is not easy. The path of being a murid is one which the Shaikh described as 'constantly bringing new challenges. When to wait, when to initiate. How to listen and how to serve.'

Later that day I went to the bookshop where I had begun the search for the book. I didn't expect good news, but the assistant greeted me with a smile as I came through the door and said, 'The book just arrived today: *Thy Sweet Love Remembered.*'

CHAPTER 4

THE PLANT

One day very late in the autumn of the year in which I had just met my Shaikh, I passed by the window of a small plant shop. I was to see him that evening and for some reason I had awakened that morning noticing that an urge to bring him something as a gift had sprung up from within. I sorted through the possibilities while performing the routine affairs of the day. Glancing into the shop window as I made my way along, I happened to notice a small and very beautiful vine-like plant. Set in a small, white ceramic planter, its sturdy green leaves displayed a shape and feeling so delicate and so interesting that I was compelled to choose it. It was ideal. I delivered it to the Shaikh, who smiled warmly, and graciously expressed his praises to God together with his kind appreciation for my thoughtfulness. The entire winter passed with no mention of the plant until one evening after his talk on Qur'an, the Shaikh called me to him. As I stopped before him, he calmly looked into my face and said:

'Your plant is dying, when can you come to see it?'

Suddenly, I was horrified. I wanted to come right away but it was not possible to be alone with him that night. Several other disciples were in his company and gathered at his apartment. I did, however, have the opportunity to be with them and to see the plant which by now had been transplanted into a larger planter by the Shaikh. It had withered to a point of near unrecognisability. My heart continued to sink as I speculated on what this development symbolised of my own inner state.

'You are the *sahib* of the plant even though you have given it to me,' said the Shaikh, now speaking directly to me as we all filed out of his apartment.

This was to say that I remained the owner and friend of the plant even though I had given it to him. This was true for all of those disciples whose plants were companions to my own in the Shaikh's apartment window. As we stood on the threshold making our exit, the Shaikh told a story. There was in this tale of teaching a bear and a man who were constant companions. The man casually glanced at the bear and said:

'You know something?'

'What?' asked the bear.

'You stink,' replied the man with dumbfounding bluntness.

'I have a cure,' said the bear in a voice of surprising calmness. 'Take this axe and hit me on the head.'

'I couldn't do that,' said the man, now feeling slightly guilty and growing nervous.

'You must or I will kill you,' said the bear with unexpected force and a glance of sobering intensity.

With much fear and little thought, the man arrived at the crossroads of the moment. He took the axe to the bear's head and dealt forth a crippling blow. Hurt, but not fallen, the bear spoke to the man with tears blurring his eyes: 'I will meet you here a year from now.'

Sure enough, a year later the man met the bear. Joyous to see that he had recuperated, the man examined the head of the bear and excitedly exclaimed; 'Its healed, its healed!'

The bear looked at the man, interrupting his clamour:

'It is true my head has healed,' he said, 'but your words still hurt.'

Bringing us to the moral, the Shaikh told us that words always go somewhere; they do not vanish into space. Sometimes thoughts as well, do not vanish. 'It was your thoughts which affected the plant,' he said looking directly at me. 'It is good that it was the plant and not your wife or sister.' He then turned to the group, gave his *salaams* and closed his door.

I arrived home that night in a state of confusion, feeling fully absorbed and stupefied by the issue of the plant. I travelled out of town on the weekend to attend a conference, and even while there, I was fully distracted by a haunting feeling which persisted until finally I decided to phone the Shaikh long-distance. Though no solution came from our conversation, I took comfort in the fact that he was available to me and that he told me that I could see him upon my return. The following Monday evening I saw the plant again at the Shaikh's apartment. He asked me what I thought of its condition and what should be done with it. I really did not know. We left his apartment and walked together in the quiet of the night. We spoke of many things in that time together. As related to the plant, I remember that he said that my being confused about the plant was like my being confused about the Needle. He also assured me that there was no need to worry. He told me of his own struggles as a *murid* (disciple) and how he had even thought of turning away from the Path. Just before I left him, he smiled and said:

'I encourage you to sleep on it. All the steps are measured and the answer will come when it is time.'

After a few more days of reflection, I called the Shaikh again and he spoke to me at length. Not truly understanding what my task was in this peculiar teaching of the plant, I asked him quite directly what its implications were related to my own personal-spiritual state. 'The way of direct question is not our way,' he said, 'For it is a way of messages all written between the lines.'

He gave a comparison of two poets each relating to a flower. One of these poets, the poet Tennyson, walked along and seeing a flower, plucked it in order to experience its fragrance and beauty. The other, the Japanese poet Kobo, saw a flower in a field but did not touch it. He saw it and that was enough. The Shaikh also mentioned that I should read the poem of Sir Thomas Moore entitled 'The Last Rose of Summer' which was written at or near the time he was to be beheaded by the King. He told me as well to understand that the plant is a reflection of the *dunya*, the present illusory world.

'This is a difficult task,' he emphasised. 'The issue of the plant is not one for the weak.'

During the next several days, I reflected on the story of the two poets. Over and over, I reviewed my conversation with the Shaikh. After a week's meditation, I thought that at last I had an insight. Speaking excitedly to the Shaikh by telephone, he cautioned me to be sure. 'Take some time, ' he said, 'Review your life, then come to see me.'

A few hours later I arrived at the door of his apartment. I brought with me several pages of notes related to my efforts to make sense of the plant. I still lacked clarity, however, on the heart of the teaching, and in my doubting I felt quite nervous. I said *zikr* (remembrances of God) as I walked towards the door. The Shaikh greeted me with warm salaams and invited me to enter. After sitting together for a while in silence, he served me a simple platter of food which he had prepared, then asked me to read my notes to him. I had also a copy of Moore's poem, which I read later after the notes. The Shaikh asked me to say what it was that I understood by the teaching of the plant and the poem by Moore. At that time I thought that the primary teaching was about the nature of attachment. I had thought about the feeling of loss which had welled up in me when the Shaikh had told me that the plant was dying.

This experience seemed to be pointing up the basic struggle of the seeker against '*dunya*-orientated' existence. *Dunya* or this world is like a plant which blossoms in flowers of materiality and stuff — of cars, clothes, house, money, reputation, idea and possession. What the Shaikh meant in saying that the plant was a reflection of the *dunya* was now apparent: *dunya* blossoms and dies, just like the plant. Those who are 'of the *dunya*', live in it, deriving all of their happiness from *dunya*-blossoms, attaching themselves and proceeding in life as if their flowers of *dunya* will never die. The Shaikh had said to me earlier that he was glad that the plant was not my wife or sister, since I had reacted to his news of the plant as though I did not understand that it could die — nay, that indeed it was dying. Had I expected a wife or sister not to die in the way that I did the plant, how much more painful would be the letting go of them, more close and more loved than the little plant to which I found myself so extremely and unknowingly attached.

> Oh silence, thou art an inestimable bliss,
> thou coverest the follies of the foolish
> and givest inspiration to the wise!
>
> *(A Persian Saying)*

When I completed my reading, the Shaikh looked at me and said: 'The plant must be solved before the writing of the story.' Immediately, I felt an ache in my heart and I wished I had not spoken. Somewhere deep inside I knew that his words were true, but hearing them was so very painful. I wanted to be done with the teaching of the plant. I wanted to think that I had found an answer but it was still there before me unsolved. The Shaikh moved across the room, picked up the plant and sat it before me. Suddenly, everything was churning inside.

'Let us look at this plant,' said the Shaikh. 'It was once a source of *mu'jizah* (miracle), for once it was green and in the very middle of winter it was shooting forth beautiful blossoms. Now it is spring and much of the plant is dying. I took great care with it. I have put it into a larger pot to give it room to grow. I gave it fertiliser, water, freedom from frost, and proper light, yet it withered and now its stem is dry. When you see the blossoms, you know the end is near. It is interesting that there are new green sprouts, the stem is dry and yet one seed put into proper soil will bloom. But which seed is it which will not bring up life? What shall we do with this plant?' he asked me again. 'You must go to the level of the plant. What good is it to throw a million dollars into Niagara Falls then lament it all through life? Shall we burn it? *Can you* burn it?'

I was silent and overwhelmingly electrified by all that was being said. I tried to take it all in as the Shaikh continued.

'Only God puts life into the Fire. What shall we do?' he asked again.

I still did not know. With startling suddenness he picked the plant up and quickly removed it from the pot.

'What must be done is to get to the roots. Sometimes that is all that can be done. Come with me.'

We moved to the sink where we removed the soil from the roots under water. It was already apparent from the condition of the roots that the plant was in a very deteriorated state. Slowly things began to fall into place as I saw how easily I had overlooked the obvious.

'When you are transplanting the plant, leave some of the old soil,' said the Shaikh, 'and don't break the roots, but know that too much water, and soil which is too rich, kills the plant. Both *'ashq* and *'ibadat* are necessary. *'Ibadat*, which is service or worship, is the nourishment to the roots. It is the water, food or fertiliser to the soil. *'Ashq*, which is love, is as the air and sunshine. The mother in caring for the child must provide it with love, but love alone is not enough. The child must be nourished.'

> Those who are near to thy Lord, disdain not to do Him worship:
> They celebrate His praises and bow down before Him.
>
> *(Qur'an 7:206)*

That evening as the Shaikh opened my understanding of the fading plant, I remember him once touching its withering roots. 'These', he said, 'are just like the seventy-two sects of Islam.' He referred to a tradition of the Prophet, peace be upon him, in which he reported that in the last days Islam would branch into seventy-two sects and only one of these would be following the right way. Later, as I reflected on the Shaikh's observation, the analogy became even more clear. The seventy-two sects, like the withering roots are those which were not given balanced care. Even though they had relationship with that which is true, somehow in their development, some important things of faith became over-emphasised to the extent that other things were under-emphasised or in some cases, completely excluded. In the final analysis, the only blossom to survive will be the one with its roots in the *sunnah*, the pattern of the Prophet, peace be upon him.

The poem by Moore which I had recited for the Shaikh was a very important part of the teaching of the plant. He recited it to me in one of our earlier conversations on the phone. When I read to him in his apartment, he recited the verses from his heart as I read from the page:

'Tis the last rose of summer,
Left blooming alone;
All her lovely companions
Are faded and gone;
No flower of her kindred,
No rosebud is nigh,
To reflect back her blushes,
Or give sigh for sigh!

I'll not leave thee, thou lone one!
To pine on the stem;
Since the lovely are sleeping,
Go, sleep thou with them.
Thus kindly I scatter
Thy leaves o'er the bed,
Where thy mates of the garden
Lie scentless and dead.

So soon may I follow,
When friendships decay,
And from Love's shining circle
The gems drop away!
When true hearts lie withered,
And fond ones are flown,
Oh! who would inhabit
This bleak world alone?

In truth, at that time I had understood very little of Moore's poem as it relates to the plant. Much later, however, after I reflected back on what the Shaikh had said, things began to fall into place and my insight began to expand.

That evening the Shaikh put the withering plant into a small paper bag together with a package of potting soil which I took with me when I left his apartment. As we concluded a discussion of Moore's poem he said to me:

'Put yourself in the place of Moore, and remember that there are few roses left. Also remember that the Prophet, peace be upon him, said, "Seek the company of the good." Also know that in the case of Moore, it is the hands of the wind which scatter the leaves.'

Before I left the Shaikh, he gave me a few words of caution related to my worldly concerns. He then assured me of his assistance in all developments of my life and said to me with a smile: 'Follow your heart, it will never whisper *haram* (the forbidden or false) to you. What you do for God, that should always be primary. Remember that with God you are everything and without Him you are nothing. Remember that without him you are less than the dust of the earth.'

Before showing me out with the words 'Go with the peace of God,' he recited to me the following lines from *Sura Iqraa,*

Iqra bismi Rabbika, alladhi khalaqq
khalaqal insana min 'alaqq
Iqra wa rabbukal adramul-ladhi
'Allamabil qalam.

Proclaim in the name of thy Lord and Cherisher,
Who created —
Created man, out of a [mere] *clot of congealed blood.*
Proclaim and thy Lord is most bountiful —
He Who taught [*the use of*] *the Pen.*

After a week's time, the mystery of the plant persisted and its teaching continued to evade me. I had removed as many dead leaves as I could and put the plant into a small pot in the sunlight. After several days, I found no change. Sitting with another of the Shaikh's disciples, I checked the plant branch by branch. Finding most of them rotting and dead, I checked the roots again. Many of these too, were dead and rotting. I salvaged one small stalk which seemed to have a faint trace of life. It seemed relieved when I freed it from the dying plant. I put it into water and waited. Looking at the other disciple, I sighed and muttered that I wondered where the story would come from. 'The story is now,' he said. 'We are living its writing.'

Soon after this, I saw the Shaikh. 'We are not yet done,' he said. 'How is the plant? How is it making *sujud* (prostration)?' Then, smiling, he made the following utterance and left me standing where I had met him:

'Do you know of the sickle and the wheat? Death sharpens the sickle and the wheat makes *sujud*, and bows low to the earth.'

> But celebrate the praises of thy Lord, and be of those who prostrate themselves in adoration, and serve thy Lord until there comes unto thee the Hour that is certain.
>
> *(Qur'an 15:98-99)*

One night I collected together the dried leaves and stalks of the plant. Everything had withered except the single stalk which was itself still in questionable condition. I put the dried pieces into a large cooking pot and took them outside to the back of the apartment where I lived. There was a very gentle spring rain that night. I started a fire in the pot and stood just underneath the eves looking into the pan. There were a thousand lessons in the fire. The Shaikh had once said that Shaikh Tussi was annihilated in his fire. Quoting him he said: ' "I was melting like a candle and like ice, nothing remained." Here,' continued the Shaikh, 'when you are at this place of Shaikh Tussi, you are outside yourself looking at yourself and here you will know the mystery of who yourself is.'

My reflections were interrupted by the shouting of my neighbour. The smell of smoke had entered the hallway and my neighbour, the lady next door, rushed to the source of smoke in the interest of saving her property from fire. The dried plant had nearly burned to ashes. As I looked into the face of my neighbour, who had arrived out of breath and puzzled by my fire in the pot, everything was suddenly much clearer for me. The teaching was in part about killing the desire for the things of this world (*dunya*) and complete detachment. One can only accumulate when completely detached and independent. Accumulation here, of course, refers to spiritual progress in the sense that the world can be enjoyed only when one has freed oneself from its absorbing distractions. When the spell of *dunya* is broken, life can be enjoyed to the fullest extent, for then one is able to see the world for what it truly is. The signs of attachment are in each case, apparent to the Shaikh but subtle for the *murid*. In fact, it is through a disciple's interaction with a Shaikh that he comes to recognise attachments which he hardly knew existed in himself. This subtlety was clearly demonstrated on another occasion where the Shaikh was dealing with us regarding *dunya* and detachment.

'I see the bitterness on one eyelash,' he said, 'so be honest with yourselves. On the Day of Judgement it is you and God, and may He, glory be to Him, remove our mistakes from our hearts.' This statement is a continuation of the same subtle teaching of the Shaikh and his work to assist us in the 'inner clean-up', for even in his prayer: 'May God remove our mistakes from our hearts' there was contained a teaching. It is that even the smallest desire for anything other than God Most High is an inner impurity. Such an impurity is actually a definition of polytheism for unity only appears when the last bit of desire and multiplicity is gone. In the words of Shaikh Sharfuddin: 'Real monotheism appears only when the *root* of polytheism has been destroyed.' In order to enter unity, one's character must come up to standard. Every movement must be wholly from God, by God and for God. There can be no attachment, no desire, no anger, no pride (not even in subtle forms), no pleasure at praise, nor pain at blame by others. In fact, unity is by definition the stage of abandonment of *dunya* (things of this world) at which the Shaikh says: 'He penetrates you and you penetrate Him.'

The plant having a life of freedom from frost in fertilised soil is the lesson of *dunya* again, since *dunya* is that place where man lives in his house, protected from winter, feeling safe. Like a well-kept house plant he is fertilised by every luxury and so insulated by mundane comforts that he forgets that death will overtake him. The present is forever fading, passing like the wind.

'So it is in the *dunya* when one has gotten all that will make him happy — then soon', says the Shaikh, 'it is all taken away.'

At one point in the teaching, the Shaikh had said to me that the plant was my thought and inner condition. His point was that inside of me some of the *dunya*-plant continued to blossom. In some subtle and perhaps unconscious way, I was nourishing some piece of it and expecting it to live. On the path to God every trace of desire for *dunya* must die. This is actually a lesson of the first step, for the teaching of the Masters throughout the ages has been one of letting go. This was the first and last diamond-set teaching of Sister Majeed, may God bless Her soul: 'You have to let go to go.' It was a teaching which then I could not fully fathom, but which now is crystal clear. One must let loose the grip in order to go forward, one must die in order to live. Everything moves in cycles just like the plant, and with the blossoms comes the nearness of the fading. Such is the teaching of the demise of great civilisations, for always their blossoming signalled their fall. This points up the crisis of the Rejecters of Faith, the *Kafireen*, those people of *dunya* who do not acknowledge the reality of the fading. Moreover, they continually take this world to be more than it truly is. When the *dunya*-blossoms fade, in every case they are shocked and full of disbelief that the end has indeed arrived.

The Shaikh had tested me by asking what the fate of the plant should be. As we watched it in its exhausted condition, he said to me: 'Be the plant and go to its level.' The teaching here is well expressed in the Dervish phrase: 'Death dies and life lives.' The plant wants to live. When I become the plant I know it; but how to help the plant to live and what to do when it seems to be dying is most difficult to answer. What can be done? What must be done? What did I learn from the Shaikh? It was simply this: One must go to the root. Wanting to live and yet not knowing how to live is the major dilemma for most men on the planet earth.

The story which the Shaikh had told of the two poets was a teaching of how to approach life. He had said to me: 'God's signs are pervasive in the universe. Learn as says Ghazali, "from the indirect observation of nature". Tennyson was one who had to pluck the flower in order to understand its mystery. His method essentially closes, and he becomes lost in analysis and arrogance. The Japanese poet, unlike Tennyson, does not challenge the mystery of God. His method opens and the fact that he *sees* carries him, for his 'seeing' by itself opens volumes to him.

Moore's poem extends the teaching of the other poets. He was as the last rose and his last desire had already been surrendered. He knew the illusoriness of the fleeting *dunya*-flower. Even though it was the wind which scattered the petals, in the case of Moore, he alone had the right to pluck the flower because of his purity of intention and his knowledge of God.

As relates to the very core of the teaching of the plant, the Shaikh had said: 'Too much water, and soil which is too rich kills the plant,' and 'both *'ashq* (love) and *'ibadat* (worship) are necessary.' The plant, at this level of the teaching, is symbolic of the person. The essence of the plant being the fragrance of its flower, symbolising the essence of the person which is the soul. In order for the seeker to grow or to make inner progress, certain basic outward conditions are necessary. The first part of the Shaikh's statement re-emphasises the fact that the seeker must find a path of balance and moderation through *dunya*. Too much *dunya* kills and detracts from the goal, as says Shaikh Attar on this point: 'Love and poverty go together.'

The second part of the Shaikh's statement is showing how *'ashq*, which is love and *'ibadat*, which is service or worship, are necessary outward conditions for the seeker's development in much the same way as are air and sunshine for the plant. The *'ashq* or love which is referred to here, however, is what might be described as 'love as the means', rather than 'love as the end'. That is to say that, at this stage, love is a necessary condition which serves as a means to the goal of 'Love as the end'. Expressed differently this means that a certain basic kind of healthy environment is necessary for the seeker to be able to receive spiritual sunshine and air or spiritual warmth, light, and breath. Without these outward conditions, inner spiritual progress cannot occur.

The Shaikh had cautioned that love is not enough. Here he referred to love (*'ashq*) as a means, for we know that love as the end, or final state of being is more than enough. But as the means or environment or atmosphere, love is important, yet not entirely sufficient. It is for this reason that once the seeker finds his way to the Path, in the way that the plant finds its way to air and sunlight, nourishment, which is worship and devotion to God (*'ibadat*), becomes equally if not more important. For the Seeker, *'ibadat* is also a means to the goal of Divine Love or annihilation in the fire, which is nothing less than Love as the End. The Seeker therefore, must actively seek opportunities for service not only in prayer or almsgiving and charity — but in every activity of life, so that each breath of life breathed and every action initiated is fully charged with the hope for the pleasure of God and nothing less ever, than service, worship or *'ibadat*.

For these reasons as well, the Shaikh said that this teaching is not one for the weak, since it is indeed a teaching of complexity, containing many teachings. 'Which is the seed', he asked, 'which will not bring up life?' It is primarily that seed which falls on the rocks. So it is for those with hardened hearts. By way of the means and God's mercy, the End is achieved and to understand this teaching, one's heart must be open.

The Shaikh had said: 'Seek the company of the good, there are few roses left.' Every seeker on the Path of God is among the lone roses, and the roses past are the true ones who have shown the way. So it is that those who can look, and who have eyes to see, will have the affirmation of Guidance. At the same time, the seeker must know that the true ones are few and soon the wind will do its final scattering.

After several weeks I took the ashes of the dried plant which I had burned in the pot and saved in a small package. I opened them to the wind like the petals of Moore's rose. Of that beautiful plant which had so mysteriously blossomed in the winter, all that remained was one single, hardened, hollow stem. That same stem which had once been vibrant with life and sprouting leaves now symbolised the entire teaching of the plant — a teaching of detachment of one's heart not only from things of the world, but from the emotional clinging to one's sometimes limited idea of how things truly are. Beyond this and more importantly, it is a teaching of the life of the heart which is known only through love and through service. So it is that the little stem came to have special meaning for me:

Hearken to this Reed forlorn
Breathing, even since t'was torn
From its rushy bed, a strain
Of impassioned love and pain.

The secret of my song, though near,
None can see and none can hear
Oh, for a friend to know the sign
And mingle all his soul with mine.

'Tis the flame of Love that fired me
'Tis the wine of Love inspired me.
Wouldst thou learn how lovers bleed,
Hearken, hearken to the Reed!

And like the reed pipe in the poem of Mawlana Rumi, it tells my heart the tale of its own separation.

CHAPTER 5

THE TWO JOURNEYS

During the very early stages of my acquaintance with the Shaikh, the activities of the world had a great hold on my life. Although I was not involved in the pursuit of any obvious wrongdoing (*haram*), I found myself at a place where I was devoting a large amount of time and energy to so-called 'good-cause' efforts which I thought at the time were purely for the pleasure of God. Almost two years after my return from Saudi Arabia, a series of opportunities to travel presented themselves. I subsequently made two journeys, the first of which was to Morocco and the other to Saudi Arabia for the second time.

Before the first journey, I spoke with the Shaikh on the telephone. His only instruction was that I should attempt to visit the Darqawieen Mosque of Fez and while there I should ask to see Muhammad Ibn al Habib. Travelling with another Muslim, I departed for Fez very late on a beautiful Friday afternoon. The plane departed on time and arrived in Casablanca the following morning. We took a bus into the city, where we discovered that there were a few hours to wait for the next bus to Fez. We checked our baggage and had lunch. The old battered bus which we were to take arrived very late that afternoon. We boarded it and, like sardines in a can, we settled down for the slow and crowded ride ahead.

The ride, I soon realised, was actually a boon. It not only gave me the opportunity to be closer to the people but also to see the sights of ancient Moroccan walls, to taste the simple food of the roadside stands and to hear the sounds of both French and Arabic, the languages of the land. I felt very much at home after only a few hours. Before boarding the bus I had been slightly worried about our luggage because I had not seen it loaded with the other baggage which was piled high as a mountain and riding the roof of the bus like the hump of a trusty camel. We arrived safely in Fez very late that night, where I found that my Western preconceptions about efficiency had helped me hold on to my worry about the luggage for the entire length of the bus ride. To my great surprise and to my learning, I found that our luggage was not at all in peril. It had arrived quite safely in Fez, in fact preceding us in its arrival and waiting in good care.

Through a series of enquiries we found our way to the hotel which was to host the meeting which brought us to Fez. It was a grand hotel with every conceivable luxury, tinted with the Arabesque. Set on a hill in the newer part of the city, it gave a spectacular view of the noble older city and its beautiful surrouding landscape. The older city at the centre, and the newer city which sprawled around it were worlds apart. The contrast between them was for me as glaring as that between the luxury of my hotel room and the desert strains of Bedouin music which came over the radio speaker near my bed as I casually turned the switch. I walked onto the balcony to admire the view in the light of the moon. The bright-green dome of a large mosque was visible across the distance and I learned upon asking that it was in fact, the Darqawieen Mosque. The pulsating heat of the night was beautiful and seemed to keep rhythm with the music from the radio inside. It had been a long day and I felt tired. I said prayers, then flopped down on the bed. I clicked off the radio and took rest for the night.

The following morning I descended to the dining room, where I met my friend for breakfast. He informed me that there would be a meeting at a nearby university which we should attend and that we could take a cab there after eating. We had only a few days stay in Fez and I was beginning to worry that I would not be able to escape my friend and the meetings for which we had come, long enough to get to the Mosque. What is more, I discovered very quickly that I would need help to reach the mosque. The old city was full of little alley-like streets — a veritable maze to a stranger like myself.

I met my friend at the front of the hotel where we took a taxi. Arriving at the university we found it absolutely deserted except for two men on the grounds who told us that no one was there. Since we were unable to find the meeting my day was free.

Suddenly God had made a way. I asked Him to forgive me, for it seemed that I was continually doubting and He was continually showing me that there really was no need for me ever to doubt Him. I returned with my friend to the hotel. There were a host of taxis and men with motor-bikes hovering at the hotel entrance, soliciting passengers. After leaving my friend, I changed my clothes and returned to the front of the hotel to search for a way into the city. I asked several of the drivers what they would charge for a ride to the Mosque. They informed me that they could only take me to the gates and that after that I would have to travel on foot. When I asked their prices, however, I was astounded by the amount they wanted.

I summoned what little Arabic I knew to squelch this injustice. 'No, no!' I said, 'Your price is too high and what is more what you are doing is not in Islam!'

'Muslim? Muslim?' queried one of the men in an accent of broken English, as he stepped into view from the rear.

'Yes,' I said. '*Insha'Allah* (God willing), but God Allah knows better who is truly Muslim.'

'You come on bike,' he said. 'Have friend at gate of *medina*, give bike to friend, we go to *Jami Masjid, inshallah*, OK?'

'How much?' I asked, still somewhat annoyed.

'No take money, Brother. Come, we go, yes?' he said in a tone of warmth which cut cleanly through my annoyance. He started the bike's motor and motioned that I get on.

We were off in a moment and soon we arrived at the city's gate. Sure enough he knew several people who were 'hanging out' so to speak, at the gate, much like the men in front of the hotel. He left his bike with one of them and we continued on foot down the narrow, shaded streets in which children played and donkeys pulled small carts and wagons.

It was just about the time of *'Asr* as we reached Masjid Sidi Ahmad, a smaller mosque on the way. We stopped to say the prayer and continued on our way. The Darqawieen Mosque was beautiful in its simplicity, with its grand arches. The floors were covered with durable and clean straw mats on which scattered groups of men sat throughout the mosque. Some sat alone with prayer beads (*tasbih*) in hand for Divine remembrance (*zikr*) and some read Qur'an. I decided to begin my search by looking into faces. I approached several of the old men who sat alone at various places in the mosque asking them in my poor Arabic if they knew Sidi Muhammad Ibn al Habib. The first man I came up to listened and slowly nodded without speaking. Others whom I approached seemed to recoil in shock at my question. Time was passing and it would soon be time for *Salatul Maghrib*, the sunset prayer. The young man who had brought me to the mosque had taken his seat in a small circle of young boys who sat with a *qari* — a reciter of Qur'an — and another man whom I later discovered to be the *Imam* (religious leader) of the mosque. I approached the circle and took a seat. After the boy who was reading finished his turn, my young companion introduced me. I said what little I could in Arabic but soon the conversation became too complex, and I could no longer speak or understand. The *Imam* asked me to recite some Qur'an.

'*Iqraa*!' he said.

I told my young companion guide to tell the *Imam* that I had an important question but he stopped the dialogue.

'Read Qur'an,' he said again, looking directly into my face.

I recited *Sura Fatiha* and the first of *Suratul Baqara*. The *Imam* turned to the young boys and said something to the group. It seemed that he was saying that they should take encouragement in meeting Muslims from the other side of the world. He turned the circle over to the *qari* and stood to leave. The *azan* was called soon after this so I left the circle to line up for prayer.

After the prayer I attempted to reach the *Imam* but it was difficult to get to him in the crowd. It just so happened that the *qari* passed as I stood there and he took me and my companion guide to a quiet corner of the mosque where the Imam was sitting. I gave my *salaams* and sat before him.

'Do you know Sidi Muhammad Ibn al Habib?' I asked in intense earnestness, looking directly into his eyes.

'Read,' he said as if he hardly heard my question.

I recited from *Suratul Hashr*, a section of the Qur'an. When I finished, he spoke to me in Arabic and my companion helped with the translation:

'The man you search for is not in Fez,' he said. 'He is in the city of Meknes.'

'Then do you know him?' I said pressing my query. 'Can you take me to him?'

'Yes, I do know him,' he replied, as a look of loving kindness came upon his face. Not noticing his use of the past tense, he added, 'I was his friend for thirty-five years. I hope to meet him tomorrow. Can you come at five o'clock?'

Struck by a sudden wave of gloom, I lowered my eyes as I

answered that I could not meet him. I was to be in meetings all day which I did not expect could be cancelled or unattended.

'Write your name and address in Fez,' he said seeming to understand my predicament. 'Have faith.'

I wrote my name on a small yellow piece of paper from my tablet and handed it to him. I stood to leave. One of the boys of the circle, the son of the *Imam*, accompanied us to the entrance and out into the crowded narrow streets.

'Please, you come tommorrow, five o'clock,' he said. 'My father he knows.'

By now I was oblivious to the words of this enthusiastic lad. I was already feeling a sense of failure and everything was beginning to seem absolutely futile. At this point I might say that Muhammad Ibn al Habib, unbeknown to me, was not on this planet. This beautiful and perfect shaikh of the Islamic Inner Path (*Tasawwuf*), well known by his countrymen, as well as among the dervishes and seekers, had been in the better world for several years.

My plan was to return to the Mosque early the next morning and continue my search. I had a feeling of urgency to carry out the Shaikh's instructions and to see where I might be taken. The young man who was my companion and guide agreed to meet me the next day at noon. He said that he would come between the hours of twelve o'clock and three. I thought it would be difficult, but I agreed. The next morning I overslept. Moreover, I awakened to find that the floor of my hotel room was entirely flooded and water was pouring from a broken pipe in the bathroom. I wondered what it all meant. As I stood there in a puddle of water I had the strangest feeling and I sensed that the Shaikh was laughing at my circumstance. I remembered a time when I had been with him working in the yard outside the Tekiya. It was very wet and the Shaikh was wearing garden boots. He stepped into a very deep puddle and while standing there he told a story:

'There were once some ducklings on a pond', he said with a smile, 'who were complaining to their teacher that all they were learning was a little "quack, quack!"

"You are now only little ducklings," said the teacher duck, "but in time you will grow. For now quack, quack is enough."

'So it is with you,' said the Shaikh as he looked into my face and laughed his usual warm infectious laugh. In that moment, I saw the utter duckling that I was and all I could do was laugh together with him.

Unable to reach the hotel desk by phone, I dropped the receiver, threw on some clothes and rushed to the lobby to report the flooding. I went to the room of my friend, brushed my teeth, cleaned up a little and went for breakfast. The manager of the hotel gave me another room to which I returned after breakfast to write some notes and reflect on the series of events. Somehow the subject of Sufis had overtaken the discussion at breakfast. Some others at the hotel for the meeting had joined our table and someone among them had introduced some essentially negative discussion about Sufis. My friend had noticed me reading a small book on the plane which was written by a man who had once been his student but who had somehow, much to his teacher's dismay become what my friend somewhat cynically referred to as an 'avowed Sufi'.

'I certainly hope that you don't get off the track with those Sufis,' he cautioned. 'What they do is *bida* (innovation) and certainly unIslamic!'

I recited for him a list of great Muslims who were well-known Sufis. Balking at my recital he grumbled in annoyance:

'Muhammad, peace be upon him, is our guide, and our only Shaikh, and that is where the matter ends!'

What he said was in fact true, yet he did not realise that the people of *Tasawwuf* or Sufism, the Path of Spiritual Islam, say exactly what he had said. It is nothing different. None the less, something in his tone caused me to lapse into silence for a while. I said nothing more to him related to the subject of *Tasawwuf* from the time of our discussion on the plane until this particular morning, when I casually mentioned Shaikh al Akbar in the midst of the breakfast chatter about Sufis.

'Shaikh al Akbar!' he gasped, nearly spraying the table with unswallowed orange juice. '*Astagfirullah*! Only Allah is *Akbar*! Only God is Great!'

I could not believe my ears. Certainly no Muslim would compare Shaikh Ibn al Arabi with Allah Who is most highly exalted above His creation and without comparison. Regarding Shaikh al Akbar, however, it is a well-known fact that he was nothing less than a towering man of God. His title, which was given to him by his own contemporaries, is, at the human level, a statement of his greatness. Among Shaikhs he was great indeed, and it is in no way a violation of faith to acknowledge the accomplishments of men. This noble Shaikh was well versed in both *Shari'ah* (divinely revealed law) and *fiqh* (jurisprudence) immersed in love of God. As a scholar and one of Islam's most prolific writers he produced fifteen volumes of commentary for general readers on the first half of the Qur'an. His other works are modestly estimated to number about eight hundred. A truly realised being, he descended by birth from the Prophet's own family. May God shower His blessings on the Prophet and ennoble the faces of his family and those who are truly with him.

I left the breakfast table feeling sick to my stomach. I was in no way ready to face the day of mundane meetings, a tour, and a twenty-sword ceremonial (of all things!) followed by a tea and late-night conference. In the unfolding of events, however, it happened that the young man who was to accompany me back to the mosque did not return. Having nothing else to do I took the tour. I enjoyed what I could of it but it was too laden with unnecessary affect and besides, I was very much distracted. I returned to my hotel room considering what had happened. I went over every detail of the trip. I pondered every face I had seen in the mosque. I wondered if I should have chosen this one, or that one? I reviewed in my reflections, the face of the *Imam* (religious leader) at the mosque. Now it all seemed so far away. I began to feel a sense of despair as I thought of returning home to tell the Shaikh that I had failed.

'What might he say?' I wondered. 'Does this mean that I have failed as a *murid*? Am I truly on this Path?'

Tired of thinking, I said prayers and some rememberances and called it a day.

The following morning I overslept again. It seemed at the time to be becoming a syndrome. My head was full of thoughts again: 'How can I get back to the Mosque? How can I negotiate that maze of this city alone?'

I went down to breakfast still in a fog. My friend recited the day's schedule as he chomped on his toast. Much to my surprise the day was relatively uncluttered. There was only one early evening meeting and another tour of the countryside and the mountains. I surrendered the idea of returning to the mosque. It seemed that there really was no way of getting back.

My belaboured musings about the day were interrupted by the voice of the waiter who had approached the table unnoticed: 'Sir, there are some people here to see you.'

'Perhaps it is the man who was supposed to come yesterday,' my friend interjected.

'Who could it be?' I asked myself as I stood up from the table. I didn't think that it was the young man from before, yet the mere fact that anyone could be calling for me puzzled me greatly. I walked to the lobby with my friend, who, now unable to contain his curiosity, was following close at my heels.

The waiter nodded in the direction of three men. It was obvious that they were from some other place. Two of the men were dressed in Moroccan *jallabiyas,* the traditional lightweight hooded garments of the country. One of the two men was an older man of charming spiritual elegance. His beard was white and his eyes were a striking blue. The other man was much younger and seemed to be more in pursuit of the old man than in pursuit of me. I had noticed him attempting to kiss the old man's hand as I entered the lobby. The third man was the youngest of the three. Dressed in European slacks, shirt, and boots, I estimated his age to be about 19. The old man was standing next to my friend speaking in Arabic. My friend, who was fluent in Arabic, assisted in the translation:

'They are inviting you to their home,' he said. 'They are also asking if you are the man who enquired about their friend when you were at the mosque.'

'I am that man,' I said.

The old man had taken a seat. I noticed that he had in his hand the exact same piece of paper which I had given to the *Imam* at the mosque the day before. He instructed one of the men to ask me how I got the name of the man I sought. I asked my friend to explain to them that my teacher in America asked me to enquire about him.

Somewhere near this time in the exchange we moved away from my friend. God caused it to come about in a very smooth and natural way so that some thing had come up which made it necessary for him to leave, much as he might otherwise have wanted to stay.

I sat down with the three men in a quiet corner of the room. I was directly before the old man, who had now taken on a very stern demeanour. He asked me a series of questions which were translated and propounded to me by the other two men. Still responding to their question about my enquiry at the mosque, I explained that Shaikh had sent me. They asked his name and I told them.

'What kind of Muslim are you?' they asked.

I recited Kalima: *Ashadu an la ilaha ill'Allah wa ashadu anna Muhammadan 'abduhu wa rasuluhu.'*

'*La*! Not Shaikhs,' cautioned the old man very strongly. 'Remember that Tijani, Alawi, Ad-Darqawi — all of these men were nothing more than Muslims. We say for each of them *Ustedh* or professor.'

Throughout this exchange I continually looked into the face of the old man who concluded his questions and looked away for a moment. The younger man in Moroccan dress stood up to leave. He attempted again to kiss the old man's hand but did not succeed as the hand was quickly removed at this gesture.

The old man now seeming satisfied with my answers looked into my face again, now with an expression of kindness. The youngest man spoke for the first time, addressing me in clear English:

'You will come with us please. You are invited to our home.'

'Yes,' I said without hesitation. 'Of course yes, let us go.'

We left the hotel lobby together and on getting outside, the old man suggested that we walk because of the difficulty in getting a taxi. Earlier the hotel entrance had been literally crowded with drivers, but now we could not find a single one. Actually, I felt relieved. Walking felt so much more natural and it gave us a chance to talk and be together at ease. We made our way off across a sandy hillside through the market square and into a busy little village.

I explained the difficulty I had in speaking before my friend and I told them the story of my journey to the mosque and how I thought that I had failed. The young man translated for the old man, who asked again how I knew of Sidi Muhammad Ibn al Habib. I explained again how I had been instructed by my Shaikh to search for him. The old man told me his name at which time the young man spoke:

'My grandfather, you see, who is the man you have met, is the Shaikh who succeeded Sidi Muhammad Ibn al Habib. He knew him well for many years and loved him very much.'

The old man looked at me smiling. He repeated his name, this time prefacing it with the respected title of Hajji and honourable surname As-Sufi. We continued walking and spoke of many things along the way. Among these things were the importance of learning and other topics which evolved out of questions from the old man about the nature of my work and the job that I held in America.

'I regret that you do not speak more Arabic,' said the young man. 'My grandfather has a great store of knowledge which could perhaps be of benefit to you. He knows a great deal about psychology. Among a great many other things he is a true scholar — and Sufism itself is, as you know, the crown of psychology. It is in fact the great psychology of the *nafs* (ego) of man.'

It was just about this time in our walk that the old man was approached by another man, a simple townsman of the village.

'Ya Sidi!' he called, approaching the old man and stopping directly before him. He spoke in a quiet voice and the old man listened, smiled and gave reply.

'This man is asking my grandfather for some advice concerning a problem with his wife,' said the young man. 'People call on him for all sorts of things, as you might guess.'

The interaction between the old man and the villager was natural and affectionate. I noticed that the man from the village stood very close when speaking to the old man and fastened a button at the neck of the old man's *jallabiya* which had begun to become undone. They quickly concluded and we walked on.

'It is only Islam,' said the old man, 'which has brought us together like this. This is the sociology which must be studied.'

We passed by a cemetery along the way and I gave greetings (*salaams*). The young man repeated his *salaams* after my own.

'This which you do', interjected the old man, 'is from *Sunnah*.'

'The heart of the Muslim', said the young man, 'should be full of peace, for God, in giving the *Sunnah*, has shown the Muslim how to live and how to die and established within his heart the certainty of *akhirat*, the life to come hereafter.

> For they have been guided [in this life] to the purest of speeches; they have been guided to the Path of Him Who is worthy of [all] praise.
>
> *(Qur'an 22:24)*

I could only look at the young man in smiling admiration. It was heartwarming to see such spiritual vibrance in a man as young as he. Looking at him I thought of myself and how I, at his age had been nothing more than a wandering Western youth. Not a bad being — but wandering none the less, in that dreadful lostness, which now seems to have a choking grip on most of the generations, both young and old alike.

We arrived at the old man's home, a quiet, perhaps ancient

dwelling with a massive door opening from the narrow street. Entering, he showed me into a comfortable room where we sat for a time to have coffee. After coffee he brought out for me pictures of himself and Shaikh Muhammad Ibn al Habib. He showed me a very special book of writings as well, which were his own works as well as commentary on things produced by Sidi Ibn al Habib. He later invited one of the English-speaking *fuqara* (dervishes) to join us. We continued to talk over mint tea and biscuits and I thanked the old man for all of his kindness as feelings of gratitude began to well up within.

'It is all to Allah,' he said in a very quiet voice.

He asked me to write to him upon my return to the United States, which I did. He answered with a very beautiful letter written in both Arabic and English. I continued to correspond with him even now after the passing of several years.

His beautiful grandson invited me to stay and be presented to his family in Meknes, which regretfully I could not do, but in our meeting a special friendship was kindled and its flame too still burns.

That afternoon when it was time to leave, the old Moroccan Shaikh saw me to his door where we exchanged salaams. The dervish whom he had invited drove me back to the hotel. Shortly after my return to the hotel I received a phone-call from the desk saying that someone had come for me. I went down to the lobby where I found the old Shaikh's grandson.

'You forgot the paper on which you wrote our addresses,' he said with a broad, warm smile, extending his hand with the paper.

'And how did you get here?' I asked, surprised that he had come so far for such a small thing.

'I walked of course,' he said, 'and it is my pleasure to do it. *Assalaamu alaikum* (Peace be upon you).'

I walked with him to the front of the hotel where I stood to watch him until he disappeared from view far up the road and over the sandy hillside.

That evening after attending the conference meeting, I rode with my friend and some other participants of the conference to the mountainside. Sitting underneath a tree near the bank of a beautiful lake, I reflected on my time in Fez. Now after having met the old Moroccan Shaikh, I felt full. I had been so full of doubt, but God had been so very merciful. Returning from the countryside to the hotel just at the approach of sunset, I noticed a striking Moroccan man, riding a gallant dark horse. Dressed in a dark cape-like garment characteristic of Morocco, he had the bearing of a dervish in his humility and simplicity of manner. The picture of him trotting along the roadside stayed with me a very long time. After a while I realised how very deeply I had identified with him. He was absolutely serene. Oh, would that I might ride my lower self in the way he rode that noble steed. Would that I might ride to the place of *baqa billah*: going onward in the realisation of the Divine, a steady ride on the crest of the ocean's wave.

The following morning I flew to Paris with my friend, then on to the United States. On the night of my return I saw the Shaikh. It just so happened that I arrived on the same evening as his Quar'anic talks. I arrived before him still carrying the shoulder bag which was my only luggage. He enquired about the journey and I told him about the general series of events which I thought had concluded in my meeting with the old Moroccan Shaikh.

'*Alhamdulillah* (Praise be to God), he said, looking into my face and smiling warmly.

'The old Shaikh came to pay *ziyarat* to you (to visit you). *Alhamdulillah*.'

I was not able to speak with the Shaikh at length about the journey at that time but I felt pleased that I was able to report that I had been sucessful in my search.

The following day I came home early from work with a feeling of incredible sickness. Suddenly, it seemed that an awesome wave of nausea rose up from nowhere to overtake me completely. Reeling from the abruptness of the change, I lay in bed thrust in a languorous abyss, entirely drained of strength and unable to fathom what had put me on my back. I remained in this condition for about a day, after which I was still quite weak, though slowly beginning to return to my senses. The voice of my wife interrupted my ponderings as I lay there attempting to overcome my perplexity:

'The Shaikh is here. He will give you a few minutes to prepare yourself.'

I summoned what little energy I had to renew my ablutions, and returned to the bed. The Shaikh entered the room wearing ordinary slacks and a sweater. He gave *salaams* and knelt at my side placing his hand on my forehead. He said a silent prayer then looked at me with his usual disarming smile. I felt better as soon as I saw him and I began to think of how amusingly trapped I was in my own melodrama.

'How are you?' he asked.

'I'm better now, *alhamdulillah*,' I said, now feeling almost embarrassed at my condition yet completely surprised by this unexpected visit.

'Your sickness is the sign of what your journey is worth,' he said in a voice of sober directness. His words struck me like a revelation. I responded in silence looking into his eyes partially in wonderment at my own lack of insight. He uncovered a small vessel and extended it for me to drink.

'How does it taste?' he enquired.

'It is sweet,' I answered, 'like the water of a deep spring.'

He noticed the cloud of puzzlement, related to my own self, which continued to hover throughout our exchange. He began to laugh a hearty laugh.

'I sensed that you laughed in the very same way when I was in Morocco,' I said. 'It was at the time when I stood in the middle of my flooded room completely overcome with the thought that I had failed in my search. It seems that the more I go, the less I know.'

'All knowledge is here,' he said pointing to the heart. 'Fast today.' The sickness is part of your purification.'

He then told the story of Shaikh Abu Bekr of Nishapur and the donkey:

> One day the Shaikh rode along on a donkey accompanied by several thousand murids. As he rode along he sank deep into a meditation where he saw himself in a noble state approaching the door of *Jannat*, the Garden of Paradise. In the moment the donkey raised his tail and sounded a most uncouth noise. Upon hearing this sound the Shaikh Abu Bekr began to wail and tear out his beard. He snatched off his turban and threw it to the ground. Later, he was asked by some of his murids what had happened. He told them of the thoughts of his meditation and how in its very midst the donkey had shown him who he truly was.

After a slight pause the Shaikh stood up to leave.

'Stay away from those who treat the Qur'an with disrespect,' he said in a tone of piercing clarity, 'and from those who madly love this *dunya* and twenty-sword salutes.'

He gave his *salaams* and quietly left the room, leaving me as surprised in his departure as I had been in his entry.

> Have we not made for him a pair of eyes and a tongue and a pair of lips? And shown him the two highways?
>
> *(Qur'an 90:8-10)*

Two weeks after my return from Morocco, I departed on the second journey, a trip to Saudi Arabia for another conference. Before leaving I met with the Shaikh. We walked together on a sultry autumn evening, which I am sure was one of the last beautiful days of autumn. What the Shaikh said to me that night as we walked the city streets, spoke to some of the very deepest longings of my heart and gave me the assurance that by God's permission they could indeed be realised. I left for the journey bursting with hope and filled with excitement. I made the intention to carry out everything I was to do and I petitioned God for His help and assistance along the way. Before completing the journey I would need to travel to two other countries: Syria and Turkey.

'Between these two cities,' said the Shaikh, 'you will find your treasure. You will pay respects to the Prophet, peace be upon him, in Medina, then you will go to the tomb of Shaikh al Akbar in Damascus and to the tomb of Hazrati Shamsi Tabriz in Konya.'

From the very outset of the journey I was beset with minor trials. The plane which I took from New York to London was unable to land due to fog. We flew to Amsterdam, where we spent several hours waiting as the plane was refuelled.We proceeded to London, where we arrived in just enough time for me to miss my connection for Saudi Arabia. The flight I had missed was the last direct flight to the city of Riyad, my destination. The next flight plan required connection and did not leave until several hours later. I waited out the day in the airport and boarded a late-afternoon flight for Jeddah, where I arrived after midnight, only to be held up by passport officials. As soon as I approached the gate, I knew intuitively that I would be delayed. Sure enough, two uniformed Saudi airport police were carefully scrutinising the travellers ahead of me in the line who were not nationals and had already confiscated several passports by the time I reached them. Mine was taken too, but the delay was cleared up in about an hour. My passport was returned and I proceeded to the departure lounge where I spent the night waiting for an early morning flight to Riyad. As I walked through the airport I passed a lone Saudi janitor. Dressed in a grey hooded garment, sandals and red and white *kufiyyeh* headdress, he mopped the floor of the corridor with a vigour the degree of which was hardly surpassed by the cadence of my tired, dragging feet.

I arrived in Riyad annoyed and exhausted after two full days of travel. I had departed for my destination a day earlier than I had really wanted, and arrived a day later than I had planned.

> Be patient, O fearful one, since all who went by this road were in your state.
>
> *Shaikh Attar*

From the airport at Riyad I bargained for a taxi, but still paid more than I should have for the trip. I decided not to fight it. I arrived at the hotel and was immediately shuttled to the conference meeting-place. I attended the opening session then escaped to my room to sleep. The conference met for five days, each of which was difficult and filled with activity. There was very little time for rest. During these days, however, the hosts of the conference treated the attendees very well from the *dunya* point of view. We were chauffeured to and from the meeting-sites, served excellent food and given reasonably good accommodation. During the week of meetings, several young Saudi students were assigned the task of confirming flight reservations of the conference attendees. I asked for a flight plan which included trips to Syria and Turkey after a stop in Medina. The conference ended on a Thursday, on which day I set out for Medina. I travelled with a small group of men who had been participants in the conference. We arrived safely, without much difficulty and were greeted by another Saudi host. We were given accommodation for the night and the next day we prayed *Jumah* at the Mosque of the Prophet. Later in the day when the crowds had subsided, we visited the Prophet's gravesite.

The group of men with whom I was travelling wanted to perform the *Umra* (the Lesser Pilgrimage) in Mecca. I should have never entertained the thought. We all travelled from Medina to Jeddah at which point I should have separated myself from them. I could have easily taken a plane from there onward to the next stage of my journey. Strange as it may seem, it never entered my mind to leave them, even though all of the signs to do it were clearly apparent. In the first place, I had already performed *Umra*. I was the only one in the group who had seen the Ka'ba. The Shaikh had urged me to visit the Prophet, but Mecca had not entered our discussion. Not disregarding the sanctity of the Ka'ba, the choice to go there was one which reeked with hindrances.

Somehow I was swept up in a group-think and I completely lost my senses.

We spent a full hour or more trying to get a taxi for the distance to Mecca. After we had finally found a man to drive us, we were stopped by the police just as we were entering the car. We were delayed for another hour as the police ticketed the driver and threatened to suspend his licence for operating an illegal taxi service. I was very disappointed that this had happened because the man had been very kind and was the only one of the drivers we had met who had given us a reasonable price. One of the men in our group who spoke Arabic well had assumed leadership in the group, and was now off with the driver attempting to rectify the situation with the director of airport police. The matter was eventually settled and we were allowed to leave. As we departed for Mecca, the plane to my other destination soared up into the sky. It would be two days before the next flight to Damascus.

The trip to Mecca was very long. When we arrived in the city we went to our hosts for Umra. There were none. They had not received a message that we were coming. After wasting another hour or two telephoning in search of the man to whom we were referred, whom we never found, we proceeded to Mecca. I finally began to get the message: the care of our caretakers had ended and we were on our own. They had sent no one to meet us in Jeddah and when we arrived in Mecca by our own initiative there was no one waiting. One of the men in the group had a friend in the city. We found him easily, made ablutions, and proceeded to the *Masjidul Haram*. The sight of the Ka'ba was uplifting. God knows, it is a magnificent house to behold but something was missing in that moment. That something was in me. As I concluded a prayer I realised, as I sat there, that God has established a *qibla* (direction) in Mecca and a *qibla* in the heart. One must come to realise their existence through one's own experience and one must discriminate by the condition which is to be faced. Suddenly it became clear to me that there are many directions but only one heart. *Sa'ee*, the Pilgrim's ritual of running back and forth between *Safa* and *Marwa*, was enlightening in the face of these thoughts. I could easily see that the running, the walking, and passing others along the way is a strong teaching about life's journey to the goal beyond the *qibla*.

Verily to the Lord is the return of all.

(Qur'an 96:8)

After *Umra* I could not find my sandals. For just a few moments I was filled with annoyance, that such a thing could happen in the Mosque of Mecca. I wanted to think that someone wanted to steal those shoes which cost little more than a dollar and which had only about 5,000 look-alikes outside the doors of the Mosque. As I walked the streets of Mecca barefoot in search of another pair of sandals, I saw my own arrogance and need for humility. What is more, I remembered that when I had last seen the Shaikh before coming onto the journey he had been wearing thong-sandals. He had told me to travel to Damascus wearing sandals or walking on bare feet.

We returned to Jeddah with the same driver who had brought us, and Saturday night found us back at the airport. There were no planes to any of our destinations. There was nothing until the next day. The first flights to Syria and Turkey were not until Monday. There were no longer any hosts and there was no place to go. The airline officials were extremely rude and there was no way to move or escape them. After spending the night in a cold corner of the airport floor, I awakened so tired that I nearly fell asleep while standing. Two of the other men in the group who were returning to London attempted to dissuade me in my plans to lay over until Monday. They were travelling to London that afternoon.

'You'll be exhausted,' said one of them. 'Look how tired you already are.'

'Not to mention how unfriendly and aggressive the airline personnel have become,' chimed in the other. 'Actually, we think that you should probably get out of the country. We don't see any reason for you to go to Syria — do you have a visa?' questioned the first man, now speaking for himself and the other.

Such was the general tenor of the discouragement which these men voiced out of concern for me. I knew that they didn't know what I had to do and there was no way that I could tell them. In spite of what I knew, I listened to them against the voice of my own better judgement. I told myself that I was indeed too tired and lapsed into some strange state where I completely lost my will to think or act. It all seemed to happen in seconds and before I knew it I was on a flight back to London with the others. I had fully cancelled my other plans and surrendered the tickets I had already obtained. I had given up and in doing so I had thrown away a rare opportunity for self-discovery in the face of trial, intrigue, and difficulty. Moreover, I threw away my chance to demonstrate my ability to perform in circumstances requiring a challengingly high level of personal initiative. In not taking this initiative I felt myself passing by the possibility for spiritual progress and greater inward peace. I was close to the goal, but to speak of closeness in this instance is like having twenty-four cents in a time of crisis at a phone-booth, when only a quarter will do. I had much to look forward to, but I missed. I let go. All I had to do was think of my soul instead of my body and attempt to survive the wait.

> The soul like the body, is in a state of progress or decline; and the Spiritual Way reveals itself only in the degree to which the traveler has overcome his faults, and weaknesses, his sleep and his inertia and each will approach near to his aim according to his effort.
>
> *Shaikh Attar*

As soon as I had surrendered my tickets I felt a wave of sickness churning from my depths. A bleak cloud of doubt hovered over me all the while I rode the plane to London. The further away we flew, the more clearly I saw myself. I grew sick with gloom and fell into an abysmal pit of depression. I could not believe my lack of effort. I was angry with myself for not trying, especially when I knew from past experience something of the fruits of faith and determination — I had done some difficult things before. Somehow in the face of this challenge, however, I forgot everything I knew. Facing myself in the realisation of how very much I had forgotten of what I had learned before, I grew even more sick with depression and deep-rooted feelings of failure.

'Was this the will of Allah?' I asked myself, 'or was it the product of my own unconscious sleepiness and lack of courage?'

On reaching London, I called across the ocean in a desperate attempt to reach the Shaikh. Someone answered to say that he had gone into a retreat *khalwat* and was unavailable. Much later, after returning, and only after everything I might have sought was gone and irretrievable, did I begin to remember the very last instruction which the Shaikh had given me before my departure:

'Remember to keep these three things,' he cautioned: 'instructive tongue, attentive ear, and faithful heart.'

The next time that I saw the Shaikh was at one of his talks on Qur'an. Shortly after I had entered and taken my seat, he said to the small assembly:

'If illumination does not come to you, perhaps it is not God's fault but your own. It may be that your heart needs more purification.'

It was almost as if he were speaking only to me. His statement answered the question which still lingered in my heart related to the will of Allah. Immediately came the answer in the often-recited Qur'anic verse which suddenly entered my mind: *la ilaha illa anta subhanaka inni kuntu minaz-zalimeen* — There is no God but Thou, glory be to Thee; I was indeed the one who committed the wrong.

After the Qur'anic talk, a small group of the Shaikh's disciples were gathered in his company. As I joined them he asked about my journey. I told him that I had been very unsuccessful.

'Shaikh al Akbar was waiting for you,' he said in a voice of utter seriousness. 'You stood him up.'

I was speechless as I sat there noticing that the feelings of gloom had begun to surface again.

'The apple falls when it is ripe,' said the Shaikh. 'Allah is the Lord of the two Easts and the two Wests. Wherever thou turn thy face there is He. You will have the same chance which you had there, here in this tekiya. Remember that there is only dust in the grave of the Prophet, peace be upon him, and dust in the other graves. Allah is God and nothing else matters. I only wanted you to hear your own heart — but isn't God the best to decide?'

It was about two weeks before I saw the Shaikh again. During this time my depression persisted and I often reflected on the things he had said and the strange course of events. I had been invited to give a talk before the Muslim community at large, something which I was really not in the frame of mind to do but I made an effort to collect some thoughts and prepare myself to speak. Just before I took the podium, the Shaikh entered the room with some very honoured guests. I approached him with *salaams* and said to him that he should be the speaker and not myself.

'Speak,' he said. 'You should speak and we will listen.'

With much reservation I gave the talk with as much thoughtfulness and enthusiasm as I could. Somewhere in the talk I told the following story:

> There was once a certain slave whose name was Ayaz. Through a certain set of circumstances, he came to be owned by the Sultan Mahmud, who grew to love him very much owing to the noble character which he as a slave possessed. Later, he came to be so highly favoured by the Sultan that he was made treasurer of all the kingdom and all the most precious and exquisite jewels and gems

were placed into his care. The other courtiers who observed this development were most disturbed by it. They were jealous and their vanity would not allow them to see how a mere slave could be given such a position and elevated to their rank. As a consequence of these feelings they were found to be more and more frequent in their complaints, especially when the Sultan was near, and they did everything that they could to discredit the noble slave.

One day one courtier in speaking to another when the Sultan was near, was heard to say: 'Do you know that the slave Ayaz goes often to the treasure house? He goes every day in fact; even on his day off he goes and he stays there for long hours. I am convinced that he must be stealing our precious jewels.'

The king could not believe his ears. 'If this is true,' he thought, 'I must see it with my own eyes.' So he went to the treasure house to observe. He had a small hole made in the wall so that he could see what occurred inside. The next time that the slave entered the treasure house the king was standing outside. He watched the slave quietly enter, close the door, and make his way to the chest. He knelt down before it, opened it very slowly and took something from it, a small parcel which apparently he had kept there. He kissed it, pressed it to his eyes, then opened it. And what could it be? It was the same garment of rags he'd worn as a slave. He took off his courtier's clothes and put on his garment and stood before the mirror.

'Do you remember who you were when you wore this?' he asked himself. 'You were nothing. You were only a slave to be sold and by the mercy of Allah the Sultan was made to see good in you which perhaps you did not deserve. So Ayaz, now that you have arrived at this place, never forget where you came from, for prosperity can make you short of memory. Do not be proud over those who are now under you and above all else, pray for the king that Allah may bless him and grant him long life . . . and remember always Ayaz. Remember.'

After these remarks to himself, he changed back into his courtier's clothes. He carefully folded the garment of rags, kissed it and placed it back inside the chest. He closed the chest, locked it and quietly walked to the door. As he left the treasure house and came outside, he looked directly into the face of the Sultan. Tears were streaming down the Sultan's cheeks as he looked at the slave, and he was hardly able to speak, so large was the lump in his throat. He smiled warmly and said: 'Oh Ayaz,' he sighed, 'until today you were the treasurer of my jewels, but now . . . you are the treasurer of my heart. You have taught me the lesson of how I too must stand in front of my King, before Whom I am nothing.'

Just before I had concluded my talk the Shaikh left. Later, when I was leaving, I came outside and to my great surprise I found him double-parked in the street, his motor running as he sat with his guests. On seeing me he signalled for me to come.

'What is the pain I see in your eyes?' he asked, as I approached the car.

'It is the trip,' I answered.

'Some *hizmet* (service)', he said with a hearty laugh, 'what went wrong?'

'I had a way . . .'

'But what?' he interjected.

'I guess like you said, I wasn't ready.'

'It is easier to get into the palace of King Khalid', he said, 'than the tombs of our Shaikhs.'

He then told me a story of a businessman who wanted to learn about *Tasawwuf* (the Mystic Path) from a dervish. The dervish accompanied the man through all of his mundane affairs but all the while they were together he was too absorbed in his business to enquire about that in which he had expressed an interest. Finally, in the taxi-cab rushing to catch a plane, he put his hand on the shoulder of the dervish and said:

'Well, we have an hour left; tell me all about *Tasawwuf*.'

'The *dunya* and the Dervish Path', said the Shaikh, 'do not easily mix. You cannot tread them together.'

Then almost like what seemed to me to be out of the blue, the Shaikh asked: 'How long did it take you to skin the sheep you sacrificed?'

Several weeks passed before I realised what this question meant.

'Learn yourself from the story of Ayaz,' he said, 'maybe you gave us a beautiful *khutba* (talk), but there is a lesson to be learned from it. Think about it for yourself and meditate on it tomorrow.'

He gave his *salaams* as he accelerated and drove away, leaving me standing there in the street. By the time the smoke from his exhaust had cleared, he was completely out of sight.

When I saw the Shaikh again he extended his last message:

'Instead of telling stories,' he said, 'let your stories tell you. Apply them to your own life. Put on the garment of poverty every day and kill the *dunya* in yourself with the knife of *Hazrati Abraham*, peace be upon him. Remember that if you choose *dunya* (this world) you get only *dunya*, but if you choose God, you get both *dunya* and *akhirat* (the hereafter).'

After a brief pause, he looked at me smiling but he spoke in unquestionable seriousness:

'To understand this,' he said, 'you (like any true seeker in search of his Lord) simply must become pregnant!'

The Shaikh's final comment left me in a state of dumbfounded amazement. My own wife was blossoming in her first pregnancy at the particular time, and thus became for me the outward representation of my own hope to be entirely pregnant with love and single-minded desire for nearness to God. This simple remark made by the Shaikh caused me to observe my wife through all the stages of pregnancy and to become more inspired and aware of the process through which inwardly, I too had to pass, before I came to delivery.

The teachings of the two journeys continued long after my return home. Every day was in fact an extension of the journey and the many lessons which came to me as a traveller unfolded slowly day by day. Months before, as I have mentioned in an earlier chapter, the Shaikh had given me a list of five things I was to remember, namely (1) self-restraint, (2) alertness, (3) hope, (4) trust, and (5) *amal* (hard work or action). Several teachings relating to these things were continuing to unfold. As I continued to think about the little note I came to see it not so much as a map to the home of the dervish, but rather a map for a murid who is seeking God and who may come to live in the state of surrender, certainty and love of God which is the fulfilment of *muridat* (discipleship) and the 'home' in which a dervish dwells along the way.

I was beginning to see the journeys primarily as a teaching of hope but earlier teachings were included as well. Lessons of faith and patience and all the many other things which the Shaikh had attempted to help me to realise in my daily experiences showed me the mercy of God in His having given me life.

The steps and stages listed in the note were now in retrospect becoming more and more apparent. All of the things the Shaikh had written in the note months earlier had been re-expressed in the instructions he gave before my departure on the second journey:

'Instructive tongue, attentive ear, and faithful heart.' In some place along the way of the journeys my faith, alertness, and self-restraint were tested by events which touched one or all of these things at once.

But what of this aspect of hope? The understanding of what it is to hope was generated by my failure. 'Things lie hidden in their opposites,' says the great Shaikh al-Alawi, 'and but for the existence of opposites, the Opposer would have no manifestation.' This peculiar nature of learning by contrast was what brought me to realise the mercy of God manifested in not one but two journeys.

> If you consider yourself honoured by the diamond, and humiliated by the stone, God is not with you.
>
> *Shaikh Attar*

For months I wondered what had caused me to be successful in the first journey and to fail in the second. How it seemed to me was not truly how it was, I later realised, for when I examined myself and was 'faithful to my heart' I came to see that the second journey would have only fostered my vanity and thus have been an obstacle in the path of my progress. 'He who didn't taste the hemlock', the Shaikh had often said, 'didn't taste the honey.' So it was that the bitterness and depression which grew out of what I had taken to be a crashing and fatal failure was, in the end, the sweetest teaching of what it is to hope.

Several months later, one drizzly afternoon, I was attempting to decide whether I should travel to the Tekiya or do one of the many other things which tugged on me in the moment. At that time I lived many miles away, which caused me to be more cautious in travelling. I was driving along in the rain filled with indecision. I turned my car around at least twice until finally I heard my heart say clearly: 'Go to the mosque!' That was the day on which I finally understood that it is never a wrong decision to go to the mosque.

When I arrived at the Tekiya, the Shaikh was upstairs in his room. I performed a few chores outside, renewed my ablutions and went into the mosque. I sat down in a corner and began to read Qur'an. During the reading I felt a presence. I looked up to see a beautiful man on the sheepskin rug before the prayer alcove (*mihrab*). He was bearded and wore a black robe and a beautiful, very tall black turban. He held prayer beads (*tasbih*) in one hand and sat nodding his head as I read. There was a beautiful smile on his face, into which I peered. He continued to smile and after a moment he was no longer there. Shortly afterwards the Shaikh came into the mosque. We sat together and I told him about the visitor. 'It will happen all of the time,' he said with a smile. Later, referring to the same occurrence, about which he asked me several questions, he said: 'You are a very lucky man.' The visitor who came bore out the truth of what the Shaikh had said to me shortly after my return from the journey: 'You will have the same chance here which you had there.' Beyond any logic or reason something had sprung into life which was not in any way related to my deserving or my effort. It was one ray from a great Sun which now is rising in my heart. Just as the song on the radio had said: 'The journey is taking place today . . .' Indeed it is.

The story of Ayaz is actually the teaching of the realisation of the fruit of hope. 'Put on the garment of poverty everyday,' the Shaikh had said, 'and kill the *dunya* in yourself with the knife of Hazreti Abraham, peace be upon him.' Within poverty is the quality of the slave, and within this is the secret, not of what one loses, but of what is to be found. The story of Ayaz is a teaching of the exalted position to which one can rise after having become a slave. Ah *taslimiyyat*! It is the slavedom of submission which leads to realisation of the fruit of hope: the taste of Unity. But before the seeker can approach the realisation of Unity — before the long journeying bird can come before the Simurgh, every foreign element of the heart must be cleared away. Such a cleansing is mirrored in the answer given by Hazreti Shemsi Tabriz to one who enquired of him: 'What is gnosis?'

'It is the life of the heart through God,' he answered. 'What is living make die — thy body I mean. What is dead, vivify — thy heart I refer to. What is present, hide — it is this world. What is absent, invite — it is the world future life. What exists, annihilate — passion. What does not exist, produce — intention. True knowledge is in the heart, while the profession of faith is on the tongue. Service is at the expense of the body: If thou wouldst escape hell, serve up thy intention; if thou desirest the Master, turn thy face towards Him for thou wilt at once find Him . . .'

As I reflected on the two journeys in the passing of time, together with my failings and successes, I came one day upon the following verses of Qur'an:

> They will say: 'Our Lord! Twice hast Thou made us without life and twice hast Thou given us life! Now we have recognized our sins: Is there any way out of this?'
>
> *(40:11)*

In this verse God has brought man from the death of non-existence to life which is the soul's first journey. Man then goes from this life through death to Resurrection in the *akhirat* which is the second and final journey. My own travel brought me to mindfulness of the journey which truly matters. Having been shown this, I began to see a great blessing in losing what I thought I had sought during my mundane travel to the Middle East. My own hypocrisy became clearly evident to myself. Upon my acknowledgement of this, a true and crystal hope began to surface from some untouched place within. This hope is not yet fulfilled completely, but is present, felt, and growing to fulfilment — and if one is truly pregnant, as suggests the Shaikh, then it is enough to grow with the passing of the days. By God's grace and by His mercy, delivery will come.

CHAPTER 6

THE CAR

After my return from the journeys I came into another long period of infrequent contact with the Shaikh. I did, however, have the opportunity to make two short but very pleasant car journeys with him to a nearby city, after which I rarely had time alone with him. Long intervals with no close personal interaction became increasingly characteristic of my relationship with him, and yet as I have said, it usually happened that during these times I was left with some challenging personal task to complete. The longer I knew him, the more subtle the tasks became.

The Qur'anic talks of the Shaikh continued through this particular interval and in the absence of his personal discourses they provided me with a great deal of inspiration and guidance. These particular talks which dealt with two of the great battles of Islam, *Badr* and *Uhud*, were extremely powerful and among the last that the Shaikh gave publicly in that community. A major theme was the nature of struggle, suffering, and trust in God Most High.

During this time personal concerns of spiritual development were addressed more openly and collectively by the Shaikh in the circle of murids and dervishes who were his disciples. This situation thrust me into a place where I reflected more on my connection with the other seekers whom I had come to know, and what the commonalities were in the journey which we shared. Suddenly, I arrived in a place where I clearly saw that I was not the Shaikh's only disciple. Moreover, I learned that I would sometimes have to speak in the presence of others or not have the opportunity to get an answer from the Shaikh without waiting several months. Something about this open forum affected my view of my own concerns, and it often happened that things which at first seemed very important did not seem at all worth saying publicly in the company of the Shaikh.

One of my most major unexpressed concerns at the time was my car. I had never really mentioned it to the Shaikh, but I was continually replacing parts, or having breakdowns, or having to go for long periods of time with the car off the road in a state of disrepair. Earlier, during the time when I was trying to fathom the teaching of the plant, one of the Shaikh's dervishes had been having car troubles much like my own. He always smiled and asked me how my car was whenever he saw me, but it was months before I made any connection between his experience and my own. Even if my car was out of order when he made enquiry, I never realised the point. One morning I received a phone-call from the Shaikh. In our conversation I mentioned that the dervish with car trouble was planning to go in search of a better working vehicle. The Shaikh suggested that I join the dervish and accompany him in his search. Following the Shaikh's direction I contacted the dervish.

We spent the afternoon in Car City, a section of the town in which there was street after street of used cars. Cars of all types and sizes, domestic and foreign, luxury and economy, sports coupés, sedans, customised wrecks, refurbished antiques, and more. Each had its claim to fame and each made its bid for a buyer. Some had been owned by famous somebodys and some by nobodys. Some were represented by their brand name, some by salesmen talking fast and making unrefusable offers, some by their shiny chrome and low mileage, and some by perhaps nothing more than a sign painted on the windscreen saying 'Good Runner'.

As we made our way along the streets that sunny summer day, being wooed as we were by cars which perhaps hoped to escape from their urban concentration camp onto some peaceful side-street or perchance into a garage, dim reflections of my own search for the Needle came to mind. The dervish looked at every possibility, asked questions, and listened patiently to salesmen. After having passed through several he turned to me in a quiet moment and said:

'How is one possibly to know which one to choose? My choice is only made more difficult by the fact that the Shaikh has already suggested to me that whatever car I choose will be short-lived, and yet there is a *right* car.'

I listened to him sympathetically but made no response. 'Which one to choose?' was the question which had come up before, as I stood in front of a cabinet of a thousand and one record needles. It is a question to test the faith of the seeker's heart and though I had already had such a test, the question of the dervish was faint in my ears that day. Because my own car was running well at the time, I detached myself in aloof observation and decided that the teaching was primarily for him.

Finally, the dervish decided on a car which he had spotted earlier. It was a simple, very battered, silver-blue economy car, which seemed to be an American replica of a Toyota or a Datsun. The salesmen stood behind the car smiling as if they were the parents of Cinderella about to inherit the wealth of a prince. Behind their smiles they were probably hoping that the bonds would be tied quickly, but it was apparent to the dervish, to them, and to myself that the Cinderella carriage was fast approaching its midnight hour. The dervish expressed serious interest in its purchase when we returned to the sales office. He asked to inspect the car again and the two of us looked under the bonnet, discussing back and forth the problems of the car with the mechanical finesse of two monkeys attempting to repair a watch with a hammer and saw. The salesmen seemed hardly to notice us. In fact, to my surprise they even suggested that the car needed a few last-minute repairs. The dervish, however, like a nervous groom, asked for time. He needed a few hours to think before making a conclusive agreement.

We left in search of a phone-booth from which the dervish attempted to reach the Shaikh. After a few tries he got through and told him about the car. The Shaikh summoned us to his apartment so we left the phone-booth and proceeded there. We waited at the door until we were fully convinced that he was not inside. We walked the hallways and finally went to the laundry room sink where we made our ablutions for the midday prayer. When we returned to the Shaikh's door he received us. He sat quietly on the floor dressed in a shirt and tie over which he wore his hooded dervish robe. He was silent for a time and when he raised his head to look at us I saw in his face an expression which seemed to be something between kindness and desperation. More clearly perhaps, I saw that he was a stranger on this planet. While I was still much in this world's grasp, for him it meant nothing at all. When he raised his head that quiet afternoon, I knew that he was passing through this life with the swiftness of a desert wind. His eyes were moist and full of light and the love within him moved his heart to speak to us in kindness and in patience. He asked where we had gone when leaving his door moments earlier. We told him and he reprimanded us for not using his rest room, which he said was our own. He asked if we had said *'Asr*, the prayers of afternoon, and we said that we had not. He showed us the direction to the east and we performed the prayer. We spoke for a time and left.

The Shaikh had told the dervish that the salesmen wanted too much for the car and to offer less. I wondered what would happen. The dervish seemed to be slightly anxious about the possible outcome, but the next time I saw him he was driving the little car. That car served the dervish and myself quite well, though it was constantly in repair. Often it was running when my own car was not and so I rode in it and benefited by its being owned by the dervish. Before the little car eventually became the pumpkin which it truly was from the very outset, it carried us on many long journeys, and was the focus of many a teaching. Beyond this, and on more than one occasion, we travelled very far in it to visit Shaikhs who had come to our country from far-away places, to teach us and help us to strengthen our faith.

In the weeks which followed my visit to Car City with the dervish my primary interaction with the Shaikh continued to come through his Qur'anic talks. The group of his disciples usually enjoyed some time with him after these meetings once a week. Most of the time we crowded into the little room which served as his office. These were more informal times in which he extended the lessons of Qur'an to the practical aspects of our lives, heard our questions and taught us by the way in which he answered us, gave examples, or told stories. This method of contact continued through most of the winter months and into the spring. Many months passed before I realised the extent to which I had benefited through these times with the Shaikh in spite of the fact that my contact was not as outwardly personal as it had been in the past. During these months continual incidents involving problems with cars were surfacing in the picture of events. In the weeks which immediately followed my trip with the dervish to Car City, I slowly awakened to the fact that I was living another teaching. One cold snowy night on my way to one of the Shaikh's talks, I passed the dervish who had bought the car. The car had completely lost all of its electrical power and would not move. Seeing that he needed help, I stopped. We attempted to start the car with jump-leads, but each time it would start, go a short distance, and then die. Finally we tied his car to my own with an old rope, and towed it to a service station not very far up the road. We crowded the dervish's family and passengers into my car and proceeded to the talks.

As we came into the meeting the Shaikh was speaking:

'Any suffering which comes to us', he said, 'is actually a blessing. We should say to God: "Give me suffering, and as much of misfortune as You will, that I might come to appreciate the suffering of the Prophet and (through my suffering) know Your overwhelming mercy (*Rahmat*)."'

Everything which the Shaikh was saying in his talks was directly related to my life and the experiences present at that time. I am sure that I clearly heard the words of the Shaikh, yet their *meaning* escaped me. Somehow I simply could not realise the scope of what was presented and its relevance for me. On the other hand, strange as it may seem, I could see very easily how what I had heard was a teaching for everyone else — especially the dervish. Weeks passed before I finally came to see that the events surrounding the car not only had personal meaning for the dervish related to his own station, but were teachings for me as well. My experiences with the dervish and the car, like other experiences which were subtly presented in my life, were each a means to my own inward expansion and evolution.

> Soon will We show them our signs in the [furthest] regions [of the earth], and in their own souls, until it becomes manifest to them that this is the Truth. Is it not enough that thy Lord doth witness all things?
>
> *(Qur'an 41:53)*

One evening just after one of the Shaikh's *tafsirs*, I approached him with a book I had uncovered amongst some old belongings I had stored away in a box. The book was an old handwritten section of Qur'an from Persia, which I thought might be valuable.

'Do you have any attachment to this book?' the Shaikh asked, as I presented it to him.

'No, not at all,' I answered, rather surprised by his question, which caught me completely off-guard.

'Good,' he said. 'I'd like to borrow it for a time. Are you sure about the book?'

'Yes,' I said. 'Please take it. Keep it for as long as you like.'

The conversation ended and that evening the Shaikh departed with the book. A few weeks passed and one afternoon I noticed that my thoughts were repeatedly turning to the book. The thought even passed through my mind that the Shaikh might keep the book. After all he had had it now for quite some time. This particular thought was incredible and I was surprised at myself when I observed it passing through my mind. I knew that the Shaikh had enough books of his own, but more importantly, I knew that he held no attachment for any of them, had no need whatever for my book and what is more, had no desire within him to possess it.

Shortly after this, at one of the talks, the Shaikh called me to himself again. 'Here is your book,' he said. 'Were you concerned about it?'

'No, not at all,' I said, answering much too quickly and lying to avoid my embarrassment.

'Are you quite sure?' he pressed.

'Yes, I am,' I said, hoping the challenge would end.

'You were worried about the book,' he said. 'I suggest you analyse your own mind. Do you remember what you were thinking one certain afternoon?'

The Shaikh had clearly seen into my heart. I had once read that one cannot be a Shaikh who cannot read the hearts of his disciples. In that moment I was completely halted in my naive tactic. Realising at last that the Shaikh truly knew, I faced him more honestly than I ever had before.

'Yes, I remember what I thought,' I said. 'Actually you have been right in all you have said and I am surprised at my own thoughts and very embarrassed.'

'There is nothing valuable in the book,' he said. 'In fact it contains a mistake. You should be more careful of what you accept. Here, please take it.'

Without looking at me he placed the book into my hands and immediately walked away. From that time forward I never related to the Shaikh by playing the false game of testing to see if he knew. In dealing with the book I achieved a greater insight into how unconscious I was about my own mundane attachments, of which the book was merely a symbol. But even more importantly, I began to understand my own tendency towards doubting and my lack of trust in my teacher. Being brought to this place of examining myself, I plainly saw how much I used my head instead of my heart.

Just a few weeks later, again at one of the talks, several people and a group of the Shaikh's disciples had come together for a meeting. The dervish who had been having car trouble was there and his troubles with his car had continued over the weeks. In fact, at that particular time his car had completely broken down and another one of the disciples had given him the loan of a car. The dervish had arrived without the borrowed car to report to its owner, in the presence of the Shaikh, that some electrical problem had developed in the car. He had seen sparks of fire underneath the bonnet which he could not diagnose. The car would not move, whatever the case, and he had been forced to leave it temporarily abandoned by the roadside.

Throughout the report of the dervish the Shaikh observed the disciple who was the owner of the car.

'Are you feeling some concern?' he asked the disciple, who immediately gave the reply:

'No, not at all — it's only a car.'

'You are not being honest with yourself!' said the Shaikh quite sharply. 'You are not ready for such a teaching for it is a teaching for a dervish and you are a *murid*.'

I immediately thought back to my experience with the book. Just as it was with this disciple, my own lips had been faster to speak than my mind to realise. I did not see my attachment, yet my attachment to the book was as apparent as the murid's attachment to the car. Moreover, in each instance it was the Shaikh's confrontation which had forced us to see exactly where we were. Before we left for home that night the Shaikh told us that the car had nothing more than the simplest problem: a worn battery cable. Sure enough, when the dervish and the disciple returned to the car, they found that the Shaikh's diagnosis was right.

From this time forward over a period of four or five months, most of my few interactions with the Shaikh were somehow involved with cars. Through this series of happenings I was brought step by step through the teaching until I finally saw the point. The first of these began when a dervish friend arrived at my door late on Saturday evening. He had been travelling several hours by car and needed a place for the night. I showed him to his room and left him to rest. About an hour after his arrival there was a quiet knocking. I casually walked to the door to answer and to my mild astonishment, I opened to find the Shaikh, who calmly greeted me with *salaams*.

'What are your plans for the evening?' he asked.

'I had not made any,' I answered. 'Is there something I can do?'

'Come,' he said. 'Let us take your car and go.'

We were inside the car in a moment. The Shaikh pointed a direction and we drove off.

'My car is out of gas,' he said. 'I'd like for you to take me back to it then see if you can find a gas station which is open.'

He gave me specific instructions as to how to approach his car as we drove towards the place where it sat at the roadside. When we reached the car, he inspected it very carefully then signalled for me to go. I left the Shaikh and drove off in search of petrol, but finding every nearby station closed I soon returned to him empty-handed.

'It is all right,' he said. '*Alhamdulillah*. Are you quite sure that you would like to stay with this task?'

'Yes, *insha 'Allah,*' I enthusiastically answered. 'I would like to very much.'

'OK,' he said, after a moment's pause. 'I want you to go to a certain dervish's home and ask him for some gas. He has some I am sure.'

This particular dervish lived about twenty-five miles from the place where the Shaikh and I were standing. We calculated the amount of time that it would take for me to get there and back. We agreed on a place for our rendezvous and I dropped the Shaikh off at a small restaurant just up the road, perhaps a mile or so from is car.

I arrived at the dervish's door at about two o'clock in the morning. After having knocked for what seemed like half an hour, he answered. He was a little sleepy but he was very cheerful, pleasant, and eager to assist. I explained to him that the Shaikh had sent me and he gave me a large can of petrol. Needless to say, it was very late when I returned to the Shaikh. I was completely wrong in calculating the time that the journey would take and by the time I came back the little restaurant was closed and the Shaikh was standing outside at the curb. We returned to his car and poured the petrol into the tank. He gave me money to replace the dervish's petrol and sent me home. Before I left him, he told me to wake the dervish who was my guest and to have him come outside where he would meet him. I did as he instructed and I did not see him again until the time of his next talk.

About two weeks after my night meeting with the Shaikh I met with him again at his apartment. I came with no greater insight into the experiences of my last meeting with him than what I'd had when I left him at the roadside, which essentially was none. For all the many hours of reflection I had given to the incident over the passing of the days, I grew no clearer and no wiser. The teaching of the car continued to evade my understanding. Finally, the Shaikh brought me to the place from which there was no evasion or escape.

'I want you to go back to the house of the dervish who gave you the gas,' he said. 'Ask him to take you to my car and tell you the story.'

I left the Shaikh and arrived at the door of the dervish about ten o'clock at night. He greeted me warmly as he had done before, and when I explained to him why I had come he smiled.

'OK,' he said. 'I guess we'd better go out to the barn.'

It was a beautifully clear and crisp winter night but spring was not far away. The dervish and I strolled across the yard underneath the branches of a large tree and into a fenced-in clearing next to which was a complex of barns. He talked to me as we walked.

'Several years ago when I was in Turkey for a time', related the dervish, 'a *murid* came quite excitedly saying that the Shaikh had bought a new car. It was actually a used car but it was a fairly nice car none the less. Certainly, it was nothing extravagant, but a car which was in good running order. It was a little surprising to us, however, because the Shaikh's previous car was quite old, and nearly a junker. Somehow it had run well for many years with no maintenance beyond gas and occasionally some oil. It had magic marker writing on the window which the Shaikh had never bothered to remove. I didn't think much about the new car, however, but I listened to the *murid*'s story. Later though, when I was back in the United States, I became more aware of the car through a series of experiences with the car and the Shaikh of which I cannot speak.'

We had come to one of the barns and stopped before a large sliding door on which there was a padlock. The dervish and I both recited a short prayer and entered the barn. As we had approached the barn it had begun to dawn on me that I was living another teaching. For the first time since my trip with the other dervish to Car City, I began to feel a real sense of personal involvement. I was really wakeful as we entered that barn, and I brought my full consciousness to attending to what the dervish had to say. I saw the Shaikh's car before me as the dervish continued with his story.

'Last winter', he said, 'the Shaikh suggested that it was time to put the car away — to bury it, so to speak. He told me what needed to be done in order to prepare it for its burial, which involved clearing the barn of its junk, and gave me a specific set of instructions on how the car should be cleaned. He also gave me specific phrases to recite, which I said whenever I entered the barn. I carried out these instructions to the letter. The Shaikh had made some comments about a weakness in one of the barn walls suggesting that it needed cement and even though I listened, I remember that I had disagreed inside.

'Related to the car, however, the only explanation that the Shaikh gave was that the car had simply gotten out of control. Such a car, he said, could not be driven by one weak in faith. He said that in fact one of the reasons for the car needing to be buried was that it was not responding as it should.'

The dervish went on to say that he buried the car by covering it with a large white cloth which served as its shroud. He locked the barn door and left. After a day or two he returned to the barn.

'When I came back into the barn,' said the dervish, 'I found that the bricks I had placed by the car were moved and the licence plate had been taken off. The shroud was as I had left it. Checking the barn door padlock, I found it completely untampered with and though there was deep snow, I saw no footprints, nor any visible signs of movement. What was most interesting, however, was that the wall which the Shaikh had suggested repairing now had a large hole in it. I repaired the hole and a month later it reappeared just as strangely as it had appeared before. Winter passed and late in the spring the Shaikh was preparing to make a journey. He said that it was time to take the car out and see. Another dervish was with me at the time and he attempted to take the car out of the barn but was unsuccessful. The car veered out of his control and smashed into the side of a wall. He gave the wheel over to the Shaikh, who then brought the car out of the barn.

'See,' said the Shaikh: 'in order to drive properly you must obey certain rules. One must be attentive to detail and when driving one must be concentrated on driving. Keep speed constant, maintain the appropriate speed for the limit and keep both hands on the wheel.'

'The Shaikh drove the car away', continued the dervish, 'and left it in the parking lot of the apartment where he lived. He was travelling out of town at the time and he returned after about one week to find that the car had been stolen. Completely unruffled, he reported the car to the police, who were more surprised than he because no such theft had ever occurred in the complex where the

Shaikh was living. Not much later the thieves were apprehended.

'The car', said the Shaikh, 'had been prepared for the *haram* (wrongdoing) it was subjected to. It should now be treated as respectfully as a mosque. Enter it with ablution and also remove your shoes.'

'From that time forward,' said the dervish, 'there were continuous episodes with the car of the Shaikh or with cars of others among his disciples.'

I remembered this particular comment of the dervish and later, after I had become fully submerged in this teaching of the car, I found upon enquiry that practically everyone in the circle of dervishes and murids had been experiencing car troubles. Out of the dozen or so cars which we then collectively owned, at least four had deteriorated and fallen apart to such an extent that they had to be replaced. My own car was the worst.

'When winter came again,' said the dervish concluding his story, 'the Shaikh instructed me to prepare the car again. "Put down the white *musalla* (prayer mat)," he said. "But do not put the car on it." So I brought the car into the barn again, cleaned it, and I put the large white cloth before it as a prayer mat. I locked the barn door with the car standing there before the *musalla*. I wondered to myself what one does when one is in the barn before the mat, but not yet permitted to stand on the mat. What does one do? There is not unlimited time for standing in the barn.'

The dervish and I left the barn and locked the door behind us. We walked back across the yard towards his house, stopping every step or two to admire the stars. He invited me to stay overnight to avoid the drive. I accepted and the following morning I left for home.

One Saturday not long after I had visited the dervish who had housed the car in the barn, another set of circumstances brought me together with him and the dervish whom I had accompanied to Car City.

It was a beautiful late-winter day and spring was just about to come. The mid-morning sunlight was bursting with warmth and a scattered cloud or two floated by on breezes of the bright blue sky. We were casually cruising down the road along the lake that day, just the three of us, together in the Shaikh's car. Strange as it may seem, I have no recollection of what our purpose or destination was. I only remember that we were under the Shaikh's direction and that the dervish who drove had both hands on the wheel. The driver was the dervish who had housed the car in the barn. I sat next to him in the front while the other dervish rode quietly alone in the back seat. The morning passed, to our collective surprise, without incident, but that little ride brought us together in a way we had not been together before. It was a good time. We laughed and talked and reflected on the experience and each of us knew more clearly than ever before that the teaching of the car was touching us all. When the time of the next talk came, the Shaikh was not present. He had sent a message that he would not be there and he had instructed the two dervishes to take charge in his absence. He had told them to share some of their experiences with the car. This instruction was one which I personally saw as a challenging teaching within itself. The group of people who attended the Qur'anic talks were to say the least, a motley crew. There was always a small number of *murids* and dervishes present who were clearly known to be disciples of the Shaikh, but there were also sincere Muslims and Christians present who were just as clearly not inclined in any way to the mystic aspects of faith. Occasionally there might even be some among us who did not profess any particular belief at all. The thought of giving a Sufi talk to this group struck me as both amusing and slightly scary.

I noticed these feelings in myself and as soon as I took a moment to analyse their surfacing, in connection with the task from the Shaikh to the two dervishes, I began to feel even more uncomfortable with myself. It suddenly struck me that I was feeling scared to be known as a Sufi. More than likely everyone in that group knew it already but giving a talk on the car, of all things, seemed at that time to be just a little bit too much. Apparently, the Shaikh knew it was not for me to do and he did not ask me. As I reflect back on that time I see how tremendously much I benefited by this simple incident. Some of those people in the group who were not in the circle of the Shaikh's disciples had known me as just a 'regular Muslim'. The mere thought of giving the talk showed me that I was trying to be two kinds of Muslim: the regular Muslim in public and the Sufi in private. So many times the Shaikh had said: 'There is nothing higher than a Muslim, one who is fully submitted to God.' I do not know what caused me to cling to this dualistic thinking but I saw that it was in me. The Shaikh had addressed this concern when speaking to a group of us months before.

'Though it is true,' he had said, 'that even in faith one evolves by degrees and stages, the true Muslim is only one. There is nothing to hide if one is a Muslim who at the same time seeks to have a loving heart and a direct experience of the beauty of Allah.'

Much later I understood this even more clearly when the Shaikh spoke to me of the people who profess to be believers in God, yet who in their basic outward (*zahir*) orientation, become very uncomfortable when the name of God is recited aloud, outside of any ritualised prayer. Even though I thought I had resolved this dualistic remnant of hypocrisy within, I noticed when the Shaikh made the comment on people of the outward that something inside of me clicked and fell into place like the final piece of an unsolved puzzle.

The first dervish to speak was the one whom I had accompanied to Car City. 'When I met the Shaikh a few years ago,' he said, 'he always asked about my car. I have had much car trouble since that time, in fact last week my car broke down and for two days it would not start. I was finally able to get it started, then the other night on the parkway the lights dimmed and the car began to die. I finally began to see that the first valley of Shaikh Attar is discovering all about our so-called car. We all have a car even if it seems that we don't, and until one comes into unity with Allah, this car has at least two aspects. There is the outer car that transports the body in this world (*dunya*), and related to it is the subtle 'inner car' made mostly of the feelings we have nurtured related to our own individual outer cars. There is another car which takes us to the hereafter (*akhirat*) and it is a car that will not die, and which never goes into disrepair. It is this car which should be sought. The Shaikh promised me that I would have such a car but he said that I would drive many a car before I achieved it.'

As I listened to the story of the dervish I understood him to be referring to a certain state of *being* in speaking of the car which takes us to the *akhirat*. During his talk he made this point clearer by telling us of an incident where he and another disciple were with the Shaikh:

'The Shaikh's old car had been left in an icy parking lot for quite some time one winter,' said the dervish. 'There was snow all over the car and a wall of ice up to the hood. No one would have believed that the car would ever have started, much less got out of that space. The Shaikh got into the car and told us to stand back. It started up instantly and in another moment he had freed the car. It seemed to us that the car flew up and over the ice. Witnessing the spectacle with our very own eyes we stood there in amazement.'

'What happens,' challenged the dervish after a slight pause, 'when you wake up in the morning on an unfamiliar road in an unfamiliar place with your car? On the way to California your car breaks down. At once you're in panic dread. Suddenly you realise for the first time that there's another car, a car inside that is just as solid and just as dense. Now in the crisis your whole attitude towards the car is a model of how you deal with the world. After you've mastered dealing with the car in the world (*dunya*), you finally get to yourself. When at last you get to yourself and to your own *nafs* (egotistical self), as manifested through your interaction with the car, you begin to learn about *the car inside yourself*. You have to learn to take this car all apart, to repair it and clean it up.

'When my brother dervish and I got entrenched in *dunya* the Shaikh's car was put into the barn. The car is comfortable inside the barn. It's warm and secure but you can't go anywhere. We're giving up our hypocrisy now and seeing our real attachment. It is our attachment which keeps us from reaching the open road.

'Besides the little car which each of us drives, there is the bigger car like that which the Shaikh drives with certainty and confidence. A car which was in preparation for years. We each have a seat in the bigger car and it rides us through the *dunya* and into *akhirat*, the world to come. This is the car which we all are on indeed. The teaching of the car turns you inside out but the only way you can discover is to drive the car from wherever you find it. Realising how identified you are with your car causes something to happen inside. You see how much you really love it. People of the world (*dunya*) seem never to have car trouble; but on this path, the car is having terrible troubles — both the car within and the car without. This is the battleground, the *Jihad al Akbar*: the greater war, the struggle with one's self.'

> When you enter the first valley, the Valley of Quest, a hundred difficulties will assail you; you will undergo a hundred trials.
>
> *Shaikh Attar*

The talk of the first dervish about his experience with the car helped my understanding very much. From that time on I had a different view of the car. That mundane invention which has come to be so much depended on by contemporary man, became for me a metaphor for a whole other world of experience, and a vehicle for travelling within. It was now very easy to see that this entire teaching was alive. It was neither intellectual nor philosophical, and no amount of reflection on the past or speculation about the future was helpful in that moment when I realised the utter 'broken-down-ness' of my car. The teaching which came was *now*, present in this moment, near. Here! The challenge to my self being to find silence somewhere in that very moment of chaos or to be overruled by my egoistical self and make a desperate escape in any one of a thousand desire-filled directions.

The following week the second dervish presented himself to the circle of people. I had the feeling that night, that much of what had been said the week before was missed. I speculated that there was perhaps too much preoccupation in the minds of some with the Shaikh's failure to be present. Somehow it seemed that something in the talk of the second dervish tapped not only into existing feelings of disappointment but also into expectations that the Shaikh should have been there to give the meeting direction. Even though we never actually discussed this issue directly, the unfolding of events seemed to force everyone to examine their real motives for being present at the talks. The Shaikh truly did have the capacity to be in harmony beyond the level of personality at which most of us were then stuck, being together in that group with true feelings of mutuality was not less than a challenge, to say the very least. It soon became clear that we were each being given an opportunity to see what did in fact bring us to the talks. Was our interest in God Almighty, in loving Him and serving each other, or was our interest only in the Shaikh?

In the face of these questions the teaching of the car was taken to a completely new level. This teaching which had been individually personal in the past now became a teaching collective. It was as if the group of us who attended the Qur'anic talks of the Shaikh were being introduced to the teaching of the city bus, which is basically just a bigger car. This bus was not running now for the second week and no one was sure exactly what the problem was. It was apparent now, however, that when the bus was running, some of us had perhaps not asked ourselves seriously enough where the bus was going at the time we climbed aboard. We assumed that the final destination was the same for all the riders, and in the ultimate sense it is. There is in reality only One Destination, but at the level of the world (*dunya*), which is exactly where we were, what happens when a bus breaks down is that people begin to talk about where they *think* the bus should go, or the particular places that they are *hoping* to reach. One soon comes to see that there are many anticipated stops along the way and people have hopes of getting off at different places.

At the Shaikh's instruction the second dervish had been appointed as a representative of the bus company, something like a tour guide, so to speak. He had been given the task of dealing with this collection of passengers and making an effort to help them see how they might utilise their time while the bus was not running, at least not in its usual way. Connecting with the talk of the dervish who had spoken the week before, he began to ask the challenging question:

'How do you know you're on *Sirat-al Mustaqeem*, the Straight Path? Even if you say all your prayers, read Qur'an and do all the nice things how do you know?'

What it seemed to me he was asking was this: 'How do you know that your car is going to make it to California if that's the journey you have set out upon?' The common reply would probably be something like: 'Well, I'm on route 66 West so I will get there eventually but also I checked the car out thoroughly before I got started. I've got an all-new electrical system, a Die-Hard battery, new brakes and top of the line radial tyres. I use the best gas and even though it doesn't snow in California, I have rust-proofed the car at least twice. I have taken every precaution.'

As one might guess, everyone became a scholar of religion when the dervish propounded the question. Qur'an was quoted, history was cited, and ancient and obscure pieces of knowledge were brought forward — all without shedding any light on the question. Many mechanics emerged in the group that night, but no one could repair the bus.

'How do you know?' the dervish asked again, and still there was no answer. Some became too 'above-it-all' to speak on a question with such an obvious answer and others among us completely withdrew.

The longer I sat there the more I realised how much we all behaved like people who are generally found on buses: close in physical proximity but actually far apart. Usually only when drawn together by some imminent crisis do they come to realise their mutual dependence and that their destinies are intertwined. So it was with us. Without the Shaikh our bus had broken down and thrown us all together. There was for me great opportunity in this crisis. Brought in to face-to-face contact with others whose understanding was slightly different from my own, I was forced to resolve my attempt to be two different kinds of Muslim. This lingering remnant of hypocrisy was finally attacked. I was surprised to realise its existence within me and relieved to win this battle, in the war upon my self.

After the dervish's talk the people in the group seemed extremely disgruntled. For some, this talk of the car was completely void of meaning and empty of purpose.

'The Shaikh is OK,' I imagined them to be thinking, 'but his disciples are all mentally disturbed.'

How interesting it was that the Shaikh appeared that night after the talk had ended. He didn't speak or make any comment on what had taken place before he came. He simply observed us as we milled around, talking to each other in scattered pairs and trios, fully absorbed in the chaos of our feelings, a clear indication of our stations at the time. None the less, the presence of the Shaikh forced us all to clearer vision, beyond the strangeness of events. Moreover, I sensed that somehow at some other level, we had begun to feel we were connected and we began to understand.

Not long after this I had occasion to be with the Shaikh. As we sat together in a car, he enquired about the talks which he had directed the dervishes to give during the time he was away. I related what I had seen and heard, together with a few of my own personal feelings and reflections.

'You only got about 5 per cent of the teaching,' he said. 'Some of what you heard was true but some of the issues are not yet finished. The question of the shrouded car in the barn is still unanswered and unclear. The dervish's analogy of the car going to California and the question "How do you know it will get there?" are both on target. The analogy of the bus is on target too. We are dealing, in the bus, with those who *know* Islam (obedience and surrender to God) but don't *live* Islam. When suddenly the electricity goes off, all faces are blank. The predictability of the car's working is not greater than the predicatability of health. In either case, we never deal with fallibility until it breaks. Unless your car breaks down you don't begin to know.'

The second dervish's question: 'How do you know that you are on the Straight Path (Sirat-al Mustaqeem)?' was all connected with the general teaching involved with our reaction to his challenge. When I spoke more about it to the Shaikh, he made it very plain and simple:

'One's *Iman* or faith and one's car are the same in some ways,' he said. 'Scratch or put just a little dent in the people's faith, then watch and see what they do.'

As God would have it my car was not running again. Before the Shaikh left me we sat for a while longer talking. Sensing that my car and my faith were both being battered, he told me a story of Hazreti Ayyub, the Prophet Job, peace be upon him. God tried him with a disease which caused the gradual deterioration of his entire body. When the disease accelerated, the prophet asked God to spare his heart that he might continue to love Him, and his tongue that he might preserve his means of *zikr* (remembrance) to his Lord. God granted this request and because of the sterling faith of Hazreti Ayyub, peace be upon him, God Most High protected him from Satan and restored him to health.

'Whether you have your car or not,' said the Shaikh, 'you still have your feet to walk by, and as long as you have a tongue and a heart you should be grateful. The car, your health, and even your tongue and heart are all the property of Allah.'

That day as I sat with the Shaikh I began to see my struggle more clearly than ever before. After months of avoiding I came to grips with my attachment and my ungratefulness to God. From that day forward I felt myself relating with more trust in God, no matter what the condition of my car which continued to have its ups and downs — with a predominance of the latter. Some weeks later it happened again that I was together with the Shaikh at the farm of one of the dervishes. I had stretched the skin of a ram I had sacrificed on the holiday of Eid, and stored it in a barn. I asked the Shaikh if he would come and see it. We entered the barn and approached the skin together.

'It was a big animal,' I said remembering the animal as it had been when alive.

'You have a big sacrifice to make,' said the Shaikh.

'It certainly died a lot easier than I am dying,' I said matter-of-factly, reflecting on my personal struggle.

The Shaikh stopped and looked into my face. 'I don't think I have ever heard anyone say that,' he said. 'You should put that statement in your book.'

The next time I saw the Shaikh, he was in the Tekiya. About two weeks had passed and we were on the very verge of spring. Several disciples were gathered around him as he sat in his usual seat by the window, looking out of it occasionally and speaking to us about whatever came to his heart to say. As we sat together that day loud noises could be heard outside, moaning from afar. Sounds like those of a chain-saw or a mower.

'Do you know what that noise is?' asked the Shaikh.

A few of us guessed possibilities but none of us really knew.

'It is the engine of the snowmobiles,' he told us. 'And do you know why it is so loud? It is because the engine has to work harder when the snow is wet and heavy as it is now. The noise of the engine expresses the desperation of the snowmobiler.'

He recited a Qur'anic verse together with an explanation: 'Allah says: "Whether you warn them or not they do not believe." The snowmobilers do not believe that spring is here, yet the signs are clear and the snow is melting.'

This was one of few group interactions that we had with the Shaikh which concerned the car. Several months passed before the teaching went forward. During these months I attempted to resolve the teaching of the plant, and I continued to reflect on the things which the Shaikh had said whenever I was with him. I entered a period of truce in the struggle with my car and for several months I coasted along quite smoothly.

One bright Saturday morning, early in the summer, I received a phone-call from the Shaikh. He didn't phone that often and I was surprised to hear his voice.

'Can you meet me today? There is something I would like for you to see.'

I answered that I could and I wrote down the address and some directions he gave. Shortly afterwards I left. The place where I was to meet him was at a large intersection very much like Car City. There were several very large car dealerships all along the street. I parked my car and began to walk along the street. I did not see the Shaikh. I walked to the end of the dealership in one direction then turned to walk the other way. As I was walking along just beginning to wonder if I had missed the Shaikh or perhaps misunderstood his instructions, I heard his *salaams* just behind me. I turned to see him stepping from around a tall metal lamp-post which probably lit the place at night. I was very happy to see him, although it seemed to me at the time that he had stepped into my view from nowhere. I didn't try to understand the manner of his arrivals or departures, and though the question sometimes came into my mind about the ways in which he might travel, for the most part I left this question alone. I intuitively knew that its discussion was beyond the place where I was in my development at the time.

I turned to meet the Shaikh and return his greetings. We walked along together as he began to speak:

'My car stopped running here in the middle of the street. Some men were kind enough to push it into this lot. The car is over there in one of the garages and the mechanics have been working on it for several hours. The problem with the car continues to escape them and with all their knowledge of automobiles they have none the less been unable to repair it. There is a restaurant nearby. I will join you there in a minute. Order something for me, and do not watch me when I cross the street.'

I went on to the restaurant and I ordered a sandwich to share and a couple of Cokes. The Shaikh arrived in a few minutes and joined me at a small table near a window which looked out onto the street. Sunbeams poured in through the glass gently lighting his face which was already radiant with light from the Sun which shone within him. My heart swelled with feeling as I took in the moment. I realised how fortunate I was to be with this noble soul who wore the natural, normal body of any other man and who sat there that day sipping an all-American Coca Cola. We were silent for a time in which I felt my heart unsynchronised, but beating closely after the beat of his heart.

'I want to extend to you an invitation,' he said. 'An invitation to be free — to be a free man. Do you not know that death is *yaqin*? It is certain and yet you deny death. You deny the breaking down of the car, yet you are living in the expectation of car trouble, and when it comes, life stops. Your work is all involved with becoming free of the traps.'

I listened and made no comment. Everything I felt he knew and he verbalised my unspoken hopes.

'I must leave now but we will be together this afternoon,' he said. 'I will go to the car and probably find the men still without a solution. But *insha'Allah*, I will drive the car.'

He gave me a few instructions before departing and soon afterwards I left. He walked back to his car, which I am sure he drove away. When I arrived at his apartment that afternoon, sure enough his car was already there and parked behind the building on the lot.

This meeting was the last one which I remember having with the Shaikh which was directly concerned with the car. Nearly two years passed before I came to a place where I thought I finally understood the teaching. During this period I noticed, as I earlier mentioned, that the car of practically every disciple went through some kind of difficulty. Some of the cars were in such bad condition that they had to be replaced. My own car had its minor problems here and there, but I entered into a period inside these two years where I had no major difficulties for more than a year. I was grateful to God for the convenience He afforded me and I never forgot that the teaching was present.

Towards the end of this period in which I had relatively no trouble with my car I made a journey with my wife and child to another state to visit my parents and near relations. Returning from the trip, we went into a chuck hole on the highway which resulted in a badly damaged tyre rim and severe shock to the inner workings of the car. I managed to change the tyre and we drove the car home but it was not performing well. Electrical difficulties soon developed and I was forced to take the car off the road again. Unable to afford the cost of repair, nor able to diagnose its problems, I left the car to sit in the driveway. I did make efforts to get any friends who were mechanically inclined to inspect it, but those who did had no solution. Spring faded, summer passed and winter arrived. Finally, realising that I could not repair the car, one of my mechanic friends and I pushed the car into the garage and left it.

Ours was a two-car family anyway and by now I had grown accustomed to using the other car, which belonged to my wife. Hers was the one which usually kept us mobile during the long periods of the other car's states of disrepair. Winter wore on and became one of the coldest I had ever known. One bone-chilling morning I went out and hopped into my wife's car. I stuck the key into the ignition as I twisted around in the seat searching for the snow brush. I turned the key and there was no response. Interestingly enough, there was no response inside of me to the lack of response of the car. There were no dread thoughts of towing or fear that the battery might be dead. For the first time ever in such a circumstance as this, my thoughts turned immediately to God. It did not really matter if the car started or not and all I could do was feel grateful for all of the benefits and means which God Most High had given me. I felt genuine gratitude for even having had a second car. Moreover, there had never been a time when my own car had broken down and God, may He be exalted, left me in the lurch. I sat there in the driveway with both hands on the wheel experiencing a sweet new joy which was swelling within me that very moment. I glanced up to look at the garage before me, which was covered with a thick white blanket of snow. Remembering my own car, which had now been stored inside the garage for months, my mind turned immediately to the Shaikh's car, which had stood for months, shrouded in white in the dervish's barn. In quiet suddenness the final piece in a teaching which had gone on for no less than three years fell gently into place. With no forewarning a crisp and simple clarity wafted into the moment like the cool evening breeze which sweeps in from the sea.

The death of the car is the perfection of faith, the opening door to flawless trust (*tawakkal*) and the first step towards realisation of the fullness of worship (*'ibadat*). The inner car is the *nafs* or the experiencing lower self which is attached, by way of feelings, to the material car outside. The outer car is simply a unifying model of the assorted worldly paraphernalia to which we become attached and thus distracted from God Most High. The death of the car is actually the process of bringing the *nafs* to rest — the spiritual state of *mutmainnah*. It is not the death of the body but the death of extreme desires and ego-centered self-gratification. It is clearing the transaction between the soul and its Creator. It is letting go completely and letting God Almighty take over.

'One must close before one opens,' the Shaikh had often said, 'and the cup must be emptied before it can be filled.'

So it is that the death of the self brings perfection of faith. The death of the self or ego is the emptying of the cup. Trust which is *tawakkal*, follows faith or *Iman*. Thus it is faith which helps one get one's foot in the door. The fullness of worship (*'ibadat*) is realised on the other side of both faith and trust so that the *emptier* the seeker, the sweeter the *ibadat*, which is the worship and service of the servant to God, the Lord Most High. The Shaikh had once said that the seeker evolves to a state of faith. Indeed, as God Almighty says: 'Ye shall surely travel from stage to stage,' and the process by which attachments are brought slowly into perspective is a development which happens degree by degree.

'One who is weak in faith cannot drive the car,' the Shaikh had once said. Indeed what he said is true, for until faith comes one is *driven* at each step, but when one arrives at last at the stage of faith, Allah alone is the Driver. The car in the barn stood before the white prayer sheet (*musalla*) only for this reason: Prayer without faith is empty. But when the car within is finally at rest and the space within is clean, the *musalla* offers the possibility of a place to perform one's *'ibadat*, at the outer level, while the cup emptied of *nafs* offers a place for true worship to happen, this time from within.

'It is the outermost out and the innermost in,' the old woman told me years before. May Allah bring me through the stages and draw me closer to the secret of that truth which she spoke.

Thus came my understanding of the teaching of the car. A teaching of struggle towards the slowly opening door of *tawakkal*, that state of simple, flawless trust. Still sitting there in my wife's car, stalled in the driveway, I ended my reflections. I casually turned the key again and the engine roared to a start. I drove out of the driveway and the teaching continued — someday, if God be willing, I will go beyond the door.

CHAPTER 7

The Park

During one of the times when my car was running fairly well,I had the opportunity to spend a day with the Shaikh. The teaching of the car was already in progress and unfolding, but at that particular time I had not realised anything more than the very surface of its depth. As is quite usual on the Path of the Seeker, it often occurs that events overlap and sometimes it happens that two or three of these may be happening at once. So it was that the teaching which came in my journey to the park, was only one of several more brief but important teachings which happened in those years in which I struggled with the car.

The Shaikh had told me, several weeks in advance, that I would be spending a day together with him and another disciple. We would go with him to a gathering of some sort where he was to address a very large group of people.

'This will be a test of your *hizmet* (service),' he said to me. 'You are to stay at my right side no matter what happens. You are to speak to no one, and when I am speaking stay as close as you can and observe the faces of those in the crowd.'

This very simple instruction struck me with mild surprise. It was the first time that the Shaikh had told me what was being tested in me before he gave the test. Generally, I had been left to realise the purpose on my own. This being the case, I made an effort to be especially alert. I made a mental note of what he had told me, then waited for my time.

When the day finally came on which we were to travel, the other disciple was unable to come, so the Shaikh and I set out alone, together just us two. It seemed to be a very long trip. After several hours driving we arrived at the home of a man who was to accompany us to the gathering, only to find that he had already gone. Having no clear directions, we were left to find the way on our own. The wife of this man, who apparently knew the Shaikh well, saw our dilemma and suggested that she might go with us and direct us to the gathering, a short distance away. In a moment she sat in the seat behind the Shaikh and myself unexpectedly now the navigator of the ship. She communicated her directions to our Captain, the Shaikh, who communicated them to me. I drove according to whatever instructions he gave, without uttering a sound.

After we had asked directions at several places, I began to realise that we were lost at sea. We had stopped at a roadside auction, a house along the road, and a small variety store, all to no avail. We spoke to a man who made his way along on a bicycle, but he too was unable to help us find the place which we sought. We stopped again along the roadside near a large open field. There was a large service station across the way. The navigator left the car in search of a map, while the Shaikh and I stood outside the car to stretch our legs. It was a beautiful summer day and the sun was smiling warmly upon us. I was studying a *sura* — a verse of the Qur'an — which I had written on a small piece of paper. The Shaikh asked me what it was that I had, so I showed him the paper and recited for him in Arabic the opening verses of *Surat-ul Fath*, the Victory:

In the name of Allah, Most Gracious Most Merciful.
Verily We have granted thee a manifest victory.
That Allah may forgive thee thy faults of the past
and those to follow; fulfil His favour to thee and
guide thee on the Straight Way; and that
Allah may help thee with powerful help.
It is He Who sent down tranquillity into
the hearts of the Believers that they
may add faith to their Faith . . .

In that moment, just as I was concluding these lines, there came the gentlest, sweetest breeze. The wheat-like plants in the field beside us bowed low their heads as the breeze swept by. I looked into the face of the Shaikh and he looked into mine.

'It is time for *zuhr* (noon prayers),' he said. 'Let us get into the car and say them.'

Just as we concluded, the woman returned. I started the car again and we drove away. After another half an hour's ride we were lost again. We stopped at another house but no one seemed to be home, so we continued on ahead. Somewhere soon thereafter we came upon a countryside grocer's shop. There was a telephone-booth just outside the door. The Shaikh made a phone-call then asked about directions from a woman in the shop.

'I am trying to locate a place called Caspian Park,' said the Shaikh. 'Can you give me any help?'

The lady paused for a moment to think, then gave directions. She seemed to know the area well. We were back in the car a few minutes later, driving along the country roads near the park. Caspian Park, the place of the gathering, was only one small part of a very large park area which we had soon entered after leaving the shop. Somehow, inside the larger park we missed a road onto which we were to turn. I noticed myself beginning to become just a little impatient. Realising that my response was not appropriate, I told myself that I must keep myself in patience. Just as this was passing through my mind the Shaikh looked at me and said:

'Are you loosing *sabr* (patience)? It seems that you are.'

He had apparently been tuned in to me all the while. My first inclination was to deny my impatience but I did not. I had learned this lesson before. Why lie? More than likely I would not be able to deceive the Shaikh on even so small a matter as this, but even if it were that I could deceive him, could I also deceive God Almighty? I did not answer the Shaikh's question; I only looked over the steering wheel not speaking. My silence spoke the truth of what I had felt.

I turned the car around again and returned to the road we had missed. On a tree near the entrance to the road, there hung a small sign which read: CASPIAN PARK. I turned left onto the road which took us into a deeply wooded area. Tall trees lined the way on either side, casting shadows which stretched long before us in the light of the afternoon sun. We rode peacefully for what only seemed a moment. Soon the quiet forest roadway burst into a clearing and we had arrived at our destination.

Frisbies floated like UFOs, children ran and shrieked in play, and there were people everywhere. The sounds of folk music filled the air, together with smells of food and beer. There was much eating, drinking, dancing, and laughter while the band played on.

The Shaikh and the woman left the car and I went on to look for a place to park. When I returned to the Shaikh to take my station at his side, several people had gathered round him. We were ushered into a building, a kind of large dining shelter where the Shaikh was seated. I remained standing at his side close as a shadow.

We were brought enough food to feed an army. The Shaikh instructed me as to what could be eaten or not. We took little but he recognised every initiative of generosity or kindness. An old man with a flushed red face and the breath of a distillery leaned over me in order to see the Shaikh. He smiled and offered me a beer which I immediately waved away. We were brought Cokes. I served the Shaikh and kept his place at the table clean. Some of the people stayed near us at the table, sitting in silence as if they had come to an oasis amidst the sand dunes of the desert.

One of these people was a weary old Catholic priest uniformed in the usual long black cassock with buttons to the neck.

The priest was reminiscent of the Beatles' Father McKenzie, a loving but lonely and tired man. He wrapped his fragile arms around the Shaikh in greeting then sat down beside him to speak. Later, when the Shaikh informed me that the old man's health was poor and that his heart had stopped twice, it all seemed clear. I could see that it was the stress of a labour of love which had stopped the priest's heart, and the mercy of God which had brought it back. I would have guessed that some of the people in the gathering had once been in his care, but were now beyond his reach. Like Father McKenzie, he too had probably spent many a night writing sermons which no one would hear. Still he would probably outlive many of his parishioners in spite of his health and they, would see him on the way to their graves. Like Eleanor Rigby whose funeral was attended only by Father McKenzie, these struggling souls might too, be attended only by the tired old priest and be buried along with their names.

After a short while we were ushered outside. The music stopped as the Shaikh moved to the bandstand platform to take his place before the microphone and the encircling crowd which had now drawn near. I kept my station beside him and in a moment I too stood peering into the faces of the people all around.

The man who had accompanied us to the platform stepped up to the microphone and introduced the Shaikh in a language which I did not know. When the Shaikh began to address the people he too spoke in this language, which I guessed was Caspian. Though I did not, in the ordinary sense understand a single word uttered by the Shaikh on the bandstand that day, I felt the message completely.

In the course of the Shaikh's speaking I was taken through a wide range of feelings. I gauged my understanding by comparing the expressions which registered on people's faces with what was occurring by the moment in my own inner reactions to the talk.

The crowd grew very silent as the Shaikh was speaking. Though he did not shout, his voice could be heard ringing throughout the entire park. He was forceful but kind. He was direct but every word was spoken in the spirit of love. All the while he spoke I stood at his side. I carefully observed as much as I could, in myself and in the crowd. Among the people I took special note of some. The first among these was a man almost directly in front of me about thirty feet away. He was on the front line of the crowd as well. He was dressed in knee-length shorts and a tee-shirt which read 'Florida is for Lovers'. He wore a little crumpled summer hat, covered in buttons, pins, and other paraphernalia. He was the stereotypical 'happy-go-lucky' or 'life-of-the-party' type, yet throughout the talk his face was without expression. He seemed far away yet I suspected he was very near and deeply touched by what he heard. There were others near him who wept openly. I wondered who was touched most within. I wondered how visible I was to the eyes that looked on me as I stood speechless on the stage, but racing with dialogue inside.

Part of the front row of the circle was made up of three very old women sitting on folding chairs. They were smug and silent, and very modestly dressed. It was apparent that they were a generation growing extinct. The younger women, their daughters perhaps, were more bold in displaying their beauty and probably much more concerned to preserve it by jogging, tennis, and regular applications of Avon cosmetics or Oil of Ulay. Some of these women were near enough to hear the Shaikh. Their children were close by, moving about with toys in hand, but silent. Some teenagers, too, moved near. There were some whose lives were obviously in distress and some of these drew near. Some continued to drink their beer while others ran away completely. The old priest stood close, not far from the women, and on the floor before us, between the Shaikh's platform and the people, there was a beautiful little retarded child. She was inconspicuous yet everyone saw her. She was near to us and at the same time far away. Aside from the Shaikh, she was perhaps the only holy person visibly present and apparently in a world all of her own.

When the Shaikh ended his talk we left the platform to go back inside. As the band resumed its playing several people stepped forward to kiss his hand. Soon thereafter I fetched the car and we departed, as we had originally come, together just us two. Later, on the road, I gave an account of what I had seen.

'What exactly did I say?' the Shaikh asked. 'How did I get them to listen? *Who* listened? Who was Muslim? How many? What were their perceptions? Were you afraid? Humiliated?'

I answered as much as I could honestly answer from my own feelings and impressions and after this retreated into silence.

'Good,' said the Shaikh. 'Now let me ask you if the day was wasted?'

'No my Shaikh, certainly not,' I quickly replied.

'Good,' he said. 'Drive further. Later on I will ask you more.'

We drove for a while longer in silence, then he spoke to me again:

'There are various kinds of *dunya* (worldly attachment), he said. 'There is worse *haram* (wrongdoing) in discos than what you have seen in the park. Many acts of kindness came forward from these people and you must know that there is hope for those who can still shed tears at the mention of God's name.'

The Shaikh also noticed the lack of desire in me to speak. He asked if I had ever heard him address non-Muslims before and I said that I had not.

'Never again will you hear me speak in public', he said, 'as I have spoken in the way that I did today. Remember that we must speak broadly on such occasions, but we must not compromise the truth in public, and to those who are willing to listen, we must speak about the word of God.'

He paused briefly then continued:

'Never forget that God teaches best how *murids* (disciples) are made. Remember the angels who confessed their lack of understanding as they witnessed the creation of Adam, peace be upon him. They knew that his descendants would wreak havoc on the earth — but Allah told them that He knew what they did not know and they realised and said:

> Subhanaka la 'ilma lana illa ma 'allamtana — Glory to Thee: [Indeed] of knowledge we have none except what Thou hast taught us.
>
> *(Qur'an 2:32)*

My mind was racing in search of the meaning of the day and all the Shaikh had said to me. We were just coming into the time of sunset and were still about an hour from home. It was time for the prayer. We had just come onto a quiet park-like roadway. It was a nice place to be at the end of the day.

'Let us stop here and say the prayer,' said the Shaikh.

We parked the car at the roadside and walked onto the grass. We stood together and sent our praises to God Most High. The prayer was sweet and when I dropped my head onto the cool, grass-covered earth, I felt myself truly a servant. For just a fleeting moment my heart was full of joy. As we walked back to the car, I began to understand. Prayer is *hizmet* (service) in the absolute. It is selfless service to God. Actually, one's entire life should be a prayer. When one prostrates one's being together with one's head, there is no greater station. The angels bring a lesson for the making of disciples because they understand what *hizmet* truly is. They know nothing except to glorify God Almighty, and their will is only what He commands.

One other conversation with the Shaikh on the day of the park stood out in my mind. When I remembered it the entire teaching of *Hizmet* slipped into focus.

Having spent so much time that day standing at the side of the Shaikh, a question regarding closeness came to my mind. I enquired as to whether when he died he would be closer to me or further away.

'I am already a dead man. I have been dead for years,' he said. 'How can one be close or far from a man who is dead?'

'It seems that the Hazreti Abu Bakr in me is overcome by the Hazreti Umar in the face of such news,' I answered.

The Shaikh understood what I hoped to convey, for when the news of the Prophet's death, upon whom be peace, came to Umar, he refused to accept it, even threatening to cut off the arms and legs of anyone who did. It was Hazreti Abu Bakr who brought Hazreti Umar and the people to recognition of the very painful truth. After praising God and thanking Him he gave the following brief address:

> O Men, if you have been worshipping Muhammad, then know that Muhammad is dead. But if you have been worshipping Allah, then know that Allah is living and never dies.

After I had responded to the question of the Shaikh, he said nothing. He looked at me a long and quiet look, then looked away. I remembered that moment clearly in the months which were to pass. Perhaps two years did pass, however, before I understood. Before the Shaikh the disciple is like the corpse in the hands of the the washerman; the Shaikh is like the corpse in the hands of God. There is a kind of death which holds the secret of *hizmet*. It is the death to everything except God Most High. All *hizmet* done is actually to God, but learning to serve others is a means to taming the rebellious, ego-focused self. The Holy Prophet, peace be upon him, has said:

> *Mawt, mawt, qabla ta mawt* — Die, die before you die.

It is the death of the ego and senses, in order to live.

Thus we conclude the teaching of *Hizmet*, the teaching of service and servitude. About it, one Shaikh has told us as simply as this:

> Whoever does *hizmet* to Allah, Allah will surely do *hizmet* to him.

CHAPTER 8

THE CAKE

Perhaps a month or two after my journey to Caspian Park, I saw the Shaikh again. It was the day of *Eid-ul Fitr* and I was among nineteen in the circle of his disciples who had gathered that day in the Tekiya for the prayers and festivities which come on this day, after thirty days of fasting in the month of Ramadan.

It was always a joy to be in the presence of the Shaikh, and because his movements were so unpredictable we were all enthusiastic when he came — and eager to absorb as much of his light as we could. This day, like most of those we spent with him, was filled with prayer, *zikr* (remembrances of God) and much *muhabbat,* or love-inspired discourse about the joys and trials of the Path.

The particular teaching which began to unfold for me that day was a brief teaching, very much like the teaching of *hizmet* at the Park. It occurred in the midst of several other teachings which continued over a longer period of time. Although I have described it as a brief teaching, its impact was powerful, to say the very least. It was a teaching which struck me at my depths, continuing to yield insights with the passing of the years.

It was late in the evening and the hands of the clock sped towards midnight. We had prayed the night prayer, *Salatul 'Isha* and several of those present had begun to move into the library, which was near the door going out. When I walked into the room the Shaikh was standing near a bookshelf holding a medium-sized white box in his hands.

'This is a gift I have received from someone who is our sister and our friend,' he said as he took a seat among us on the floor. 'But this gift is also for *murids.*'

He opened the box, from which he brought forth a very beautiful chocolate cake. *Oohs* and *ahhhs* resounded throughout the room and for a moment everyone was bright and full of cheer. He held the cake on his lap and gave the question:

'What shall we do with it?'

He continued questioning in what was for me, a curious tone of voice, somewhere just in between cold seriousness and joking:

'What if it is that the cake is not really for the *murids,*' he said, 'but only for me?'

No one uttered the faintest sound but everyone was thinking and wondering just what was going on. One disciple laughed. Another said: 'Oh, I think that this is simple. How thick is the cake? Let's divide it into nineteen pieces.'

When I heard this remark, the Qur'anic verse 'Over it are nineteen' floated through my thoughts. This verse, which appears only once in the Qur'an, is the numerical formula for *Bismillahir Rahmanir Raheem* (In the name of God Most Gracious, Most Merciful). It is also the number which proves, scientifically, the divine origin of the book. I am sure that the full scope and meaning of this verse was clearly beyond my understanding, yet whenever I heard it, read it, or thought of it, I was struck with a deep sense of wonderment and mystery. So was I struck that night.

The Shaikh, however, responded to the remark with the following story which involved two cats and a monkey: It seems that the three animals had been given some cheese which was to be equally divided among them. The monkey took charge of this division because he happened to have a set of scales in his possession by which he could measure and weigh the pieces. He set the pieces on the scales, then casually ate bits from one side or the other, supposedly to balance the pieces. The cats, it seems, were very slow learners and it was not until the monkey had eaten nearly all of their cheese that they realised what was happening.

'Who wants the cake?' asked the Shaikh in a voice of challenge, immediately after telling the story.

'Perhaps it has fruit inside,' he continued. 'What is the inside like? It could be any of a thousand delicious possibilities. Do you think this lovely cake was baked by our friend or did she buy it in a store?'

We all thought it was bought but the Shaikh told us that he thought it was home-baked. The doubts that filled the room regarding this simple matter were more thick than the cake and could be cut with a knife. The Shaikh continued with the teaching.

'Who would like some?' he asked again.

A hushed silence crept across the room and still no one spoke a word.

'Enjoying the cake is just another of life's pleasures,' said the Shaikh. 'It is like the pleasure of skinny-dipping in the ocean: you dip into the beautiful and relaxing salt waters and it is a healing — like thousands of little rolfing masters, massaging you, or like a chiropractor. The water leaves you tingling and heals the scars of your body. You come out of the ocean and feel the warm sun on your body then you lay in the shade and have a nice two-hour nap. When you wake up you feel so good. You go down to the café and have a nice, ice-cold *pina colada.* Do any of you know how this is?

The silence persisted while a heavy tension crept across the room like the morning fog across a field. The hour grew very late. I was tired and I thought I had seen the point.

Suddenly another murid who also thought he had got the point burst into a soliloquy of desperate self-flagellation. Feeling guilty he pounced upon himself with unceasing incrimination. He was stopped by the Shaikh:

'This is not the point,' he said. 'There is a very fine line between pride and self-recrimination. You must come to understand that you cannot punish yourself as you are doing now. Humility in the true sense of submission to God is neither proud nor self-destructive. One Sufi Master has put it well: "Neither say 'I need something', nor say 'I need nothing'; say only 'Allah' and you will see marvels." '

There was a moment's pause and the Shaikh continued:

'You seem to all be falling asleep. How can you be sleepy in a *muhabbat* (discourse) related to love of Allah? Perhaps there is fruit inside this cake. Is there anyone who wants this cake?'

There were no more squeals of joy, no *oohs* nor *ahhhs.* Finally, I raised out of my silence.

'You may take my part,' I said. If part of the cake is mine you have my permission to do with it whatever you like.'

The Shaikh made no reply to my arrogant generosity. I sank back into my corner.

'I will try to eat some,' said one of the dervishes from the back of the room.

'Can you eat the whole cake?' challenged the Shaikh.

'I can only try,' answered the dervish.

'Can you guarantee that you can eat the whole cake?' pressed the Shaikh again.

'I can only guarantee that I can try,' said the dervish.

'What then shall we do with the cake?' asked the Shaikh still again, now addressing the group. Nineteen blank faces looked in his direction but still no answer came. There was another moment's pause in which I looked down at the floor. When I looked up again the Shaikh had plunged both of his hands into the cake. In a few seconds the beautiful cake was kneaded into a lumpy blob of chocolate crumbs and frosting. Everyone woke up.

Something about the smashing of the cake raised me slightly from my lethargic posture.

'It never occurred to me to smash the cake,' I said, speaking honestly but still aloof.

'It is nice to sit back in silence and be wise,' said the Shaikh, 'but you are not on a pedestal and you are not separate from the rest of mankind.'

The Shaikh, of course, was speaking to me quite directly and his words came down upon me like a ton of falling bricks. There was no escape and no way out except to go through the floor. Being unable to do so, I sat with my head drooping low, as if it were a wilting summer flower out of water in its vase.

Somewhere earlier in the evening I had nearly snapped off the head of a dervish with whom I had disagreed about some small thing he had said concerning me in the course of the Shaikh's teaching. I had never been out of good manners in the presence of the Shaikh but that night, something subterranean was touched in my self and suddenly, my ego had flared up and out spreading fumes all over the room. The Shaikh had said nothing at the time but he certainly noticed. But now, when the bricks were falling down on me, not a single stone was left unturned.

'There was a sting in your voice which was quite disturbing,' he said. 'Did you notice it in yourself? It was directed not only against the dervish but also against myself and the entire group.'

I wanted to flee and had I been able to find my legs I might have done it. All I could think of at the time was running away; sitting there, attempting to let in the words of the Shaikh was my most courageous act of the year. A remnant of false pride was fully exposed and my insides felt as much a blob as the squashed and crumbled cake.

'The very heart of Islam', said the Shaikh, now addressing the group, 'is smashing the cake. When the idols were smashed in the Ka'ba, the people then saw them for the wood and stone they were. That wood and stone is no different from your desires and your job. You can experience the ultimate pleasures of love without even laying a finger. Or you can be like the animals going through a life filled with only the basics of eating, drinking, sleeping, and reproduction.'

He asked if anyone had ever seen a bull on a farm and for the first time since the discourse began there was some laughter in the room. In the midst of the laughter, the dervish whom I had snapped up asked a serious question. He had understood the significance of what the Shaikh had done in smashing the cake.

'Why', he asked, 'do I feel physical pain when the cake in my life is smashed?'

The Shaikh, who was very effective in teaching through humour, lifted his hands as if he held a stone in each and smashed them together.

'This', he had earlier told us, 'is how to castrate a camel.'

In this gesture the dervish got his answer and any others who remembered about the camel also understood. Certainly the point is clear: namely that whenever one cuts off that to which one is attached, one naturally feels pain. The degree of pain is in fact a sign of how strong the attachment may be.

'Who would like to eat the cake now?' asked Shaikh, his hands still messy and covered with chocolate. No one uttered a sound and no one made a move.

'Are you all sleepy again?' he asked. 'How can you be sleepy in a discussion about Allah? One who is a Sufi eats little, sleeps little and wastes little time.'

There was another pause and again silence filled the room. The Shaikh closed his eyes as if deep in thought. After a few moments he spoke.

'Have you ever read the saying on the cup of a Burger King shake?'

We chuckled as he continued:

I'm Sir Shake-a-lot
I love a good shake
Whenever I have one
I shiver and quake.

'This little verse sent me into a three-hour meditation,' he said. 'I sat shaking and quivering in the love of Allah. No pleasures can come near to this. You must overcome your sleepiness. Don't you see that we cannot even reconstruct a dead cake? Yet Allah, glory be to Him, has made us alive from nothing. When I opened the box there were *ooohs* and *ahhhs* for the beautiful cake, when there should only be *ooohs* and *ahhhs* for Allah.'

The Shaikh recited the following verse of Qur'an in Arabic then gave its translation:

> The trumpet will be sounded then men
> will come running from their graves,
> rushing to their Lord. They will say:
> "Ah woe unto us! Who has raised us from
> our sleeping places?" And the answer will
> come: "This is what [Allah] The Most Gracious
> had promised and the word of the
> apostles was true.
>
> *(36:51–52)*

On concluding the verses, he handed over to us the box of the crumbled remains of the cake and ordered us to go outside and eat them. We were in fact eating the teaching and it was not a joyful eating.

When we saw the Shaikh again, a few days later the *teaching* was concluded.

"Do you have to swim the channel to enjoy it? Must you eat every fish? Why all this talk of ultimate pleasures? It is to wake you up. Nothing is more gross than two lovers over-fulfilling their desires. Did you notice that as soon as you begin to eat the cake you lose your desire for it? The anticipation is better than the over-fulfilment and when the cake is crushed, no one wants to eat it. The issue of the cake is one of rudeness and coarseness versus refinement. To enjoy the cake without eating: that is the challenge. When I have chocolate pudding, just a spoonful is enough. After a single mouthful the taste buds are saturated, so just a taste is all you need.

'The question *is* what is *your* cake? And how do you learn to smash it? You need not be like the man in the countryside who could only appreciate a flower by plucking it.'

The Shaikh had once told us a story of an older Shaikh in his country who kept a garden full of beautiful flowers. He spoke of the care given the flowers by the Shaikh, and went on to say how few people in this country could really appreciate a flower. I did not understand then, but after the smashing of the cake, it became a little more clear. It was significant for me that the cake was smashed on the day of *Eid*, the holiday which comes after a month of fasting. The teaching of the cake is the lesson of Ramadan in brief: Learn to control your desires! It is rooting out low desires and putting the *nafs*, or ego, into balance.

'Until we are rid of our crudeness,' said the Shaikh, 'walking the earth like elephants, how can we hear? Hazreti Rumi said: ". . . Shems is coming from the East, listen to the footsteps of light . . . ." But how can you meet Shems coming from the East? Only by keeping your eyes open. The only way that you can see is to open your eyes to the universe and the creation around you. The signs are there.'

The Shaikh had also said, regarding desire, that:

"No matter how you drink, your lips are dry."

I took this to mean that the seeker must recognise his own thirst and understand wherefrom his desire proceeds. There is the desire of the *nafs*, the low and unrefined, and the desire of the high, which is the fire of *Ashq* or love. Both of these are states of unquenchability. The lesson of the cake is really about discriminating and ordering one's wants so that one may move from the low state to the high. Such a process is known as spiritual refinement.

'If Allah isn't put first,' said the Shaikh, 'we will not be satisfied — no matter how much we have. *Dunya* (the world) is fine. Just put Allah first. When you put the desire for a house first, for a promotion — for whatever, you may be successful and life will pass, but know that after life passes, there is no return and no amount of tears will bring any of us back. Don't put anything before Allah or He may give you the satisfaction of your desires.'

The word for refinement on the Mystic Path of Islam is *adab*. It is a state of culture, of elevated dignity and full humanisation. It is both a process and a state, for in the former sense it is the subjugation of the lower to the higher, the gross to the subtle, the body to the soul. It is a movement by degrees from beast to human; a growing out of one's egotistical self and into one's beginning stages of spiritual ascension. One who achieves it graduates from the school of hypocrisy and looking good-on-the-surface. One with *adab* has cultivated the very best of the natural impulses of the heart, and brought forth, with radiant fullness, the secret already placed within by the mercy of God Most High. *Adab* is a state of power, and purity of both character and being, the fruit of struggle and mastery of self.

All of the lessons in this story are related to the end I have just described. The cake, the flower plucked by the poet, the lighted footsteps of Shemsi Tabriz, the stories of the beach and sensual comforts craved for by the *nafs*, the cake itself, its final smashing, and later our eating it. All of these are lessons on the way to *adab*.

There is a calligraphic rendering in the Tekiya which in Arabic reads: '*Adab Ya Hu*'. During one of the Shaikh's discourses, he asked about its meaning. Someone in the assembly answered: 'It means Good manners, Oh God.' That person was right in his answer for that is exactly the meaning. It is to behave in the best way, since one is always in the sight of God. There was for me a subtle teaching as well in the Shaikh's story of the Shepherd and Moses, peace be upon him, It is that God is near, forgiving and ever ready to foster what is good. His signs are there, as the Shaikh did also say, for those who can open their eyes. Everything in Allah's creation is moving towards its refinement and fullest development. It is this understanding, by the mercy of God, which caused the following verses to rise in my heart:

In every cloud and drop of rain,
The message speaks so clear, so plain.
In every little grain of sand . . .
The lines across my open hand,
In the rays which dance around the Sun,
The many a reflection of the One.
In rocks unprogressing, at least seeming so,
Yet these too are growing with all things that grow,
Into diamonds, rubies and gems which shine;
Within these and myself a thousand signs,
Directing and guiding me to the Light,
Opening my heart to the Source of Sight.
The Illuminant Lamp's Eternal glow,
Lights the globe of my heart as it comes to know,
The exalted state of the lowly slave;
The joy of the madman in stupor who raves,
By the light which pierced his darkened soul . . .
Strike the match of surrender
See the Flame of the Goal.

Thus we conclude the teaching of the cake; a teaching of refinement and routing the *nafs*. It is a teaching from the Shaikh, one person in the rapidly shrinking community of people of true spiritual refinement. People who truly know how to live, who know how to walk in peace with themselves and the creation around them. Who know how to taste and enjoy and not be overwhelmed — save only by Love Divine. Who know the thirst of the higher ones and tasted the shake — who sip deep from ecstasy's cup, then shiver and quake.

CHAPTER 9

The Fishbowl Trilogy

I

Late one autumn, in my early days on the Path, long before the teaching of the cake, I became involved with a very large and dilapidated barn-like building which stood boldly on a corner of the Tekiya grounds. This building was itself both the source and the symbol of a group of related teachings which extended over several years of my journey, up to and through my struggles to acquire that spiritual refinement known by some seekers as *adab.*

All of the teachings of this series generally involved some activity shared by the Shaikh's disciples. Like fish of the sea, we moved as a school through waters of the lessons, somehow interdependent in our learning yet simultaneously left to sink or swim on our own. Like fish in a bowl we entered into a space where we became increasingly visible by way of motives and behaviour, both to ourselves and to others looking on. Swimming through these teachings under the direction and care of our teacher, the learnings became as clear as the glass of the goldfish bowl.

The Shaikh had given the instruction to one of the dervishes to have the building toppled. Within a few days the boards and beams of the building rested in one awesome and colossal mountainous heap.

'Save the lumber which is useful,' ordered the Shaikh. 'As for the rest, burn it.'

The task seemed impossible. Many of the beams were so heavy that it took several men to lift them a few feet off the ground. The job was even further complicated by the other rubble and large wood scraps which were either nailed to the beams or had fallen on top of them when the building collapsed. None the less, we followed the Shaikh's instruction and soon a flaming bonfire was set a short distance away from the fallen barn. The fire burned almost twenty-four hours a day and whenever disciples came to the Tekiya the fire was burning and there was work to be done. The woodpile seemed imperishable and for months it seemed not to show the slightest sign of diminishment. The first winter came and through the coldest days of zero weather both the fire and woodpile persisted. One afternoon the Shaikh stood near the woodpile on top of a small snowbank. Gracefully draped in his black dervish robe, the folds of which hung low and in contrast to the whiteness of the snow, he quietly observed the flames of the fire as we worked. Still overwhelmed by the seeming endlessness of the woodpile in the midst of which I then stood, I half-muttered an inquisitive plea. There were boards whichever way I turned.

'Where do I start and how will we ever finish the burning?' I asked, not noticing the loose boards directly at my feet, nor the scope of my question.

'You start where you are,' said the Shaikh with a smile, 'and you work with what is near. Eventually you will reach the end.'

We both laughed and I continued to work. As I reflected on the simple comment of the Shaikh, the woodpile came to have an entirely different meaning. It was not long after this that I happened to be at the woodpile again with a small crew of disciples. We had struggled to throw a large, awkward piece into the fire. It took three or four of us to toss it, and when it landed in the fire we laughed with relief and some very slight feeling of joy from our success in working together. One of the dervishes among us commented in the midst of the laughter:

'These pieces of wood are like *nafs* (ego-desires). It's like what we throw into this fire outside corresponds with what we need to throw out from the woodpile of *nafs* inside.'

What the dervish said struck a deep note of truth in me, and I took the silence which fell on the group to be a further indication that each heart present had witnessed the same truth. This ordinary experience together with the unadorned remark of the Shaikh transformed the woodpile into a treasure and source of continued teaching. Anytime that I approached it I learned something. I gained great insight into the struggles of other murids and how their struggles paralleled my own. Moreover, I learned the basics of co-operation and mutual compassion through work and shared effort with other spiritual seekers. I saw all the many ways that different individuals approached the challenges of the woodpile, and through all of these things I learned about myself.

One of the strangest of many incidents connected with the woodpile involved the heavy hardwood beams which needed to be saved. The Shaikh had instructed us to carry the beams to the perimeters of the grounds and to make a border by elevating them on stones or smaller blocks of wood. Similarly, some were used as benches at other places in the grounds. This task too seemed impossible, and whenever a group of disciples were able to move one of these beams even one or two feet, we felt an overwhelming, disproportionate, and glowing sense of achievement. Over the passing weeks, however, we had made some progress, and by pushing, rolling, shoving, dragging, or some combination of means — we had moved several of these huge beams and the border was taking shape.

One day late in the spring, the Shaikh was observing us at work. The fire was still burning and several of us were struggling with a beam.

'It should only take one person to move a beam,' he said to us, 'and if you approach it correctly you'll see how it is done.'

Smiles of disbelief and half-doubting crept across our faces. We wondered how it could be done, but something about having heard it as a possibility made the task seem easier. When we put aside our speculations and hesitancy and made some attempt simply to work with whatever was at hand, everything moved more smoothly and quickly. Soon after this, perhaps a day or two later, a group of disciples arrived at the Tekiya to find that several of the heaviest beams had been set up as benches, and not one of them was within thirty feet of the fire or the woodpile. One or two in fact, were in the farthest corners of the Tekiya grounds. We thought that perhaps the Shaikh had moved them, but he hadn't been around. Later, when one of the dervishes arrived to help with the work, we enquired about the beams.

'I moved them,' he confessed with a quiet air of unaffected humility. 'I tried what the Shaikh suggested and I discovered it was true.'

We bombarded the dervish with questions concerning exactly how it was done.

'Really it is easy,' he said, 'but I cannot fully explain it. You must be convinced that it can happen, then stop thinking and begin to act. A little effort will take you a long way and this is as much as I can say.'

Every one of us was inspired by the initiative of the dervish. Though no one expressed their admiration openly, all of our faces registered surprise as we stood gawkishly smiling with wide-open eyes. I would guess that after that day every disciple who had been there when the dervish told his story made secret visits to the woodpile to try their hand with a giant beam. I do know that I made my own escapes there and I will leave it to the reader's imagination to picture how I looked launching my efforts in the quiet darkness of the night. Without saying whether I lifted the beams or not, I will mention two greater discoveries, each to a greater or lesser extent a product of my effort: the first was the deeper meaning of self-confrontation or inward struggle and the second was *La haula wa la quwwata illa bi'llah* — There is no power nor strength except God Almighty, glory be to Him.

The woodpile burned intermittently for a year. I remember the red glow of the coals burning in the snowy nights of two winters. Thousands of meditations were generated by that fire, then one day it was gone. The glow of the flames, tended by some lone dervish in the night, was no longer there. All was dark now when I looked out from the Tekiya at night, but the stars still lit the heavens and that flame which had once been set to the woodpile was now quietly aglow in my heart.

II

In my early days on the Path, there was work to be done, no matter which way I looked. After we had toppled an old barn near the Tekiya, I thought that there would be much less work and much more sitting for remembrance (*zikr*) and spiritual discourse (*muhabbat*). I was fully prepared to sit with the Shaikh for hours, fully absorbed and entranced by mystic teachings, repeating *zikr* and spiritual quatrains (*qasidas*) until I floated off into some ecstatic realm of cosmic reverie. Unfortunately, I was mistaken in this idea and I soon learned that the Mystic Path is a rough road, the greater length of which is traversed in struggle and if one endures and God is merciful, there are occasional reassuring moments of bliss.

When the first winter in the era of the woodpile passed, the melting snows revealed a surprising heap of vintage junk which had been overlooked while we dealt with clearing the fallen barn. Among these useless relics there was an old wooden flatbed trailer, about half the size of a small pick-up truck. It had two old tyres for wheels, one of which was long since flat. On another corner of the grounds, very near to the Tekiya, and not very far from the junkpile was another small building which I had early discovered was an outhouse, frequented only by disciples. Set neatly and inconspicuously in a small cluster of trees, it stood through the first winter of the woodpile. Naturally, with the feeling of renewal which comes with the spring we felt a greater sense of energy which was immediately noticed and mobilised by the Shaikh. He directed us to clear away the junkpile, and in a few days it was accomplished. Anything which would burn was thrown into the woodpile fire and the metal was cut into scraps and carted away on a truck belonging to one of the dervishes.

Later, when the Shaikh was with us again, he called another small group of us together for the assignment of another task.

'We must move this outhouse,' he said. 'Perhaps this trailer will be of some use.'

There was muffled laughter, probably signalling the doubt which sprang up on our faces. The Shaikh's remark had all of the irony that most humour has, for I remember that I was smiling and I suspected that not within a century would anyone among us that day, except the Shaikh, have ever thought to utilise that old trailer.

'You have weak faith!' said the Shaikh, as we began to push the trailer, finding to our own astonishment, not only that it did not crumble into pieces, but that it moved. The trailer was in fact much stronger than we thought, but we still had our doubts. When finally we rolled up in front of the outhouse, the Shaikh had told us no less than three times that our faith was weak. By the time he had spoken thrice, the cock of our doubts had crowed a thousand times.

'We must move the outhouse to the other side of the grounds,' directed the Shaikh, while pointing out a general area across the way.

Somehow, from some seemingly unknown place, a suggestion came to us to put the house onto the trailer and move it in one piece. I suspect that most of those present, if asked where that idea came from, would have said: 'I thought that the Shaikh wanted it on the trailer,' but as I now reflect back on that day, I cannot with any clarity remember that any such idea or suggestion came forth from him directly all the while that we were together. Secretly, I suspected that the suggestion came from within each one of us who was there, but regardless of where it came from, it overtook us none the less.

Like clones from a science-fiction film, we, like many of those from our modern culture, were entirely programmed by our own ideas of what *we thought* should be. Thus our stumblings with the trailer and the outhouse were largely a manifestation of our very own inward foolish whims. Later I understood how characteristic we were of new seekers on this path. Beginning disciples, like space clones, usually tend to rush in where other robots fear to tread. There we were, we heroes, fully committed to rescuing that monument to decrepitude; indeed there we were hovering around the outhouse and working with vigour — our doubt slowly giving way to a belief that the old building could in fact be freed and loaded onto the trailer. We moved the trailer back and forth, like a checker on a board, attempting to decide what location would yield its optimal use. There being no carpenter among us, we struggled for hours to move the building from its foundation. We freed it only to find our pathway to the trailer largely blocked by the trees, and ourselves faced with deciding whether to saw a tree or the outhouse.

Somehow, by some means entirely beyond my understanding, we managed to get one end of the little building on the back of the trailer. This apparent triumph was very short-lived, for the outhouse was not yet anywhere near the area which the Shaikh had pointed out. Moreover, the outhouse was still only half-way onto the trailer. We accomplished getting it up there by way of great effort only to discover that it was too heavy for us to push over a slight incline. A wave of silence descended on the group as we sank deeper into gloom. We pushed and pulled and shoved and rocked but the contraption did not move. We retreated and returned to give it one final and culminating heave. The outhouse shifted and one of its boards sounded a loud and weary crack. The trailer itself, however, had not moved an inch. All the while the Shaikh looked on. Suddenly, one of the dervishes among us bolted forward to the side of the outhouse. With a deliberate, silent fury he began to rip it all apart, tearing down its walls. Then out of the silence rang the voice of the Shaikh:

'*Alhamdulillah!*' he said. 'I thought you would never realise.'

The words of the Shaikh brought sighs of relief. We had all been tense but hadn't noticed how much until after he had spoken. Everyone seemed calmer now, and much more relaxed.

'I'm still confused,' said the dervish, addressing the Shaikh. 'How is it that you know when to break it and when you don't?'

'That is part of what makes me the Shaikh,' came the reply, 'for if I didn't know the answer, I could not make *murids* (disciples). Let me illustrate by telling a story.'

The Shaikh told us the story of the deer and the wolf. It involved some deer who were at the edge of a large and ditch-like ravine. They were quite convinced that they could not make it across, but when they noticed that they were about to be overcome by approaching wolves they discovered energy which they did not know they possessed and jumped to safety across the ditch.

'It is about the potential of man, *unused,*' said the Shaikh. 'Man won't do it unless its life and death.'

We collected the scraps of the outhouse and put them on the fire. The roof and a few other boards seemed like they might have some use so we put them on the trailer and pushed them across the grounds to the designated place. The Shaikh was constantly asking us questions about the value of the roof. It was not clear at the time but later I understood more fully, as I reflected on his words of caution:

'Remember that the trailer is your Islam (surrender to God), and the house your *Shari'ah* (pattern of divine law). Reflect upon the verses from the Prophet Jesus, peace be upon him, concerning the weak house built on the sandcliffs, but know as well that there can also be a weak house built upon strong rock.'

A quiet silence came over the group again. Everyone was struck by the clarity and wisdom of the Shaikh. His words set in our hearts with all the warmth and glow of the Sun, as it sets on the horizon at the end of the day. He smiled and spoke again.

'One knows when to break by first making careful observation. Observation would have clearly shown us that the outhouse would not make it. Now we must build another, for it is not temporary, it is here to stay. In fact, you do not know how much you need it. As long as there are *murids,* there will be need for an outhouse.'

We made our ablutions and entered the Tekiya. We had gathered inside before the call to prayer (*azan*). The Shaikh said these few words in his discourse which I reflected upon for months: 'United we fall, divided we stand.'

III

In my early days on the Path, after the era of the woodpile, I sat one day in the Tekiya reflecting on my life. It was late summer and we were in the final days of *Ramadan*. Several murids and dervishes were gathered for *itikaf*, the time of retreat in the last ten days of the fast. The Shaikh was present and had left clean white sheets for a few disciples, which were worn like cloaks, as he himself did occasionally when his dervish robe was not at hand. Those who spent these days in retreat were known as *mutakifs* and committed themselves to general silence, and more voluntary acts of devotion (*'ibadat*) beyond the fasting, consisting mostly of prayer, Qur'an reading and *zikr*.

I was among those mantled in white, and I pondered the meaning of this development — but only for a moment. Some remote remnant of pride distracted me from my reflection, for I felt very much identified with the Shaikh and honoured that I could be like him, even in this small way. Moreover, I hoped that in these days, a small part of his true piety and love of God would be reflected in my own heart. The white cloak was the symbol of this hope and I orientated myself to the silence with a plan of days filled with no activity beyond my prayer and meditation. The Tekiya's mosque would be my own Cave of Hira.

One afternoon during this time I came outside for a walk. It was a bright and sunny day made all the more perfect by a gentle south-west breeze. I passed near the place where the old barn had stood and been toppled, and the resulting woodpile set aflame. The entire area was now covered with wild grass and weeds as tall as small trees, except in the place where the fire had been set. Here nothing grew, and scattered ashes and coals lay all about, long since cooled by a past season's snow. I reflected on that pile of wood which had once seemed so endless — completely perished now. I wondered if I too might ever see such a perishing, born of struggle with my lower self perhaps, and the raging fire of love.

My pondering was interrupted by the Shaikh, who looked at the weeds, then looked at me. He moved his hand in a slicing motion and pointed to a sickle which lay nearby on the ground. Following his suggestion, I took up the tool and began to swing. I worked without speaking while the Shaikh stood looking on. I had only taken a stroke or two before there came a sense of *deja vu*. The toppling of the weeds was the very same teaching as the toppling of the barn, nearly a year since past. My struggle had not ended with the clearing of the woodpile and the impossible giant beams. Now I saw that after the more obvious personal misdirection and wrongdoing (*haram*) is dealt with and the larger ego desires overcome, new and smaller ego desires come to the surface, like the sprouting of the weeds.

After working with the sickle for a very short while, I had chopped down many weeds, but there were many still to cut. A slight churning discomfort began to surface as I noticed their number and considered how long I would be there, should I have to clear the patch single-handedly. I looked at the Shaikh with the same desperation I had felt once before at the woodpile, then I remembered what he had said:

'You start where you are and you work with what is near. Eventually you will reach the end.'

I smiled at myself and with this in mind, I gave up the thinking and quietly continued to chop.

As other disciples drifted out of the Tekiya to enjoy the sunshine and be near the Shaikh, he silently directed them to the weeds. Soon a sizeable crew had been formed. Some were digging, some chopping, and some carrying the weeds to be stacked in a pile to dry and later set on fire. Everyone worked in quiet harmony and some delightful feeling of joy I had felt somewhere before came alive in me again. The Shaikh, too, had once more shown us the fruits of mutual sharing and co-operation, and without a single word he had fostered love in the group. Very soon the barn site was nicely cleared and one of the last remaining eyesores had been removed from the grounds of the Tekiya. Neither the barn, nor the weeds, however, had gone without providing us many teachings. From among these, I will cite those which seemed the clearest to me:

First, I learned about the nature of false piety and honest work. The remembrance (*zikr*) I did while chopping weeds was much more honest and profound than what I had done in my cloak of white. When I put it on again, after chopping down the weeds, I wore it with more of the humility it deserved. Every time I had gone to the Tekiya with some pious goal — for *zikr* or *muhabbat*, I had most often ended up doing some kind of work instead. I remember, too, how terrible we sounded in our early days, reciting *zikr* together as we sat in a circle, but the more we worked and struggled both together and alone, the more pleasing was our sound. Next, I learned about my lack of *tawakkal* or trust. Allah was continually revealing to me that He was in charge, but I could not recognise this while I over-relied on my thinking. I usually went forward whenever I let go. Finally, I learned a brief but important lesson about self-purification. Namely, that *haram* (wrong doing) and its remnants are the weeds of the self. They must not only be chopped down but attacked at the roots.

EPILOGUE

Itikaf too soon drew to a close and with it passed the month of *Ramadan*. Things were quiet for a while, then one day late in the autumn we gathered in the Tekiya for another of the Shaikh's discourses. He was speaking on the subject of *'amal* — work — and describing to us its relationship to the seeker's state of faith.

"*Amal* must precede faith,' he said. 'Your state of faith evolves to certainty. Says Allah in Qur'an: "Ye shall surely travel from stage to stage."'

The Shaikh had spoken often on the subject of *'amal*. I could easily remember him mentioning it repeatedly over the years. Something about this particular discourse, however, jarred my memory of a more recent experience on this subject, which I had nearly forgotten. That experience and what was conveyed by the Shaikh is the central teaching of the trilogy. Each story is in fact a description of how the Shaikh had directed his disciples through three mundane situations towards the end of understanding one very important point.

One night before *Ramadan* began, we had been with the Shaikh at the Tekiya. It was late and the Shaikh was escorting someone else who was leaving, so we walked with him, as was our custom, down the hill from the Tekiya, to the roadside where we left our cars. There was a great deal of discussion and several questions were asked of the Shaikh as we made our way along. All of this resulted in his asking us if we had read *The Report to the Academy of Sciences*, a story by Franz Kafka. Since no one of us knew the story he told it to us in brief. The story is related by an ape who had been captured from the jungles of his homeland and taken aboard a ship for the purposes of being delivered to a zoo. The story opens with the ape standing at the lectern before the Academy of Sciences, wearing glasses and a conservative, dapper suit. He takes his paper from his briefcase and begins to read. He tells the story of his being captured and how when he had been faced with the horrible prospect of spending the rest of his life imprisoned in the zoo, he determined to escape this fate by becoming like his captors. While in his cage he began to imitate their tones and movements. This development created some interest on the ship with the result that he was put into the company of the Captain for his entertainment. By the time the ship reached the shore he had fully mastered a great deal of his captor's knowledge. In fact, he was soon speaking and after one year he was dining at the table with the Captain and the priest. After two years he had earned a university degree, and in five years attained the level of college professor. The ape continued in this endeavour and in sustaining his effort to escape the terrible fate of the zoo, became after ten years, a member of the French Academy of Sciences. On being asked what made him put forth such an effort whereby he had for all intents and purposes, nearly transformed himself from one species to another, he answered very simply: 'I had no choice.'

'The point of this story,' said the Shaikh, 'is to act and make *'amal.* When one reaches the place where one must do, having no choice, surprising things can be accomplished.

He also spoke of *'ilm* or knowledge as something which should be pursued. He talked about the large amounts of our given potential which go unused and how our unused brains become masses of amorphous tissue.

'Only the one who has *'ilm* can say that it need not be sought,' he told us.

Finally, he spoke against laziness which is the central deterrent to *'amal.* The Shaikh, I might mention, was qualified to speak in this regard because he was a master of outer academic knowledge and sciences, as well as a master of inward knowledge and the science of Reality within.

'The Path of *Tasawwuf,* the Mystic Path,' said the Shaikh, 'is not a path for the lazy. He reprimanded us for not learning Qur'an, literally asking us how many *suras,* or chapters, we knew.

'Memorising *suras* opens other parts of the mind,' he said. 'What you must understand is that if Allah's gifts to us are misused, or still worse, if they are unused, we lose them.'

He mentioned the verses from *Surat-ul Baqara* about those who say that they believe in God but actually do not believe.

'Such a level of belief as this belongs to the mosque or church,' he said, 'but not to *Tasawwuf.'*

The Shaikh had often quoted Shaikh Tussi as saying:

Not before the last mosque under the sun
lies ruined will our holy work be done
And the true believer will not appear in the world
Before the Faith and Disbelief are one.

For the first time I began to glimpse a meaning of this baffling statement. It is opposing unfirm belief grounded only in given facts, but not in inward knowing, the lack of which actually makes the one in such a state much like the hypocrite who says he believes when with others who say it, but when out of their environment and company says something else.

Continuing on the subject of laziness and *'amal* the Shaikh told us of Hazreti Umar, may God be pleased with him, who saw a group of men sleeping under a tree. 'Are you Muslims?' he asked them.

'Yes,' came the reply.

'If you were Muslims,' said Umar, 'you would be out ploughing that field over there, or working in the garden, but you would certainly not be sleeping!'

'Two things', said the Shaikh, 'which the Prophet, upon whom be peace, feared for his *ummat* (nation) were big bellies and laziness. In *Ramadan* you should remember this. Don't turn the night into the day. Eat simpler. If you experience any misfortune, you should just say *alhamdulillah* (Praise be to God)!'

'Beware of laziness!' the Shaikh cautioned us while shaking his finger. 'People in the desert travelled in caravans through the heat and worked long hours in the fields.

'Forgive in *Ramadan,* be gentle, be kind. Let your faces be smiling with no sign of tension. Always remember though, the story of *'amal* and the ape. Listen carefully to what I say because I want you never to forget.'

CHAPTER 10

THE THIRD JOURNEY

I

The easier days of my Tariqat travel, like the honeyed years of childhood, passed all too swiftly. Along the Path the teachings came and went, with all the perenniality of the changing seasons. But no matter how complex or enduring any of the teachings seemed at first, sooner or later their days passed into nights where I in my journey, sat alone and looked into myself. I savoured the learnings, much as I savoured the sweetness of the lilacs which lined the hill along the Tekiya's walkway. A fragrance made all the sweeter perhaps, by the long wait of winter, but always gone too soon in spring. So lovely it was, that delicate and luscious scent which filled the air and my heart; which lingered ever so briefly and only for a moment.

Again, as before, the weeks stretched into months in which I had no contact with the Shaikh. He had moved to another city in the early winter past. After his departure I fell into a void of silence . . . long days of quiet except for the noise of my worldly affairs. Whenever the Shaikh was present I surfaced from my inward oceans. For whatever pain I felt by way of separation, being with him was none the less a joy, and the warmth of his smile and gentle wisdom always caused me to forget my mundane concerns. The loving heart of this man was a veritable moon in which was reflected the brilliant *nur*, or light of Muhammad, by which were lighted my footsteps towards Truth.

The Shaikh set forward on his journey one cold but clear and crispy Friday afternoon. It was early in the month of January on one of the mildest days of winter. In speaking to us that day he had placed much emphasis on love for the Prophet, peace be upon him, and love for *ahlil bait*, the spiritual family and house of the Prophet. He also told us clearly that our spiritual progress was impossible without *tawakkal*, which is trust or reliance on God alone. This was not new, for he had spoken often of *tawakkal*, but somehow it was different that day. I listened in ways I had not done, at earlier times on the Path. More than anything, I was struck by his parting words, which gave the point of all he had tried to teach us. That night I made the entry in my journal:

> The Shaikh left today. As he drove off he rolled down his window and said to us: 'Before you were in my care by Allah's permission, but now I leave you alone in His care. Your *tawakkal* is to Him only.'

He gave farewell salaams, wishing us peace and God's blessing as he drove off with his window still open. It was a painful weaning. The heart of every disciple trailed after him as if it were a tin can tied to the bumper of the car of newly-weds. We were certainly no less empty in that moment, and collectively rattling our loss. We knew we'd continue to receive his direction and see him from time to time, but we also knew that from that moment on, something would be different from what we had known before. Somehow we endured as the months sped by, and I found myself surprised when I realised that the lilacs had come and gone and Ramadan was near again.

There was a great deal of anticipation in the circle of disciples that year, for we were to have a special guest. A noble Shaikh and gnostic from another country who was also a *hafiz* — that is, one who knew the entire Qur'an by heart — was to be with us for the month.

Little did I know how central a role this distinguished visitor would play in my struggles to reach *tawakkal*, the state of trust. My own Shaikh had counselled me about him and told me of his elevated station:

'I am hardly worthy to tie the shoestrings of this man,' said the Shaikh. 'Surely a heart which contains the secrets which his does cannot help but be a lover of Allah.'

About a week and a half before *Ramadan*, when the time for the arrival of our guest Shaikh Ahmet drew near, I had the good fortune of meeting him at the local airport, where I rendezvoused with two other dervishes. This man was conspicuously unassuming and deeply modest in both humility and naturalness. He wore a simple but nicely tailored suit and his eyes were pools of warmth and kindness. His smile was infectious, his beard and moustache very well-trimmed and both completely white. His hand was occupied with a set of prayer beads (*tasbih*) and his heart was full of love, to such an extent that it could be felt by anyone who cared to notice. I greeted him and placed the rose I had brought into his hand. He returned the greeting and gracefully accepted the flower, then with a smile he turned for his luggage. The dervishes retrieved it and we left for the Tekiya. When we arrived, all of the disciples had gathered to welcome our guest. We said prayers, had tea, and a brief conversation, then we showed him to his room and left to take rest for the night.

Later that week, I made my usual trek to the Tekiya to spend a night in *khalwat*. This is a time for quiet prayer and meditation and reflection on God Most High. I had left a little early on this particular night as one of the disciples had planned a dinner for the visiting Shaikh. Thinking that I had missed it, I stopped to apologise for my absence, only to find that the mealtime had been changed to a later hour. I decided to wait at the Tekiya. I made my way up the walk and stepped around the side of the building. There, to my surprise, was the Shaikh walking the grounds with a disciple. Happy to see him I rushed to give him my greeting. He kissed my face and gave me his blessing. Later, he walked with me and, as we went, he asked me several things concerning my writing. He advised me to pay careful attention to the unfolding of events during *Ramadan*. I told him about the dinner and we left the Tekiya together with Shaikh Ahmet to share in the meal. It was a beautiful time and everyone's heart was lightened by the good company and good food. We returned to the Tekiya that night for prayers and remembrance (*zikr*). After loving discourse (*muhabbat*) with the Shaikhs, some of us departed while others remained for reflection and voluntary prayers of the night.

The next morning several disciples had gathered again to see our Shaikh. He was very affectionate with our guest Shaikh Ahmet, and one had only to look to see that they were in complete harmony with each other. I cannot remember any of what our Shaikh said to us that day, I only remember how happy I was to see him and how little time there was. Rushing to catch a plane, he hastened away from us down the hill to the roadside, with our hearts trailing after him once again. He got into a car with one of the disciples and in a moment he was gone.

The following night the Tekiya was extremely quiet. A handful of disciples were sitting around with Shaikh Ahmet just before the time of *Isha,* the night prayer. He excused himself and returned after a minute or two with a suitcase. He sat down smiling and motioned for us to gather around. Opening the case, he took from it several beautiful pieces of calligraphic art, several unusual rings, beautiful scarves, prayer beads, and finally, some books with very interesting calligraphy printed on the covers. He gave each one of us a gift of some kind and something for our wives as well. Now it should be understood that Shaikh Ahmet did not speak English, yet we communicated very well. We spoke with common words from the Qur'an and a few words of Turkish, his native tongue. Although there was no one fluent in our company that night, there were murids among us who were very knowledgeable of Turkish, and all the while Shaikh Ahmet Effendi was present, they had helped to decipher messages between him and us.

The books which Shaikh Ahmet brought were of great interest to us all, for they were practical books on sufism, the Islamic Mystic Path of *Tasawwuf,* written in English. We gained great benefit from these books during the time of his visit. He would on frequent occasions ask someone to read from them when we gathered. Thus they were shared and became a source of learning for us all. Beyond this sharing, however, these books were of deeply special significance to me. When Shaikh Ahmet brought forward the books, he gave them to me to examine. When I noticed the author's name I was dumbfounded, for that name was the very same name of the Grandshaikh who five years earlier had contacted me through his dervish during my first Middle eastern journey. Moreover, when I opened the book, there on the very first page was a full-blown photo of the Grandshaikh and another of his successor, Shaikh Nun. I was the only one present that night, besides our guest, who knew anything at all about either of these men. That photograph was exactly the same as the one which, years before, the Stranger had given into my care. It had been an affirmation of our meeting, and a reminder of things to come. I had corresponded with the Stranger for several years, and I had not shown the photograph to anyone, except for one disciple to whom I was very close.

Overcome with excitement, I muttered and stammered as I attempted to communicate to Shaikh Ahmet what I knew about the men whose pictures were in the books. Understanding, but with no surprise, he simply looked at me and smiled. Then he told me that Shaikh Nun would be visiting our Tekiya the following year. Looking into Shaikh Ahmet's face as he told me, I knew with deep certainty that an important cycle was being completed. Moreover, I knew that meeting the Grandshaikh's successor would only mark the beginning of a whole new series of adventures.

The title of these books was *Mercy Oceans*. Indeed God Most High was showing me, at every step, that His mercy is more vast and unfathomable than the sea, and full of wondrous secrets. Only by His mercy had I boarded the *Tariqat* dinghy and set sail on a journey for places unknown. A sailor now, I rode the waves, carried forward by this hope: to become a diver who would surface with the pearl, and all praise belongs to God, the Lord of all the worlds.

Shaikh Ahmet was, from the very outset, at home in the Tekiya. He was clearly established in the Path of God, and the signs of devotion were apparent in his being. He recognised, better than we did, what attitude one should take in the house of God. He recognised as well, much about our spiritual states and collective stages of development. Having come to us with a purpose clearly known to himself and to our Shaikh, he immediately but gently established his programme, by means of which he might observe us and assist us along the way. Throughout his stay he led the prayers and *zikr* and was naturally at ease as our religious leader. I noticed that he, like our own Shaikh, slept very little. He rose especially early for *Fajr*, the morning prayer, and came into the mosque in the latter part of the night, about an hour before the dawn. He would say a few prostrations of *Tahajjud*, the voluntary prayers of night, then sit in silent *zikr* in the prayer alcove (*mihrab*) until the sky showed signs of light. The *zikr* of the morning were for me especially sweet, and after them Shaikh Ahmet would sing *ilahis*, or little rhyming songs of praise. In the times between the prayers throughout the day he scheduled Arabic lessons. He had brought with him a few copies of a small but challenging Qur'anic primer, which was reproduced so that everyone might have a copy. Each student was tested and received instruction according to what he knew. Those who knew nothing began with Arabic alphabet letters, those who were in the middle began there, and those who knew the letters and a little basic grammar went directly to the Qur'an.

These lessons with Shaikh Ahmet were a central point of focus in most of our interactions. Whenever I think of those days, the picture of him is clear, for he was found in the Tekiya's *muhabbat* room most of the time, when he was not in prayer. He kept near him a little podium on which we placed our books when we sat before him for our instruction, and he also had with him a record of attendance. No disciple or dervish in the circle, whether local or a traveller, escaped these lessons. The Turkish word '*yok*', which means 'no', became a favourite word among the disciples. Shaikh Ahmet would casually say this word whenever he gave an 'X' for a lesson missed by anyone among us. We would in turn use the word with each other when we playfully asked another disciple if he or she had gone for their lesson. So it was that long after the visiting Shaikh left us, whenever someone uttered '*Yok*!' it always made me smile.

When *Ramadan* began, Shaikh Ahmet put increasing emphasis on learning Qur'an. In addition to the Arabic lessons, Qur'an reading was established and as is the custom in *Ramadan*, he recited a section each day, usually in the mornings. His *qirat*, or style of Qur'anic chanting was lovely and clear, and each morning some of us would gather to listen. In the evenings just before prayers, we would sit with him and recite short *suras* of the Qur'an and other basic invocations, in unison as a group. Our days were quite full and busy and towards the end of the month, when he announced a test on the recitation of prayers and short *suras*, everyone felt the challenge. In the face of an examination, each disciple was forced to look at how they had utilised their time, and whether or not they had seized upon any one of many opportunities to learn something from our guest.

I know that in the personal sense, I was presented chance after chance and teaching upon teaching. Whenever I sat before Shaikh Effendi for my lesson, he was showing me the way. I wanted so much to impress him and show him what I knew, though now I realise that really I knew nothing. After overcoming my doubt that he was in fact a *hafiz* — that is, one who truly knew the Book — I learned to let him take the lead. Where this doubt came from, especially in the light of what I had been clearly told about him by my Shaikh, was amazing. Still the doubt was there, and Shaikh Ahmet utilised it to bring me fully to my senses. Often when I began reading he would nod off to sleep, or so it seemed, yet if I uttered a single word or letter incorrectly, he corrected me without ever opening his eyes. This simple experience with him brought me to realise the wisdom of a saying I had often heard as a child: 'Every shut-eye ain't sleep and every goodbye ain't gone.'

Now, in an entirely different context, I understood these words with shocking new fullness. Reaching this place after so much doubting, I repeatedly found myself with no other choice except simply to give up. Only at this place, the point where finally I surrendered, did I ever go forward and at last, begin to learn. This learning was both inward and outward. In this case, outward in terms of the lessons in style and form of recitation. All of this was valuable but merely the 'bones' of Qur'an. Inwardly, however, I learned by means of the feeling which swelled up in my heart, which directed me now to wholly new and different meanings. Only by surrender and by my heart, did I have my first taste of the sweetness of the 'marrow' of the book.

> Someone asked Shems-eddin: What is gnosis? It is the life of the heart through God, he answered . . . True knowledge is in the heart, while profession of faith is on the tongue.
>
> *('The Whirling Ecstasy' by Aflaki)*

One day after a lesson, I sat alone in the Tekiya with Shaikh Ahmet. He took out a small book of *ilahis* and began to chant a most exotic and enchanting melody. Struck dumb with wonder and sheer delight, I listened. Half-way through the verses, he began to weep. His tears flowed up like torrents of a rushing volcanic stream, burning with inexplicable love and feeling. Unable to distinguish between the scope of his joy or depth of his sadness, I sat quietly before him not knowing what to do. Completely overtaken, spellbound and swollen with feeling, I found myself unable, none the less, to produce a single tear. Later, when he told me that the verses had been composed by his Shaikh, I fell into a deep depression. When I thought of my love for my own Shaikh, it seemed all too inadequate and incomplete as compared with that of the noble-hearted Shaikh Ahmet who sat weeping red-hot tears of love.

Not long after this encounter with Shaikh Ahmet, I had occasion to speak with my Shaikh on the phone. I told him of my experience and how little I had seen in common between myself and Shaikh Ahmet. On hearing my complaints against myself, he cautioned me severely, saying that I did not know with any certainty who I was or what station I might hold. Then he lovingly told me:

'What you expect in this moment is not for you to have or to be. You are concerned that you did not sneeze, when it is Shaikh Ahmet who has the flu.'

In much the same way that I was taught by Shaikh Ahmet, every disciple in our circle was likewise taught. His programme brought him into regular close contact with each and every one of us, and over a period of weeks we evidenced through our effort and response in interaction with him exactly what was the level and nature of our desire, faith, and trust. Each one of us received a teaching individually suited to the idiosyncrasies of our own personal inward struggles, but we also received his teaching on some occasions, by our identification with the struggle of one or another disciple, leading ultimately, to some broader lesson or issue of spiritual progress on the Path for us collectively as a group.

As our time with Shaikh Ahmet grew shorter, the realisation began to dawn on me that soon he would be gone. He reminded us gently, but continually that he was going away, but I seemed never to have listened. Then one day as we stood for the prayer, I finally *heard* his message. Gesturing for me to lead instead of himself, smiling, he looked into my eyes and said '*ana musafir*' — 'I am a traveller.' Thus he conveyed that his way of being with us was not now, and never had been, in any way static or fixed. With much the same swiftness of passing as the lilacs, Shaikh Ahmet came and left us much too quickly and all too soon. It seemed that he had been with us for just a brief and fleeting moment, then climbed aboard a plane and disappeared into the blue. His sweet fragrance lingered with me like that of gentle springtime blossoms, and every prayer that he had taught me was like a precious petal of the rose.

Shaikh Ahmet's departure left me stunned and semi-dazed, yet this feeling was not new. I had felt this way so often over the years, that I took it as an aspect of my normal state of mind. The life of a disciple is always full of changes and challenges to how one has learned *to think that things are*. Having arrived at this familiar place, I reviewed the recent events of my life as connected with Shaikh Ahmet and tried to understand what I should have gained by his having come into my life. What was the benefit of Arabic lessons, the heavy emphasis on Qur'an and nearly two months of nightly recitations of prayers and invocations whose meaning few of us understood and did not really care to know?

After turning these questions around in my mind for nearly two months, a door was suddenly flung open and answers began to come. An unexpected gathering was called by our Shaikh. Soon I came to see that what had seemed to be the end was just another beginning, and though Shaikh Ahmet had gone from the Tekiya, he had not gone from my life. This gathering called by the Shaikh was only the first in a series of events to follow, which unfolded to me the mysteries of my own seeking heart, and by and by, I was to meet Shaikh Ahmet Effendi again.

Our Shaikh told us clearly, in no uncertain terms, that his main purpose in calling us together was to inform us that we had failed miserably in the test of *tawakkal* (trust). A report on our progress, or lack of such, had come to him directly from Shaikh Ahmet, not long after he had left us. Shaikh Ahmet had also said that our manners and *hizmet* (service) were beyond reproach, yet we had absolutely no interest in learning Qur'an or its related Arabic fundamentals. Continuing, the Shaikh told us that Muslims are a small group of people growing more and more rare, diminishing like the beautiful wolf, being driven to extinction and overtaken by the power of *dunya*, the world.

'Forget about *dunya*,' he warned us. 'Forget about your success or failure. Forget about your goals! Use your time wisely, the boat can be missed and there will come a time when the doors of the ark will close. Becoming a *shaheed* is your concern, becoming a witness for Allah.'

I remembered this warning as I heard the plane door close with a familiar but sudden 'whoosh' sound. One year had passed since Shaikh Ahmet had left us and I was now on my way to perform *Hajj*. I was to visit several cities en route to Mecca, one of which was Konya, Shaikh Ahmet's native city. I had seen my own Shaikh before I set out on the journey, and he had given me an itinerary which told me where to go and who to see. He also gave me some encouraging words of hope, saying:

'I want you to become a dervish. In fact I will make you a dervish upon your return and I will set the *kulah* (dervish hat) on your head.' These words, too, were much a part of the unfolding events and greater teachings. The Shaikh knew my heart completely, and like most beginning disciples, that heart of mine was filled with folly and vain hopes for what really does not matter: wishes for advancement on the spiritual path, for some rank, for a title, some badge or cloak — none of which have anything to do with the heart of a dervish or one who is called a *Faqir*, one who is poor in possessions but rich in God.

In the first part of this journey I arrived in Belgrade, Yugoslavia. I made my way from the airport to the train depot by bus. Once in the depot it seemed I was entirely helpless. Everything was written in Slavic and no one spoke any English, not even policemen, nor those who served in information booths. As God would have it, some young boy noticed the prayer beads which I held. After passing to and fro before me several times, I suspect to scrutinise me further, he disappeared into the crowd. Almost out of nowhere, he seemed to reappear with a man whom I later learned was his father.

'*Hu-u-u-u*', they whispered in unison as they presented before me in respectful demeanour (*niyaz*) identifying themselves as dervishes. They spoke no English but we communicated somehow and together we boarded the train. As the sun set gently behind the red tile roof of some typical but lovely little Yugoslav house, the train dragged slowly through the picturesque and mountainous hillside. The following morning the dervish and his son disembarked. They put me into the care of another person who boarded the train from their hometown, and with that person's help I was delivered directly to the doorstep of the Tekiya at Prizren.

If it were that journeys had such a thing as a heart, then my stay in Prizren would be that heart and every moment I spent there, a heartbeat of love. I felt at home and at peace and sad to leave. The morning of my arrival I was greeted by Mima Hanim, wife of Shaikh Jami. She and Shaikh Jami had spent much time with us in the States, so I felt at ease on seeing her again. She greeted me warmly and asked about my family and other disciples of our circle, mentioning them by name, one after another.

Later Shaikh Jami Effendi came and we sat together for breakfast. One of the first things I remember hearing was that Shaikh Nun had been there in Prizren only a day before my arrival. I found it interesting how these men, the Shaikhs, moved about. Though I didn't focus on it very much at the time, I somehow hoped I would meet this man who perhaps knew the secret of the Stranger who had brought me his own Shaikh's message years before, from what seemed out of the blue. But my days in Prizren were stimulating and full so I didn't give much time to these thoughts of Shaikh Nun. Every day I sat with Shaikh Jami Effendi for at least one meal at his home, sometimes more. On other occasions, I sat at the place of dining (*sofra*) with the dervishes. It was in Prizren that I began to learn what a dervish truly is. I lived among them, and saw them at work and at play. I felt the heat from the flame of their devotion and the burning joy of the fire in their *zikr*. These men were nothing less than the salt of the earth. Their hearts were ablaze with love, they were completely committed to God, and their loyalty to their Shaikh was fully established. Their demeanour was impeccable, their humility so natural and unpretentious, their service so loving and generous, one could not help but love them and want to be like them, or so it was with me.

While in Prizren I learned about Hazreti Pir Sayyid Ahmed Rufai and the Rufai Shaikhs of the Kosova province. Both Shaikh Jami and my Shaikh were in this line to Hazreti Pir.

During my time in Prizren Shaikh Jami was working daily on translating South Slavic documents on the life of Hazreti Pir into Albanian and English. Part of my *hizmet* (service) was to share in the editing and typing of what he had prepared. It was through this work that I learned about the life of Hazreti Pir and his outstanding spiritual qualities. The dervishes of Prizren, the loving daily *muhabbat* (discourse) of Shaikh Jami, the incredible *zikr*, the miraculous life events of Hazreti Pir Ahmed Rufai, the light of the Prizren Tekiya, all combined to have their effect. One day as I was stepping out of the Tekiya with Shaikh Jami, the force of it all descended to my heart. I was overcome in the moment again and again and thunderstruck with light. I felt such tremendous love for Hazreti Pir. It flowed up in rushes from deep inside me. I felt as if I knew him. Standing just outside the Tekiya's door, I attempted to communicate my experience to Shaikh Jami. It seemed as if he already knew. I told him that I would like to be connected with Hazreti Pir and he smiled.

'When I come again to the States,' he said, 'I will give you the *bayat* (invitation pledge) of a Rufai Dervish. I could give it to you now but I think it will be better to do this when others of your circle are present and also so that your Shaikh may know. But do not worry, you will be protected in your journey and your *bayats* from your Shaikh and myself will serve you all your life, as if they were *zulfikar*, the double-edged sword of the Prophet, the peace of God be upon him.

This day was one of the most beautiful and important of my life. So much love came, in so many ways. I was full of joy and hope. As the time drew near for my departure from Prizren, Shaikh Jami drew me closer to himself. I spent many hours together with him alone, or with him and one or two dervishes. Towards the end of my stay he gave me advice for my travel after Prizren and helped me prepare to leave.

On the day before I left, I became very sick. I had overeaten at the *sofra,* but unavoidably so. The dervishes had essentially forced me to eat most of the food on the table. Anyone who has travelled in the East knows the impossibility of attempting to escape their enthusiastic and generous hospitality. Somehow my stamina was low that day and I was throwing up and weak with diarrhoea. I avoided the Shaikh because I didn't want him to know. In between my visits to the toilet, I reflected on my state. I wondered why I was getting sick at this time, as I was preparing to leave. I wanted very much to stay, but what an awkward way to do it. After my second visit to the toilet I was suddenly relieved. A great sense of wellness came over my entire body. Feeling better now, I came into the *muhabbat* room where Shaikh Jami and some others were gathered. Of course, the Shaikh asked me about what had happened and where I had been so I told him. He said that it was not the food or others would be sick too, 'but perhaps', he said, 'your stomach is not used to eating this way.'

Shaikh Jami was so very kind. He offered me every help and said that he would not send me away sick. I told him that I thought there must be some lesson in my sickness which I had not yet come to know. He responded with the following story:

> There were two men praying in the mosque, each on his knees making long supplications to God. The man who finished first stopped to listen to what the other prayed for, only to hear a long list of complaints about ailments: 'Allah, my feet are aching, heal them; my back is sore, can you heal it and I have headaches, can you cure them? And here on the side of my neck is an ache, and this shoulder . . . when I move it, the arthritis is so bad . . .' The supplicant continued in this way until the man listening finally interrupted by slapping him sharply on the back saying: 'Actually, it would be easier to ask God to make a new man.'

'If people were not sick,' said the Shaikh as he looked on me with kindness, 'they would not come to the Tekiya. The Tekiya is just like a hospital. We want to make you a new man. You have brought a light to Prizren and we will never forget you. Likewise, you have benefited much. By the editing you gave as *hizmet*, you have also gained, for really it is gain enough for a *murid* to learn about his *Pir* (a fully perfected Master who guides the *murid* through the Shaikh). Go now my son and take rest. We must rise early in the morning.'

In my room again, I stood at the window which looked over the street and surrounding hillside. Feeling my departure from the city near, I reflected on my visit, my time with Shaikh Jami, the dervishes and the people there. How lovely was our meeting, yet how brief those days, fleeting as if they were only seconds. I lay on my bed of sheepskins listening to the sounds of the sultry Prizren night: friendly chatter of neighbourhood folk in their houses, the exotic cadence of Turkish music growing fainter, as I drifted into sleep.

At the window again before sunrise, I whispered farewell to the Prizren night, as she retreated into dawn. The melodic cry of some distant *muezzin* — the caller to prayer — touched me with its sweetness as darkness faded into light. As I turned from the window to make ready for the prayer, a *Rubaiyat* verse often recited by my Shaikh floated through my thoughts:

Alike for those who Today prepare
And those that after a tomorrow stare
A muezzin from the tower of darkness cries
'Fools! your reward is neither here nor there'.

I went into the Tekiya with Shaikh Jami to give my *salaams* and say prayers for travel. When we stepped outside again, everyone had gathered: Mima Hanim, the Shaikh's mother Arifa Hanim, his daughters, his younger son and a few dervishes. We stood all together for pictures and soon thereafter we were in the Shaikh's car and driving down the road.

The day of my departure from Prizren was a lovely day. The sun shone brightly and skies were clear, with puffs of clouds tossed casually here and there, like pillows on a wide blue carpet. With the Shaikh at the wheel, and me beside him, his son and dervishes Yakub and Fatmir in the rear, we sped along the dangerous mountain roads without a single care in the world. All windows open, it seemed we were sailing . . . the breeze in our faces, the rays of sun dancing to *ilahis* we sang at the top of our lungs. The three-hour ride to Skopje seemed as if it were minutes. Almost before I knew it, I was aboard the bus and waving goodbye.

The bus ride to Ohrid was pleasant. I made my way from the bus depot, past the pier of Lake Ohrid, through an old cobblestone lane of shops. Following landmarks I had been given by dervishes in Prizren, I was soon at the Tekiya's gate. In the grounds I was greeted by a friendly man who assisted me with my ablutions then sat with me to talk. When I asked his name, he only told me Arif, but I soon discovered that this unassuming man was in fact a Shaikh from a town called Struga, not very far from Ohrid. Shaikh Arif informed me that Shaikh Yahya, the presiding Shaikh at Ohrid, would arrive at the time of *Asr*, the afternoon prayer. He therefore took me into the Tekiya where I waited for the Shaikh to arrive. The Tekiya's edifice was very striking. I took particular note of it because I knew that Hazreti Pir Hayyati Sultan had built most of it by his very own hands, nearly five hundred years before. Its interior was primarily wood. In the *muhabbat* room, large planks were used as floorboards held in place by distinct black nails with large heads, which were also made by Hazreti Pir Hayyati. The planks had the feel of barn board but were much stronger. Grey, but nearly bleached to whiteness by centuries of care, the boards lay neath the fluffy sheepskin prayer mats which were scattered around the room. There were lots of windows which opened to a view of the courtyard, the tomb of the Pir, and a very tiny cemetery along the Tekiya's side. The windows were delicate with lots of panes, and with wooden frames and knobs by which they could be opened. Stark simplicity and impeccable cleanliness were the things I sensed most strongly. Inside the prayer room, which one descended into down two or three steps from the *muhabbat* room, I felt a sense of timelessness. Stylized plaques and calligraphic renderings of names of God, His prophets, or Qur'anic verses were all about the ancient, softly lit room.

Just before the time of prayer, people began to arrive, the first of whom was Dervish Yakub. When this long-standing seeker seated himself on the floor beneath the clock on the wall, it seemed as though he had always been there, for he was nearly as ancient as the Tekiya itself. Very soon after this Shaikh Yahya arrived with a few other dervishes. Among them was a muezzin called Dervish Irfan, a smiling, lively, most likeable man who filled the room with his warmth and the melodious strains of his call.

After the prayer, I left with the Shaikh for his home. Shaikh Yahya and his wife had visited our Tekiya and had been guests in my home in the States, so our meeting was a kind of reunion. I answered the Shaikh's enquiries concerning my journey, as we walked along, him pushing the bike which was ordinarily his means of transport. At his home I met his family, which included his wife, son, son-in-law, and three daughters, who had all somehow heard of my arrival and gathered there to greet me. We had a pleasant meal and sat around the table sharing stories, using fragments of Turkish, French, and English to communicate. It was good to be with them and the evening passed by quickly.

The following morning the Shaikh and I rose about an hour before dawn and made our way to the Tekiya. The streets were empty at that hour and the echo of our footsteps, striking cadence on the cement, was the only sound I heard. At the Tekiya, the Shaikh took me upstairs where there was another gathering-place. The focus of the room was a cooking fireplace with a large, flat, stone surface on which a fire could be built underneath a chimney, fashioned above it like a hood. Long, covered benches stretched along the walls on either side of the room and a bright, orange-brown-coloured carpet spanned the space in between. After the prayer we returned to this room for coffee and morning conversations (*muhabbat*). The kinder, which the Shaikh had earlier lighted had settled to a glowing heap of coals around the old-fashioned coffee pot which had brewed as we had prayed. Shaikh Yahya directed me to a seat next to himself, and three dervishes flanked him on the other side. Each of them was dressed in a long, black dervish robe and very tall, light-brown *kulah*, a dervish hat. The Shaikh was dressed similarly except that his *kulah* had the characteristic black sash wrapped about it in neat turns. They made a beautiful picture as they sat there in lotus position, silent but present, natural but completely unobtrusive. The morning rays of sunlight shone in through the windows and reflected off of the tray full of small Turkish cups held by one of two dervishes who stood gracefully poised in the respectful posture of *niyaz* in the centre of the floor, awaiting the Shaikh's signal to serve us. Receiving it, they began circling the room together, one carrying the tray, the other pouring. They were as precise as drill team soldiers, but so much more graceful and humble in demeanour. Seeing them made me think of *sakis* (cup-bearers) pouring the wine of ecstasy. When all of the rounds were completed, the dervishes who had served us served each other. Each one poured with *niyaz* and flawless, loving good manner. We spent a good portion of the morning discussing Qur'an, with the Shaikh examining me for verses I knew and pointing out others which I should learn. We returned to his home just before noon for lunch. We sat outside at a small table enjoying the moment and laughing at a neighbour's chicken who ran all about.

After prayers at noon (*zuhr*), the Shaikh took me into the tomb of Hazreti Pir Hayyati. It was a beautiful experience. Nearly twelve Shaikhs are laid to rest in that building. Most of these are in a wide room outside the central room of the tomb occupied only by the Pir. I noticed throughout my journey that I felt more life with those already gone to *akhirat*, the hereafter, than those walking around on the earth. Each time I found my way to the resting place of some noble *Wali* (a saintly being), I felt as if I were meeting a good friend again after a long separation.

Shaikha Ana was an exception, for she was a *Wali* who had not yet left the planet. Completely refined, it seemed to me a wonder she remained here. She had no attachments and was only held here by a thread of ego-less body-shell and the order of God Almighty. She was the light of Ohrid for me. I found in her a penetrating, luminous presence, a vibrating life, and flowing depth. She was at the same time natural, at ease, full of love. She looked into my eyes in the moment we met and placing her hand tenderly on my own, she touched my very soul. She was as my own mother, drawing me into her heart. The daughter of a Shaikh, and the wife of a Shaikh, she was a direct descendant of Hazreti Pir Hayyati. I took great benefit from the time I spent with her. We sat together for tea and talked. I conveyed to her the greeting of my own Shaikh, who had been as much her son as her dervish. I then conveyed the greetings of other disciples. She in turn, showed me photos of various Shaikhs and other artefacts of the Path. As our visit was nearing its end, having seen the signs of devotion apparent in her, I asked, in naive desperation, how it is that one who is a *murid* ever comes to that state of love called *'ashq*. Her eyes brightened and she flashed a smile as she leaned closer to answer.

'Come back after one year my son, and then I will, God willing, give you the answer.'

I had now spent a good deal of time with Shaikh Yahya. I had paid a visit to Hazreti Pir and been able to see Shaikha Ana. Having done these things I felt ready to depart from Ohrid. The Shaikh, however, did not want me to leave. It was difficult to explain to him but finally, he acceded. Later that afternoon his son Hudai came to me with a ticket for the bus from Ohrid to Skopje, where I would make a connecting bus for Turkey. That night I accompanied the Shaikh to the home of a man called Dervish Haidar, for a ceremony known as *mevlud*. There was much brotherly feeling among these simple-living people of the Path and I felt myself at home. After the night prayer, a fine meal of limas and meat was served at the *sofra* — the dining-place. The people of Macedonia seem to like beans at dinner. I had them in Prizren as well as in Ohrid. This simple, useful, inexpensive food reminded me of days of my own urban childhood and the large pots of limas that my mother often made. Among these *faqirs*, these people of poverty, I felt that same unaffected homeliness I felt with my family as a child.

Later that night, the Shaikh and I walked the quiet streets together again, joined by one of his dervishes. The dervish parted company with us at a certain intersection and the Shaikh and I continued alone. When we reached the Shaikh's home, we found everyone awake. Everyone was there including the Shaikh's son-in-law and grandchildren. I was very surprised to find them gathered around the table smiling. They all knew that I would be leaving in the morning and wanted to be with me for a while. It was a beautiful coming together. Jalal, the Shaikh's son-in-law, had seemed to take a great liking to me and showed me exceptional warmth. I liked him too and took this liking as a sign from God that, unworthy as I am, He showed His kindness none the less and sent me a friend in each place I went. We all exchanged *salaams* and said our goodbyes for the night. Early the next morning the Shaikh and I went to the Tekiya. I left my bag at the Shaikh's home thinking I would return for it, but by the time we had completed morning prayers, it was nearly time for me to be at the bus depot. I attempted to communicate to the Shaikh that I had left the bag, but he seemed quite unconcerned. That old test of *tawakkal* was coming up again. But was it *really* my lack of trust or did the Shaikh not understand? Just as I was about to board the bus, the Shaikh's daughters drove up with the bag. The Shaikh had apparently already asked them to bring it. Taking the bag from one of his daughters, he handed it over to me without uttering a word. By the time I had taken my seat aboard the bus, the Shaikh's wife had arrived and was standing beside him. They were joined by their daughters, and my new friend Jalal, and Shaikh Qadri, whom I met at Shaikha Ana's. Framed in my window was the lovely picture they made, standing together and waving *salaams*. Whenever I think of Ohrid that picture comes to mind, reminding me of the kindness they showed me while I was there. I gave my *niyaz* as the bus pulled out of the depot and onto the road, and smiled at myself as I felt my bag beside me in the seat.

II

It was a pleasant ride back to Skopje where I purchased a ticket for Istanbul. Outside, the bus was already in its boarding zone, with the driver and several passengers huddled at its side, attempting to load their baggage. The atmosphere was normal, with children playing and skipping about, happy to be taking a journey, their mothers hoping they would not run out in front of the bus, or even better perhaps, by some blessing of Heaven, that they would all fall alseep immediately, once aboard and in their seats. The luggage compartment having been stuffed, some people carried their smaller things into the bus, walking sideways down the aisle. Always, too, there was the exceptional person, with a locker or suitcase which they 'could not do without', crowding and bumping and forcing it to fit in some unlikely, impossible space. Turkish music came over the speakers, interrupted only occasionally by some remark from the driver.

The bus-ride to Turkey was long, nearly twenty-four hours, but it was interesting to see the land and the people. That is always the joy of travel: to see and feel the people as they live and move about in their own familiar surroundings. The Turkish people aboard the bus gave me a preview of their ways. They were warm and loving and down to earth, quick to smile and mindful of God. One family befriended me right away and when the bus stopped in a roadside, park-like area, they fed me from their provisions, not permitting me to eat from my own. They instructed their children to kiss my hand and address me as Uncle, not because I was particularly special, but simply because I was an adult and a Muslim. I was deeply impressed by the refinement of these people: their good manners so natural and straight from the heart, just exactly the way it should be. Experiencing this forced me into a good amount of self-examination and made me hope to improve my own personal condition.

The bus made several stops along the way so that people could stretch, or have a soda or refreshment at some stand by the road, or tend to other needs. Our longest stop was at the Bulgarian border where we all disembarked for their custom's inspection. The inspectors were rude and unnecessarily slow, unpacking nearly every bag and box, leaving our luggage dishevelled for us to deal with however we might. As passengers in a foreign land, our prevailing strategy was to close our mouths and keep our patience until the ordeal came to an end. Once through customs, however, everyone seemed to relax and the remainder of the journey was easy. We reached the Turkish border sometime after midnight and passed through customs with relatively little delay. The Turkish inspectors were a great deal more pleasant than their Bulgarian counterparts. They were appropriately serious but not overbearing and they welcomed us into the country. I felt as though I was returning home and not entering a land of strangers. The bus rolled quietly through the night and by morning we were nearing Istanbul.

The morning sun sat on the horizon like an orange-red ball, beautiful and bold against the soft, blue backdrop of the sky. The smell of the sea was in the air as we made our approach to the city. Stretches of water could be seen from the roadside from the outskirts, continuing directly into the city proper. The Bosphorus Sea with its Golden Horn is only one of the wonders of Istanbul. One can see sailboats and swimmers and fishermen. There are beautiful mosques everywhere — magnificent ones on hillsides, on islands, in the streets and side-streets; great ones and small ones, famous and obscure. From the depot, I made my way walking along the streets. There were pavement vendors, *baklava* shops, restaurants, cars, buses and tourists from all around the world. I was trying to find my way to Shaikh Muzzafer whom I'd also met in the States. He had visited out Tekiya with several of his dervishes and blessed us with the light of his presence.

He owned a bookshop near the mosque as Beyazit Jami, which was not too difficult to find. Arriving there, I met the man who assisted him in the store, Dervish Ibrahim. With the dervish's help I was able to find an inexpensive hotel room nearby. I spent my time visiting the Shaikh or sitting with his dervishes who frequented the shop. In fact they filled the shop to such an extent when the Shaikh was there that someone shopping for a book could hardly enter. A tea vendor passed through regularly with a tray of clinking cups and a teapot. We drank tea and laughed and exchanged mutual stories we had heard about the Path. It was in Shaikh Muzzafer's store that I met a man who told me that Shaikh Nun had recently been in Istanbul and had now gone on to Konya. I stayed in Istanbul two days until Thursday night, which was the night of the Halveti *zikr*. More than two hundred dervishes gathered in the Tekiya for this weekly event. It was a joyful celebration to be among that sea of souls. It was so moving, so delightful and uplifting, such a dance of the heart, there are really no words to describe it.

After a short trip to Ankara and a visit to the tomb of the Great Shaikh Hajji Bayram Wali, I arrived in the city of Konya. Taking a little taxi-bus known as a *dolmush*, I arrived at a small square just a short way from the mosque of Shemsi Tebriz, may God bless him, the revered teacher of Hazreti Jalaluddin Rumi. I performed my abolutions then entered. The tomb occupied an area of its own, slightly above the floor, enclosed by a railing. I approached as near as I could to give my *salaams* and say a prayer for this illumined soul. Many reflections came to my heart and I thanked God Almighty for allowing a disciple as unworthy as myself to follow in the footprints of this noble being of light. The *azan* was sounded and I stood for prayer. I had hoped to see Shaikh Ahmet as he was the keeper of the tomb and also an *Imam*. He was not present, however, so after the prayer I left the mosque thinking about how I might find him. I took a seat on a bench just outside the mosque, sitting for a moment to observe the people and reflect on where I was, happy to be in Konya, home of the Whirling Dervishes. I remembered Shaikh Ahmet's time with us in the Tekiya at home, the Qur'an lessons and his report to our Shaikh concerning our unwillingness to learn. I remembered his departure from us and how we missed him when he had gone. As I sat there in my musings, I was approached by two young boys. Curious about me, they asked my name and where I had travelled from. I answered, then asked them if they knew Shaikh Ahmet.

'Khoja Ahmet?' they replied almost in unison.

I nodded yes.

'We know,' they answered, 'Come, we take.'

I took up my bag and followed the boys along the street, around a corner through a narrow row of buildings, and up a dimly lit flight of stairs. I had seen a sign saying: Turksoy Apts. I remembered the name from correspondence. It was the right place, only about five minutes from the mosque. The boys were already knocking at the door and in a moment Shaikh Ahmet was standing there, smiling that warm, familiar smile, inviting me in.

As we sat for tea, I conveyed *salaams* from my Shaikh and fellow disciples. Shaikh Ahmet enquired about every disciple, taking down his photo album to point them out, asking 'How is this one? That one?' I answered that each was well. I told him about my journey to Prizren and Istanbul and my plans for travelling onward to Damascus, then to Mecca for Hajj. I expressed my hopes to stay a few days in Konya in order to spend time in the mosque of Hazreti Shems, the tombs of Hazreti Rumi and Sadruddin Konevi, the noted Shaikh and murid of Shaikh al Akbar. When I mentioned to Shaikh Ahmet that Shaikh Nun had been in Prizren, he told me that he had also been in Konya but had returned to Istanbul.

'It is my suggestion', said Shaikh Ahmet, 'that you spend one day in Konya and return immediately to Istanbul. My son Mustapha will travel with you and take you to Shaikh Nun.'

The following day Shaikh Ahmet gave me the grand tour of Konya. It seemed we walked from one end of the city to the other. We saw every historical site of any relevance. We talked of mosques and Tekiya, and of dervishes, and of Hazreti Jalaluddin. We spent time in the Tekiya-turned-museum, and saw much of what I had hoped to see. Late that evening, accompanied by Mustafa, I returned by bus to Istanbul. I spent the next morning with Mustafa as he attended to his affairs. Beyond his talents as a calligrapher, he was, like his father, a very talented *hafiz* (preserver) and *qari* (reciter of Qur'an). Much of his work therefore was involved with youth and Qur'an schools operated from mosques. His work completed, we took a series of buses by which we eventually arrived at the outskirts of the city. We stopped at a small shop where we purchased a loaf of bread and some cheese. From here we made our way up a steep hillside on which was located a very beautiful, newly built house which served as a Tekiya for Shaikh Nun. Mustafa showed me around and encouraged me to make myself at home. We spoke for a while, then he departed saying that the Shaikh would arrive later that night, God willing.

I spent the afternoon alone, relatively peacefully, wondering when I would meet the Shaikh. Later that afternoon a dervish arrived who said he had been sent to bring me to the Shaikh. When the dervish and I reached our destination, the Shaikh was not there. We did receive a message, however, that the Shaikh would see me the following morning. I stayed in the care of the dervish for the remainder of the evening. He served me dinner and took me to a mosque near his apartment for prayers. The following morning the dervish took me to a simply furnished urban dwelling, the home of Shaikh Nun's brother who greeted us at the door. The kindly gentleman directed me into the parlour where I took a seat.

'The Shaikh is performing the voluntary prayers of the morning,' he said. 'He will be with you in a few minutes.'

The Shaikh entered only moments later. I stood to greet him, giving *niyaz* and advancing to kiss his hand. His presence filled the room and one could easily see that he was a man of light. His eyes shone with love and piercing clarity and the long, silver-white hairs of his beard stretched forth around and beneath his face like rays of sunlight. A neat, white, globe-shaped turban was his characteristic headdress, and a full-length, green, cape-like garment was his robe.

'My name is Muhyiddin, Shaikh Effendi,' I said.

'You are Shaikh Muhyiddin,' he said smiling.

'I am sorry Shaikh Effendi, but I am only a *murid*,' I said, not sure if I was being told of my potential or corrected for some arrogance obvious to the Shaikh but not to myself.

'I know who you are,' he said, 'and I know what to call you, but let us talk of other things for now.'

The Shaikh told me that I would be spending time with him as he conducted a series of talks in mosques around the city. We would spend time at the tombs of the saintly beings and attend a remembrance celebration at a local Tekiya.

'I know as well that you have special questions and we will speak of these tonight. I must attend to other matters now.'

During my stay in Istanbul I spent most of my time in the company of Shaikh Nun. In being with him I gained a very clear sense of how incredible the pace of a Shaikh is as we moved, by God's wisdom, in what seemed to me the most unpredictable patterns. During this time I explored the mystery of the dervish who had been sent to me by Grandshaikh Daghistani from the unseen world, six years earlier, during my first journey to the East.

'For all these years,' said Shaikh Nun, 'I have carried an *amanat* (a trust) which in truth belongs to you. I was happy to carry this burden, but now I am much relieved that you are here to claim it.'

When I enquired how such a thing had come about, the Shaikh said to me:

'The Grandshaikh was a hunter of souls. He saw you in the eternal place called *Ezel* and chose you for his own.'

I was amazed by these words. It was all so incredible. I tried to let it in and the Shaikh fed me in spoonfuls, degree by degree.

On the day before I left, I was together with Shaikh Nun at the hillside Tekiya where Mustafa had first brought me. On this day, he presented me with a long personal *muhabbat*, a discourse, concerning the chain of Shaikhs of Naqshbandi Tariqat. The Shaikh explained to me the role of *Tariqat* in the heart's purification and in promoting inner-orientated spiritual Islam. He gave me the name of each and every one of the *awliya* (saintly shaikhs) between himself and the Prophet, peace be upon him. He told me it was the day I was to receive the trust. Understanding, so I thought, I enquired what the implications were. I explained that I had other Tariqat involvements and that I was happy to have my own Shaikh as my guide. Shaikh Nun assured me that I needn't feel any concern. When I showed him a photograph of my Shaikh, he said:

'I have seen him before. He is good, without question. He is a son of the Grandshaikh.'

In truth, I had no idea what my Shaikh being a son of the Grandshaikh meant. I did, however, make these two assumptions: first, that my Shaikh was somehow connected to Grandshaikh Daghistani, and secondly that acceptance of the Naqshbandi initiation pledge (*bayat*) was an advancement. So it was that I took the *bayat* to my mind in good conscience. However, as soon as the Shaikh removed his hand from my own, a dark, heavy cloud of doubt descended to my head. Suddenly, I felt a nervous sense of foreboding. I wondered if I had made a mistake.

I remained in the Shaikh's company for one more day. Taking leave from his circle, he assured me all would be well but still that cloud came. As much as I tried to dispel it, get from underneath it, or forget it, I could not. That cloud followed me throughout the remainder of my journey. It followed me through the streets of Damascus, around the Ka'ba in Mecca, and through the streets of Medina where the Prophet once lived and walked.

Shaikh Nun had given me instructions for how I should travel to Syria and also gave me the assistance of his two representatives (*muqaddims*) there. These two kindly men maintained the tomb of Grandshaikh Daghistani, and lived in his former home, a simple dwelling among the poor, high on a rocky hillside. Shaikh Nun sent me directly to the mosque and tomb of Shaikh Muhyiddin Ibn Arabi, also known as Shaikh al Akbar. From the tomb and mosque of Grandshaikh Daghistani I made my way almost daily, to the mosque of Shaikh al Akbar for prayers. Damascus, for me, was spiritually vibrant, but politically tense. With the help of the *muqaddims*, Abdus-Salam and Ibrahim, I was able to visit the Ommayid Mosque wherein is the tomb of Hazreti Yahya, upon whom be peace, who is John the Baptist. I visited the tombs of several companions of the Prophet, peace be upon him, including Hazreti Bilal Habashi, the first *muezzin* or caller to prayer, and that of Hazreti Zainul Abideen, the grandson of Hazreti Ali and several other saintly souls. Having accomplished these things I felt myself ready to leave. I took a plane to Jeddah where I joined two other murids from home and together we performed the rites of Hajj. They remained for a short stay in Medina after the Hajj and I took a flight to New York. I arrived home after having been gone about six weeks. It was good to be back. Shaikh Jami and my Shaikh were both around together with a host of disciples. They had gathered at the home of one of the dervishes shortly after my return. When I entered, they all stood and sang. It was a wonderful welcome. It was so loving and so warm. There were the smiling faces of two Shaikhs and my brother and sister disciples on the Path. My heart was full for a moment but then there came the cloud. This was obviously not the time to approach the Shaikh with a 'true confession', but I knew I would have to face him, sooner or later. I dreaded the moment with a sense of horror.

A few days later Shaikh Jami came to our home for lunch. Our own Shaikh was away and Shaikh Jami was with us to help us prepare for *Matem*, the ten days commemorating the slaughter at Kerbala of Imam Hussain, the grandson of Prophet Muhammad together with his family and companions. Shaikh Jami was easy to talk to. I related to him the entire story of my dilemma and the *bayat* (pledge) I had taken with Shaikh Nun. He listened patiently but reacted with a great sense of distress. His face grew sombre and the atmosphere of the room grew heavy and thick. All of this only increased my personal sense of distress and feelings of depression and loss. Noticing my state, Shaikh Jami frowned and touched me as he leaned closer to speak:

'I can't imagine Shaikh Nun doing this to you. When he came to Prizren, I thought him to be an honourable Shaikh. Now I have my doubts. Have you any idea what should be done?'

'Perhaps I could write a letter to Shaikh Nun,' I said. 'I could ask him to lift the *bayat*.'

'I will speak to your Shaikh about this,' said Shaikh Jami. 'Then we will see.'

A few days later the Shaikh returned to the Tekiya for the beginning of *Matem*. I approached him near the roadside at the bottom of the hill. Filled with trepidation, my heart beating in my throat, I attempted to speak:

'Shaikh Effendi, I-I-I suppose you spoke with Shaikh Jami?'

'Yes, of course,' he said, 'and I must tell you that from this moment on, you are no longer my *murid*! Shaikh Nun is your *rehber* (guide) now. You will continue to be in *Tariqat* and you will be welcome in this Tekiya, but from this time forward my relationship to you will be only that of a brother.'

Completely pulverised and speechless, I stood there before him in an awkward, dumbstruck heap. His words fell on my heart like bolts of thunder. Reading my thoughts he continued:

'I do not agree with Shaikh Jami about a letter asking for revocation of the *bayat*. You should not play games with *Tasawwuf* (the Mystic Path). In fact, I suggest that you write to Shaikh Nun and thank him. I wanted to make you a dervish, but actually he has promoted you and made you *his* dervish. Still, I find it interesting that you are the only one out of five of my *murids* who has travelled to Turkey and fallen into this trap. They are only trying to take you away from your own Hazreti Pir Hayyati. But perhaps, this is all the *hikmat* (wisdom) of Allah. I must go now. *Assalaamu alaikum*.'

He left me at the roadside demolished, as if I were struck by lightning. Each word he had spoken threw me deeper into shock, and reduced the charred remains of my world to a ruin of smouldering ash.

The Shaikh was with us for the opening of *Matem*, then left us in the care of Shaikh Jami. Shaikh Jami remained in the Tekiya the entire ten days. Each afternoon he conducted *muhabbat* (discourse) concerning the events of Kerbala. We followed Imam Hussein, may God be pleased with him, and the seventy-two *shaheeds* (martyrs) who were with him through the days leading to their devastating slaughter at the hands of Yazid. Although there was no noble cause for the pain in my own heart, it was sufficiently deep to help me identify with the greater suffering of Hazreti Imam Hussein. I began to glimpse the single-minded dedication and selfless sacrifice demanded of those souls who stand in the service of truth. In some ways my pain deepened, for in my mind I had been a traitor to my Shaikh, the person on the planet who loved me the most. No one knew me more completely, no one had ever accepted me so unconditionally. Never, had I been more true to myself, never more open or more vulnerable to another with no strings attached. The love of my Shaikh asked nothing for itself. It just shone on me, with as much generosity and lack of discrimination as rays of sunlight, no matter what my condition or state. In a spiritual sense, my Shaikh was a mother and a father, protecting, guiding and nourishing my inward potential. He was a sun and moon for me: a barren planet earth without him, revolving with no purpose. Oh how I ached. I passed the days of *Matem* in private chaos. I told no one of my painful circumstance. I did not know how to share it. I did not have Shaikh Ahmet's red-hot tears of love, but now I had my very own agony ocean. I cried its waters, weeping in the darkness of my nights, and filled it to overflowing with ice-blue tears of loss.

> Every heartache and suffering that enters your body and heart pulls you by the ear to the promised Abode. He has afflicted you from every direction to pull you back to the Directionless.
> *('The Sufi Path of Love: The Spiritual Teachings of Rumi' by William C. Chittick)*

Shaikh Jami left the Tekiya after *Matem* to attend to *Tariqat* issues in other places. A *hadrah* (gathering) had been scheduled for New York City, but it would not be until November, which was two months away. As it turned out, I saw neither my Shaikh nor Shaikh Jami until that gathering. I carried my burden through the days, expecting no resolution. During that time, however, I did write a letter to my Shaikh. It was the most difficult letter I had ever written. In the letter I poured out my heart in sincere apology and regret, asking him to keep me as his *murid*.

I did not hear anything until the time of the New York City *hadrah*. It had been announced that several dervishes would be installed as *wakeels* (chief/subordinates to Shaikhs) at this meeting. Shaikh Jami would be presiding. I expected when travelling to New York for the ceremony that I would not see Shaikh Jami for a long time after this. Since neither my Shaikh nor Shaikh Jami had said anything concerning Shaikh Nun, I took it that I would not receive the Rufai *bayat* which Shaikh Jami had spoken of in Prizren. I thought that my fate would be to continue in bewilderment. When we had arrived in New York, Shaikh Jami called me to him for a talk:

'I only want to ask you where your heart is,' he said, 'I want you to know that your Shaikh and I love you very much. We want you as our dervish, and so does Hazreti Pir.'

'Shaikh Effendi,' I said. 'I feel such deep affection for Hazreti

Pir. I was so touched by him in Prizren. I love you and my Shaikh. Without you I am just lost.'

'Then you must complete a special task,' said Shaikh Jami. 'When it is completed later tonight I will make you a Rufai Dervish.'

It was a surprising meeting. Shaikh Jami was so full of love. When I had finished the task he sent me upstairs to another room. As soon as I entered, I looked directly into the face of my Shaikh. He was sitting with some dervishes around a dinner table. Taking a piece of cake from his plate, he extended his hand towards me. For a second I was frozen but I rushed forward as he nodded, to receive the cake. He directed me to an empty chair where I sat across from him at the table.

'I received your letter,' he said, 'and I accept your apologies. We have many things to discuss, however. You have much to learn about *Tariqat*.' I told him of my earlier discussion with Shaikh Jami and he gave me his approval to go forward. That night I received the second blade of my *zulfikar* (double-edged sword), the Rufai Dervish *bayat*. That heavy, dark cloud which had followed me from Turkey, finally began to lift, but my troubles were not entirely over.

Not long after this, I had a very lengthy and important talk with my Shaikh. In this talk he clarified for me several issues of *Tariqat*. He taught me many things concerning pirs and Shaikhs and the nature of *bayats*. He reminded me of my own *Pir*, Hazreti Hayyati.

'This was your first credential,' he said. 'This is your first golden *silsila* (chain) through me, to Hazreti Pir. You will have no peace without honouring this first opening. This is your first link, and whatever comes later is on top of this. This is your responsibility for all your life. You see, you didn't come to Shaikh Nun from the street, you came to him already an equal partner to anyone in his circle. Your circumstance is like that of the Franciscan priest who became a Dominican. It is an issue of conversion of a convert. Perhaps, you should write a letter to Shaikh Nun now. You may let him know that I am not ready to carry your responsibility, for I am already carrying the *sanjak* (flag) given me by our *pir*. I entrust you to the judgement of his own heart. You must ask him what *Tariqat* you should separate from, but know that I cannot carry the responsibility for interrupting your golden *silsila* to Hazreti Pir Hayyati.'

Suddenly, my heart grew heavy again. My dilemma was not

fully resolved. I still was stuck somehow between two Shaikhs on either side of the ocean.

'You must also know', continued the Shaikh, 'that your bewilderment is not caused by me. What has happened to you is by Allah's design to help you on to *ma'rifat* (knowing realisation).

I took these words concerning *ma'rifat* to refer to some very distant future. I hardly felt myself to be in *Tariqat*, the stage where the Path opens, so I could not relate to some station even beyond *Haqiqat*, the stage of seeing the truth. But fortunately, by now I do know this: *murids* understand very little as they traverse the Path. Actually, understanding is in some ways not the *murid*'s concern. Theirs is the job of service and submission without question. In the end, God willing, the answers will come and everything will be clear. So it was I wrote my first letter to Shaikh Nun, seeking to find a way out. I respectfully asked him to take back the *bayat*.

Within one month Shaikh Nun responded with forcefulness and power. Essentially he said: 'No way! And what is more, you had better realise this is not a children's game!'

When I approached my Shaikh drooping in desperation, to inform him of the letter, he continued to leave me on my own for the most part, to struggle with the dilemma and the resulting distress and conflict. He reminded me of some of his earlier advices:

'As I told you before,' he said, 'I cannot carry the responsibility for interrupting your first golden *silsila* to Hazreti Pir. I remind you that I never asked you to reconsider your Naqshbandi *bayat* with Shaikh Nun. In fact, I told you that you had been promoted. I continue to entrust you to the judgement of Shaikh Nun's heart.'

'What shall I do about the *hizmet*?' I asked the Shaikh, still in desperation. 'All of it together is really very heavy. What should I do?'

'Your dilemma is sort of like cuisines,' he responded, entirely unmoved by my whining plea. 'Whether French, Italian, or German the basic ingredients, much like your *hizmet*, are essentially the same, yet each is different. Each is delicious on its own, but if eaten all together, one gets indigestion. So yours is the problem of which to abandon, and which to keep. You must find out from Shaikh Nun which *Tariqat* to separate from. Write to him again.'

Then in a still more serious tone, the Shaikh concluded his advice:

'You are now passing through a very deep valley dealing with *tawakkal* (trust). Do you know that presently there is no *mutawakkal* (disciple in the state of trust) in our entire circle?'

So it was I sat to write again. This time, I implored God's assistance. Feeling the full weight of my dilemma between the Shaikhs, I put my heart and soul into the writing. When I dropped this letter into the post-box I repeated prayers of peace (*salawat*) on Hazreti Muhammad and gave the decision in the matter completely to God.

This time about two months passed before I received Shaikh Nun's reply. His letter arrived in the spring of the year. Shaikh Nun was more gentle in his second letter. He explained the commonality of *zikr* to all *tariqats* with the *zikr* method of his *tariqat* only being different in that it is done silently in the heart. He also explained his harshness of tone in the first letter, telling me that Shaikhs do not like to see *murids* run from their dilemmas. He sent loving salaams to my Shaikh and closed with an invitation for us to visit him. The lilacs which lined the hill along the Tekiya's walkway were just coming into bloom. I had carried my dilemma through the still days of winter and wondered if spring would ever ever come. Suddenly, it seemed, the lilacs were touching my heart again with their fragrance, lifting my spirits and renewing my sense of hope. When I spoke to the Shaikh that fragrance was still with me.

'When you write Shaikh Nun again,' he said, 'you must tell him that we have received his gracious letter with the explanation of the beautiful hizmet which he gave to you in Istanbul. Tell him that I am moved by his kindness and generosity in sharing such a treasure with us. Tell him that we graciously accept his instructions about zikr of the heart in order to enrich the beauty of the fellowship between *Tariqats*.

'You have my permission to follow his instructions and as a sign of our love and respect to him, we are all going to share the benefit of what he has told you. Tell our Beloved Hajji Shaikh Nun Effendi that his invitation to us is most kind and that we shall use the first opportunity to visit the *ahlil bait* (family of the Prophet) and to kiss his hand which is holding the *sanjak shereef* (noble flag) and spreading the truth of Allah's unity over distant lands. We shall look forward to having the benefit of sitting in his presence and being illuminated by the *nuran nabi* (light of the Prophet) radiating from his shadow. Tell Shaikh Effendi that we understand that *zikr* without heart is like a rose without fragrance, and we take much wisdom from his lesson.

'Send to him my *salaam* with *ashqi niyaz* (loving respect). I kiss his hand, putting it on his heart and forehead as an expression of my love and deep respect to Naqshbandi Tariqat and to his *sheriful maqam* (noble station). Tell Shaikh Effendi that his instruction brings back many memories of my life. The dry leaves of the passing days have covered the roads of our journey through this *dunya* (world). His instructions are coming like the breeze, lifting the dry leaves and bringing that young boy with curly hair who used to sit in his grandmother's presence learning lessons of *hizmet*, to sit here now and share the *sherif* (one's rightful place) with me in our Tekiya. Tell him that I thank him for the sherbet of refreshment which he brought in the desert through which he is travelling, thirsty for love of Allah.

'Send *salaams* and *ashqi niyaz* with the whole *jamatul fuqara* (community of the poor) gathered around the flag of the Prophet, in his land.'

I conveyed all of this to Shaikh Nun as my Shaikh had asked. This particular experience stayed with me for a very long time. Even after some years had passed I wondered if it was really ended. I felt such deep disappointment in myself and I was embarrassed for having fallen into the dilemma of being caught between the Shaikhs. Although it seemed to be over, and the Shaikh had told me that it was, I continued to feel some remnant of guilt and lingering doubt. In a conversation with the Shaikh, the subject came up:

'Shaikh Nun is very wise,' he said. As you see, anything can happen. You are fortunate, however, for even if you felt your loyalties divided between us, your loyalties to Allah and His Prophet, peace be upon him, were always unsplit. So you see, the issue of *tawakkal* (trust) is continually coming up. It is simply not a one-time issue. It continues to be treated until it is set firmly in the heart and there is willing surrender. Then things begin to happen. Shaikh Nun and I purposely kept you in a state of bewilderment. You wonder now if it is concluded. You need not continually blame yourself. I know that you were only seeking to solve another mystery. You must know now that in truth, it was all concluded at the outset. You were not rejected by either of the *Pirs*. Both of them saw you in *Ezel*, that eternal place of Endless Time.'

So it was that the teachings of the Third Journey slowly drew to a close. It had seemed a never-ending story. The mystery of the Grandshaikh had stretched across more than seven years of my life. Seeking to understand the mystery of his contact, I almost lost my Shaikh. During the time of Shaikh Ahmet's visit, one of our Shaikh's last *muhabbats* (discourses) had spelled the whole thing out:

'You have made it this far from *before* Time,' he said. 'Now your only concern should be with *after* Endless Time. Whoever is concerned about *dunya,* this world, gets *dunya.* Whoever is concerned about *akhirat,* the hereafter, gets *akhirat.* But also know that you cannot approach the *batin* (unseen) world of inner meaning until there is no longer a speck of pride in you. What is the big deal if you have an aching tooth or trouble with your eye. Beware that you put your troubles in front of Allah, giving them higher regard than you give to him. Be grateful and know that your affliction in *dunya* is a gift from Allah. Know that *Qiyyamat* is not a fairy-tale, that day when the sun will melt and people will pray that the earth would swallow them up, rather than have to face the horrors of its destruction and the consequences of their deeds.'

The whole spiritual journey is concerned with the travelling of the soul from Eternity to Eternity, or as the Shaikh described it, from Endless Time before the soul descends to life on the planet, to Endless Time after the soul's ascent back to Eternity. It is the seeker's recognition of his condition as a traveller which gives him insight into this truth. Were the seeker able to see life from a divine perspective he or she would understand clearly how this life, with all its sweetness and affliction, is passing with the swiftness of the wind. 'Time is moving at the speed of time,' the Shaikh once said. It is indeed, for it will be only a moment before we are standing in Eternity again. This being the case, the present moment here on the planet is our most valuable asset. Now, there is time, though it may only be a moment, and how it is used is the lesson I spent years attempting to learn. I may not know it yet. The mystery of the Grandshaikh was a beautiful experience, but understanding it should not really have been my concern. It was not the intention of the Grandshaikh to direct me to himself, the point was always God Almighty, whether I understood or not. In this regard, I came across the following advice of a seeker who had reached the journey's goal. The entire work of all true Shaikhs and the objective of *Tariqat* is contained within it. May Allah give us ears to hear and motivation (*himma*) to take proper action:

'Get to the heart of the issue,' he said, 'for life is too short! Forget

> about goals, trances, hankering after revelation, flight, celestial travel, miracles and spiritual spectacles. Just persevere in trying to establish the imprint of Allah in the heart and brain so as to banish from your person the sensualist, slothful, Satanic darkness and dirt of worldly thoughts through the "energy" and light of the Sun of His Majestic name Allah. *Zikr* does change things, it really works, and one day the "click" will come.'
>
> *('Irfan' by Faqir Nur Muhammad)*

This advice brought all of the fragments together: the visit of Shaikh Ahmet and his instructions in Qur'an; Shaikh Jami in *Matem*, teaching about Imam Hussein; Grandshaikh Daghistani attempting to show me that Eternity is real; Shaikh Nun teaching the unity of *Tariqats* and the beauty of silent *zikr*; and my own Shaikh teaching about vanity and tricks of ego, about dedication, singleness of purpose, loyalty, forgiveness, and love. The advice above which concludes the lesson of my third journey, is enough for any disciple who can hear it and establish it in life. Let the seeker understand that God Almighty is the only guide and the only One to be sought. The dilemma presented me by the Shaikhs at this stage of my journey was to help me to see that as long as I desire to be the dervish of this Shaikh or that Shaikh I am missing the point. The joint lesson of Shaikh Nun and my own Shaikh was all to help me to become nothing less than a dervish of God Most High, may He forever be exalted.

CHAPTER 11

THE FIRE

Qulna ya naru kuni bardan
'We said, "Oh Fire! Be thou Cool"!'

Early in the autumn of my seventh year on the Path, a special gathering was called by the Shaikh. A ceremony was to be held for the opening of a new Tekiya. It was a happy and festive occasion, for we were still in the days of *Eid*. Both Shaikh Jami and my own Shaikh were there, at least part of the time, and there was a feeling of closeness and community and friendship from the heart. The long, summer-like days were enduring and there were blue skies overhead. The circle of disciples was expanding, the *zikr* was sweet, and this newly built house was itself signalling change and growth. Far off the beaten track, this building sat, nestled in the woodlands of the rural Canadian East. Its lumber had in fact been milled from the trees of those very woods, and its construction carried out entirely by a few unskilled but dedicated disciples. Working under the dervish assigned there in behalf of the Shaikh, disciples made journeys from their respective cities to participate in the service (*hizmet*) and blessing (*barakat*) of the work.

Travelling with two other disciples, I sat in the front seat a contented passenger, happy to be making the trip. We had set out on our journey in the early morning hours in order to make the early arrival time specified by the Shaikh. We made our way along without incident, laughing and talking and even enjoying occasional intervals of silence. The Canadian landscape passed by us like a spectacular film, touching our hearts with the beauty of its hills and breathtaking waterways. The trees whisked by like giant, graceful bouquets of flowers. Their leaf-blossoms, a dancing array of pastels of yellow, orange, brown, and red, which communed with my soul by their beauty in the softness of the morning light.

We reached the Tekiya just before noon. Shaikh Jami greeted us warmly, together with some disciples who had arrived there before us. A few of us sat down to talk with him and partake of his discourse (*muhabbat*). We were joined by some visitors who had come from the Ottawa Mosque, and later by the Shaikh, who had been walking the grounds and speaking with some of his disciples. He joined with Shaikh Jami in the *muhabbat*, baffling us as usual with his knowledge and insight, and pushing us to the painful recognition of just how far we had yet to go.

The usual prayers and *zikr* of the day were said and because it was Friday, the *Jumah* service was held. *Jumah* (Friday prayer) was followed by the opening ceremonies. Simple and straightforward, the ceremonies focused on dedicating the house to the service of God, to the example of all the Prophets, and to the Unity of Faith, that primordial declaration: there is no god but God. After the ceremonies we retreated outside to have some lunch, after which we turned our attention to work. There were some among us who had intended to perform sacrifices while there, as is the custom at the time of *Eid*. Some assisted in getting the sheep which would be sacrificed (*qurbans*), and others among us who were knowledgeable of the procedure gave help in tying the animal's limbs, and skinning and dressing the carcasses after they had been slain. The Shaikhs stood together with all of us encircling the person carrying out the sacrifice. During the *zikr*: *La ilaha ill' Allah* (There is no god but God), which we said as the sacrificer drew the knife, the seriousness of it all fell upon me again. A verse of Qur'an came into my mind, in focus as sharp as the blade of the knife:

> It is not their meat nor their blood, that reaches to Allah: It is your piety that reaches Him. He has thus made them subject to you, that you may glorify Allah for His guidance to you and proclaim the good news to all who do right.
>
> *(22: 37)*

During the afternoon the Shaikh had announced a sheep roast for the evening. A large cooking tripod had been erected, a fire built and one of the sheep prepared. By the time of sunset the last *qurban* was nearly finished, and the sheep to be roasted was already turning above the fiery flames. We said *Salatul Maghrib*, the sunset prayer, then returned outside to the cooking place. The feeling was much like being around a campfire. It warmed us as the coolness of the night crept in, and there was laughter and play and the kind of ease in the air which comes after the day's work is done. Shadows passed across the faces of some as the dancing flames threw light. Perhaps, I thought, it threw light as well, on some dark mystery or memory of their past, or by the grace of God, on their present or future. Sitting by any fireside, staring into the flames always seemed to stimulate in me a hundred thousand thoughts. I wondered, as I watched my brother and sister seekers, what was happening for them. Both the Shaikhs were serving us that night, they were the chefs and carvers who prepared the food in loving kindness and gave each of us a plate. The presence of both Shaikh Jami and our Shaikh serving us around that fire, certainly brought up many feelings in me. I watched these men of light moving with naturalness and ease, each as warm as the flames and more full of light. There to help us remove the darkness from our own lives and hearts, and to kindle the flames of our fires within. Shaikh Jami was to travel by plane to New York City that night. He would, however, be with us again during *Matem*, the time of commemoration of events leading to the death of Imam Hussain, before returning to his home overseas. As I looked into the fire I remembered the time of *Matem*, nearly a year since passed. I remembered the Shaikh's painful words as he left me at the Tekiya's roadside in a state of total loss. I remembered Shaikh Jami's loving support and the months of letters back and forth across the ocean to Shaikh Nun, with my own Shaikh's *irshad* (direction) and counsel in between. It was a time when I was in the midst of the fire and all the things I valued most seemed to be going up in smoke. It was a time of cleansing and of growth, and each day of it a teaching to help me to be better. Praise and thanks to God for the lessons which come only out of pain and suffering. Truly, as some wise person has said: 'It is the fire which purifies.'

> As long as Mary did not feel the pain of childbirth, she did not go toward the tree of good fortune. *And the pangs of childbirth drove her to the trunk of the palm tree* (Qur'an 19:23). That pain took her

> to the tree, and the barren tree bore fruit. The body is like Mary, and each of us has a Jesus within him. If the pain appears, our Jesus will be born. But if no pain comes, Jesus will return to his Origin on that same hidden road by which he came. We will be deprived of him and reap no benefit.
>
> *(Hazreti Rumi)*

The dancing flames of our cooking fire having done their dance, lay down to rest on their bed of glowing coals. The main course of our meal completed, we retreated to the Tekiya for the coolness of prayer and the flaming hot desert of our *zikr*. It was a night of power, remembrance, and celebration in the true Sufi tradition. Oh the *zikr* was sweet that night! Together, all of us, with our two beloved Shaikhs, our hearts did a joyful dance all along the seashore of the Endless Ocean of Light.

Everyone rose early the following day. We said the prayers and *zikr* of the morning, had breakfast, then went outside to begin work. The Shaikh had ordered that an old dilapidated building, a small barn of sorts, be levelled. The building stood on the edge of a large clearing about three hundred feet away from the Tekiya. A line of tall trees, companioned by a series of fenceposts, connected the two structures and spanned the distance between them.

I was among a group of disciples who worked enthusiastically to pull the building down. In the clearing, at short distances from the barn, two bonfires were built. Some disciples helped by dragging the fallen boards and beams to the bonfires while some worked at other tasks nearer to the Tekiya. The day grew hot and the sun beat down upon us. The nearest bonfire, too, radiated waves of heat which cast their squiggly shadows on the ground and left us pouring with sweat. We worked late into the morning and the building was not yet completely fallen. Soon we would begin to lose workers as some disciples had already been given the Shaikh's permission to depart. The Shaikh, however, had told the *wakeel* (representative) that the building would be levelled on this day, and though few disciples knew that he had said this, some among us had begun to feel a sense of futility in completing the task and naggings of defeat. Accompanied by one of his representatives with whom he'd been walking, the Shaikh came up the drive into the area of the barn. As any disciple probably would have predicted, it was in the moment of the Shaikh's arrival that things began to happen.

> Moses said to his household: 'Surely I have seen a fire. I will bring to you from it some news, or I will bring to you therefrom a burning firebrand so that you may warm yourselves.'
>
> *(Qur'an 27:7)*

Speaking directly to his *wakeel*, the Shaikh enquired:

'Why should we not burn it Hajji Sahib? How else can I keep my promise that it will be levelled today. It would take too long otherwise.'

There was a moment's silence. The dervish looked at the Shaikh as he continued speaking while those of us who had been nearest to the barn circled around him.

'Hmmm,' said the Shaikh as he pointed out the line of trees going directly to the Tekiya. 'But the Tekiya may burn. I must ask you though; after all, it is your house.'

Unflinching, the dervish looked at the Shaikh.

'It's OK,' he said, and no other words were spoken.

The Shaikh called for matches, and stooping he set fire to a handful of hay which lay underneath the fallen boards. He then directed one of his disciples to continue setting fire to the hay and what is more, to say that it was his own match which lit the fire, if he were questioned by police. The fire having now been set, the Shaikh immediately left, passing the two other groups of disciples as he disappeared into the Tekiya. In a matter of minutes the fire at the barn-site was raging with a roar which shook the earth. Frozen in that moment, all our eyes were upon that fire as orange and blue flames burst fiercely from the toppled heap, leaping fifty feet into the air. The fire sucked in air as if it were a huge and hungry vacuum compelled to consume, violently ablaze, spitting puffy tufts of flame which seared the parched bark of the trees, then burst apart like fireworks of July.

> But when he came to the [fire], a voice was heard: 'Blessed are those in the fire and those around, and glory to God, the Lord of the Worlds.'
>
> *(Qur'an 27:8)*

Just before the Shaikh had gone into the Tekiya, he uttered, in what seemed a voice of perplexity, to a group of disciples not near to the barn-site that 'some strange dude had lit the fire'.

At the barn-site, the flames continued to rage as all disciples were standing looking on, their eyes filled and inescapably caught by the spectacle before them. As fingers of the flames continued reaching into the trees, one *murid* presented to ask the *wakeel* if he could cut down the tree so that it would not spread to the others.

'No,' the *wakeel* answered. 'Do not touch anything.'

Meanwhile in the group of disciples who had heard the Shaikh's remark, there were also questions of what should be done. Two among them responding to their own inner voices, jumped into a car and raced away, in swift pursuit of help.

'We are going to call the fire department!' one of them yelled, leaning from the window.

'Wait!' someone yelled to them, as they disappeared at the end of the drive. In my own heart I yelled with that person, for much as I understood the need of those disciples to follow their hearts, I did not want the fire engines to come. Here the pandemonium began, for everyone was attempting to hear their own inner voice and decide what must be done. What would happen if one waited and the Tekiya was destroyed? As one stood there before the fire, witnessing it jumping into the trees could one believe that the Shaikh knew what he had done? Was God Most High in control? Was the Shaikh? Am I in control as I stand here watching all of this? Am I doubting even though I may seem calm, or do I truly know that all is well, even though it really makes no sense?

Every disciple present was forced into a kind of self-examination by which could be monitored his or her own personal level of doubt.

> Set not fire to the thicket, and keep silence my heart; draw in your tongue, for your tongue is a flame.
>
> *(Hazreti Rumi)*

The trees which stood nearest to the flames and were most likely to burn lost hardly a single leaf. Dry as they were, they continued to stand and show forth the colours of autumn. Their trunks, though blackened by the soot of the fire, were completely intact and unharmed. It was as if they were throwing off the flames, or carrying something within them in the moment, which brought them coolness in the midst of the heat, keeping the fire at bay.

There was a certain moment which came when every disciple knew that everything was under control. The fire was entirely in the power of God Almighty, and they had each witnessed it miraculously working before their eyes and in their hearts, no matter their doubts. When the firemen arrived, there was not a flame in any tree and though there was still remaining a flame or two on the barn-site, there was obviously not any danger. Doing their job, however, in they all rushed. With engine and pumper, helmets, boots, hoses, axes and picks, they laid siege to a fire which a child might ordinarily approach, with a marshmallow at the end of a stick.

'You were extremely lucky, Mister,' said one of the firemen to the very *murid* who had been directed to confess if he were questioned. 'If this fire got bigger, at this time of year, it could set fire to all those trees.'

Just before leaving, one of the firemen enquired of the *wakeel* who lived there, if he had been issued a permit for starting a fire.

'No,' he replied. 'What are the repercussions?'

'Well really it's not up to us to decide that. It's just our job to put out the fire, but we'll report back to you.'

Later, as the events were reported to the Shaikh, I heard him enquire of someone:

'Why did you not tell the firemen to walk more gently over my burning heart?'

The teaching of the fire raised a great many questions. For many who were not near the barn-site, there were questions about who started the fire, since they may have been too far away to know. There was the question of whether one should be practical or not when one sees real-life danger. There were questions too concerning the firemen and whether or not they should have been called. When some later learned that the Shaikh had lit the fire, there were still even more questions burning within them. The fire, in short, brought several issues to the forefront, namely those of faith and trust (*tawakkal*), of love and purification, and abandonment and loss. Spiritual development as related to any of these issues was necessarily a product of one's own perceptions and personal experience during the unfolding of events as well as one's idiosyncratic inner state and proximity to the site of the fire.

In the mystic discussion of the Qur'anic verse by Siraj-Edin where Hazreti Musa, the Prophet Moses, upon whom be peace, brings news of the fire to his household, three degrees of faith are revealed: *'Ilmul Yaqin*, the knowledge of certainty; *aynul yaqin*, the eye of certainty; and *haqqul yaqin*, the truth of certainty. Taking the fire to represent Divine Truth, those in the degree of *'ilmul yaqin* were in the lowest degree of faith. Such were those who received news of the fire from the Prophet Moses after he had seen the burning bush. *'Ilmul yaqin*, therefore, represented that kind of knowledge which came from hearing the fire described.

Those in the degree of certainty (*aynul yaqin*) were in the second degree of faith. These were those whose knowledge of the fire had come from seeing the light of its flames, having been shown the firebrand. The highest degree belonged to those whose knowledge came from being burnt in it. These were those in the degree of the truth of certainty (*haqqul yaqin*) who were permitted to 'warm themselves' or even to 'be consumed'.

The teaching of the Fire which our Shaikh gave to us at the barn-site, was in many ways like the teaching of Moses, peace be upon him. There was much in paradox. There was the conflict of perceptions, the failure of logic, the secret opportunity hidden in panic and distress and the baffling mysterious wonder of the creeping, grasping flames. Much like the people of Moses, there was, among us *murids*, so much struggle against doubt. There were some among us in the lowest degree of faith, much like the souls in the degree of knowledge of certainty (*'ilmul yaqin*). These were those among us who upon hearing of the fire, found that without witnessing the event, they were unable to believe it had happened as it did. Many of these were completely without trust (*tawakkal*) and may even have thought the Shaikh to be a trickster.

Those disciples in the second degree of faith were similar to those in the degree of the eye of certainty (*aynul yaqin*). These were those who had to actually witness the fire, to actually see the trees safe before they could believe. Among these, there were those who stood watching the fire with the opportunity present before them in the raging fire to renovate their inner condition and improve their state of faith. Some were able to make that leap of the moment, while others stood waiting their decision till there was clearly no risk, and their opportunity had fled.

Finally, there were those disciples in the highest degree, like the people of the Prophet Moses in the degree of the truth of certainty (*haqqul yaqin*). These were those who lived in a state of faith (*Iman*) and trust (*tawakkal*) and whose belief was not determined by their witnessing or not. In the teaching of the burning barn given by the Shaikh, one could be warmed by the firebrand whether standing close or far from the barn-site. Nearness and proximity to the fire Divine is not measured by metres or miles. It is a measure of mercy and openness of heart, and that so it seemed to me, is what the Shaikh had tried to teach us.

Just as the firemen departed, the Shaikh came back to the barn-site. All that remained was the gaping hole which had been the foundation, now filled with charred debris and ash. Inspecting one area of the site, he questioned us about what had occurred and listened to our responses. One of the disciples asked:

'Shaikh Effendi, why is it that when I am standing and seeing the miracle, I am convinced and full of faith, yet when the miracle passes, it seems I am back where I was before?'

'You just need more miracles,' said the Shaikh with a smile as he moved away from the barn-site. Taking a seat on top of a large stack of cement blocks, he continued speaking to us. Across the grounds could be seen the other two pockets of disciples who drew nearer to the Shaikh as they noticed him ready to speak. He said many things while he sat there, but one of his comments struck me, somehow, more deeply than the rest:

'There are old traditional Shaikhs in *Tariqat* and you may take that way if you like. Each one of you will be able to move at the pace which you choose, but I am a Shaikh of this century and you must step quickly if you want to walk with me.'

I wondered what it was about this remark which affected me so much. I know that as the Shaikh spoke these words I felt the desire and longing within myself to be among those who would walk together with him. I wondered how these words, too, were connected to the fire. The greater part of the afternoon was spent with us gathered around the Shaikh both at the fire site and inside the Tekiya. We were deeply engaged in sharing our views about the events of the day and in absorbing the Shaikh's loving discourse (*muhabbat*). On this occasion the Shaikh allowed disciples to express their views and feelings, and by this we learned from each other and took benefit from differing views and perspectives of the chain of events of the day. As we sat in the Tekiya just before the time of sunset, the barn-site could be seen across the way. There was one little column of smoke rising from the smouldering remains. As I sat listening to my fellow seekers turning the day's mystery around, searching their hearts, sharing their views and hoping to ask the Shaikh that question which would remove the veil, I remembered some part of a story-poem by Hazreti Rumi which was also entitled 'The Question':

One dervish to another: What was your vision
of God's presence?

THE FIRE

I haven't seen anything.
But for the sake of conversation, I'll tell you a story.

God's presence is there in front of me, a fire on the left,
a lovely stream on the right.
One group walks toward the fire, into the fire, another
toward the sweet flowing water.
No one knows which are blessed and which are not.
Whoever walks into the fire appears suddenly in the stream.
A head goes under on the water surface, that head
pokes out of the fire.
Most people guard against going into the fire,
and so end up in it.
Those who love the water of pleasure and make it their devotion
are cheated with this reversal.
The trickery goes further.
The voice of the fire tells the truth *saying* I am not fire.
I am fountainhead. Come into me and don't mind the sparks.

If you are a friend of God, fire is your water.
You should wish to have a hundred thousand sets of mothwings,
so you could burn them away, one set a night.
The moth sees light and goes into the fire. You should see fire
and go toward the light. Fire is what of God is world-consuming.
Water, world-protecting.
Somehow each gives the appearance of the other. To these eyes
you have now
What looks like water burns. What looks like
fire is a great relief to be inside . . .
You've seen a magician make a bowl of rice
seem a dish full of tiny, live worms.
Before an assembly with one breath he made the floor swarm
with scorpions that weren't there.
How much more amazing God's tricks.
Generation after generation lies down, defeated, they think,
but they're like a woman underneath a man, circling him.
One molecule-mote-second thinking of God's reversal of comfort
and pain
is better than any attending ritual. That splinter
of intelligence is substance.
The fire and water themselves:
Accidental, done with mirrors.

In this poem was the answer to my question about walking with the Shaikh:

'Most people guard against going into the fire, and so end up in it.'

There before the raging fire which jumped into the trees, there were so many thoughts of perishing and loss. But the way of the Shaikh is the way of walking into the fire. Those who step quickly, in footsteps of faith, will be as cool as Hazreti Ibrahim (Prophet Abraham) in the fiery furnace of Nimrod. The fire is *really* the only place of safety. When will I learn?

> If you are a friend of God, fire is your water. You should wish to have a hundred thousand sets of mothwings so you could burn them away, one set a night.

But alas, there are not a hundred thousand nights. Truly, the time is now, The firebrand may come and go. Looking out onto the barn-site, hours after the fire, there was a tiny glowing flame where the little column of smoke had been. How amazing that it was there. The fireman had been so full of worry. Firemen who knew so much about fire and yet so little. Water doesn't change the fire of love, the flame of love won't die.

The Sweet Romance grows sweet
To its essence,
The ether fades beyond
Its presence,
Beyond the Beyond
Where is that do you know?
Beyond the Wave,
The Silent Flow.

May God give us eyes to see things by way of truth without veils (*haqiqat*). May he show me the heart of my Shaikh as if it were a branch torn off that flaming bush which my Lord showed to Moses so that he might come to know and understand true love: that love raging, with burning flames which consume us and yet we do not perish. The flower fades but the fragrance endures in the hearts of all who touched it.

CHAPTER 12

THE SWORD

Gladiatores vincendum or moriendum erat
'The Gladiators must conquer or die.'

Late in the summer of my sixth year on the Path an instruction was issued by the Shaikh to all of his disciples. He requested that each of his disciples bring to him, as a gift, a sword, dagger, or knife. Nothing was specified concerning the design or quality of the weapons to be found, nor were we told why we were being given such a task. Each person was to make their selection without the help or advice of others. The choice was a personal one. Immediately upon hearing the instructions, a picture came into my mind of the sword I was to find. Accompanied by some other disciples, I set out to complete the task early one Saturday morning, making my way along the hot pavement of a little urban street of shops. In a small second-hand store I enquired of the owner if he happened to have any swords. He looked at me with a quizzical expression for a second or two, then disappeared into another room. Momentarily, he returned with a long, cylinder-shaped package, wrapped in white cloth.

'I think you will like these,' he said, as he put the package down and began to unwrap it in slow, methodical turns. Inside there were three unusual pieces: a beautiful Japanese dagger with a curved blade, a nearly one-hundred-year-old German sword bayonet, and a very small but graceful silver knife. None of these matched the sword I had in mind but the German sword was closest. It was smaller than the sword I'd hoped for, not as finely crafted and balanced and not as sharp. In short, it was less perfect than my ideal, but somehow I knew clearly none the less that it was mine. When I drew it from its sheath I was one with it. It seemed a natural extension of my own arm. It was not unwieldy, not too long but not too short, and I believed I could fight with it if necessary, and that it would serve me well. I chose it knowing nothing more about swords or knives than what I felt. I opened my senses to listen, and I followed the indications of the moment, not allowing myself to be distracted by unexpected tiny doubts, or whispering questions I could not answer. The teaching had begun and it continued through and beyond the teaching of the fire, for three years along the Path.

All of the Shaikh's disciples worked intently on this task, relentlessly descending on out-of-the-way antique shops, modern cutlery centres in shopping precincts, army-and-navy stores, hardware shops, hunting suppliers and gunshops in search of appropriate weapons, in cities where they lived. What was produced from this effort was simply amazing. It was an arsenal for warriors, a dazzling array of swords and daggers of all types: French, German, Italian, Japanese, and Syrian. Many were finely crafted and beautiful, with ornate hilts and blades. Most were practical and of simple good quality, and each and every one hairsplitting sharp and polished gleaming bright. I looked on in wonder as I lay my sword down with the others brought to the upstairs *muhabbat* (discourse) room of the Tekiya, where they would be seen and inspected by the Shaikh. From among the many, the Shaikh chose only one of the swords to be hung in the *muhabbat* room of the Tekiya. He chose a sword from India, striking, long, and graceful, with exquisite silver inlay inscription. Unquestionably impressive, yet understatedly subtle in its sleek, black-with-gold-trim sheath, it took its place on the wall near the *Sherif*, the seat of the Shaikh, as if it had always been there. But each sword, dagger, or knife which was brought found its place. Many of them were displayed on the walls of the Shaikh's own apartment, and others on walls of the Tekiyas or Khanqas, by a design and order known only to the Shaikh. This exercise was among the deepest, most unusual, and most important lessons given by the Shaikh. Almost two years passed before he gave any *muhabbat* (discourse) directly concerned with swords, yet during these years the most powerful, heart-rending teachings were transmitted, concerned mostly with human relationships, love, and attachment. One exception concerning *muhabbat* directly focused on swords, however, was a poem by Lermontov recited to us during a *hadrah* conducted a month or two after we had presented the swords. Interestingly, it came inside of a devastatingly touching *muhabbat* on love. Its title was 'My Dagger':

> *I give you my love, my dagger made of steel*
> *My whole and entire love I transfer to you,*
> *my sharp, cold friend.*
> *You were made by the blacksmith and Cherkez*
> *shaped you for the battle. In the moment of*
> *departure, you were given me by a hand*
> *as gentle as a lily and for the first time,*
> *not blood fell on you*
> *But a tear — a jewel of my sorrow.*
> *You were a sign of love, pure and clean*
> *and not a useless gift. I am going*
> *to remain as sharp as you*
> *my friend made of steel.*

During the time of the swords, the Shaikh had opened to us an ongoing *irshad* (teaching) concerning Mu'min and Heather. A real-life saga of love and pain, it was an advanced twentieth-century teaching of far-reaching implications. Televised by closed-circuit on channel *Tariqat,* it was the soap opera of our own lives, unfolded in segments directed by the Shaikh. With whisperings of the potential loss to be faced by an entire Western culture, the issues of the story exposed us to ourselves, pushing us to face our own personally distracting desires and longings of the heart. Passing before the backdrop of the drama of relationships and the dance of human love, the following were the themes: passion, desire, security and fulfilment, false love and true love, attachment and separation, disappointment, betrayal, and loss. The Shaikh was too close for comfort and generating too much heat. Most disciples escaped or fled, denying that any of the players in the story were even remotely related to themselves or to their lives along the Path. The cast of characters was essentially four:

MU'MIN: One of the Shaikh's finest and most beloved *murids,* he is the noble-hearted husband of Heather. From an imperfect past, yet deeply refined, he is a man of great spiritual potential who loves Heather more fully and completely than he has loved anyone or anything before. Tragically constant, he opens himself to a love which brings nothing but catastrophe to his life, his heart and soul. Relegated to the ranks of the half-living, walking dead, he struggles to overcome the grief, turmoil, and disappointed hopes brought to him by Heather.

HEATHER: Estranged wife of Mu'min. Homely, fragile, and seeming to be in need of care, she is beneath her cloak of vulnerability, a desperate *femme fatale*. Whenever she is scared, hurt, angry, or frightened, she escapes into her passions, no holds barred. An inescapable victim of her own desires, she is always with the transient; always fleeing boredom. Enraptured by the shell and shadow of love, she is afraid of love itself. She encounters in Mu'min the only love which has ever touched upon her own potential to truly love, and having glimpsed it, she is running scared. Fleeing the flame of Mu'min's devotion, she races headlong into the raging flames of her own inner chaos, while smashing Mu'min's heart to bits.

JUAN: Drug-dealer, deceiver, and master of dazzle and glitter, he is the protagonist in the play. Devious, spineless, he is a lover of illusion and delusion, a suggester and perpetrator of evil intrigue who makes war on whoever falls prey to his seduction.

THE SHAIKH: The Master teacher, the guide, light from the light of the Prophets, director to the true, servant of Allah, heart of love, and gateway to the light.

The drama unfolds in four acts:

ACT ONE: Scene 1

Mu'min meets Heather. Attracted by her simplicity and frailty, his heart is touched and he wants to care for her. No onlooker could understand what he sees in her, a bright young man, a talented architect, successful in his work, spiritually vibrant, now in love with Heather. She is a woman of no great beauty, no spiritual interest, no great ambition, and yet she and Mu'min come together. Entering love's stage of infatuation Mu'min can see only Heather. The spark becoming a flame, he passes into love's stage of affection and his heart becomes attached. Much like Majnun, Mu'min if asked what he saw in someone as commonly plain as Heather, would likely reply:

'To see the beauty of Layla, one must see with the eyes of Majnun, likewise, to see my beloved Heather, one must see with the eyes of Mu'min.'

So it was that the courtship began, followed by marriage and a period of real joy and happiness for the two.

ACT ONE: Scene 2

Two years have passed and Mu'min's heart is more full of love than ever. The flame which was once only a spark is now a burning fire. Heather, however, is becoming restless and suddenly things are changing. With no warning she is involved with Juan, a man from her past. Mu'min comes home to find himself locked out while Juan is inside with Heather. He rages outside the door while Juan, cringing with fear, crawls underneath the bed. Ironically, Heather calls the police and lo and behold, Mu'min is taken away! Devastated, Mu'min dies the first death of the heart. Soon after this Heather tells Mu'min that she is moving out. After moving in with Juan, she calls Mu'min saying that she still loves him and misses him. In a voice of sincerity, she invites Mu'min to her place. Before the conversation ends, however, she tells him that their visit can only be a brief thirty minutes for Juan will soon be there.

'You must decide,' yells Mu'min, lashing out in anger, hurt and frustration, 'it is either him or me! Choose now!'

Heather responds with a long silence and Mu'min hangs up. Feeling terribly distraught, he goes to the Shaikh asking: 'Should I call her back?'

Meanwhile, things worsen for Heather. After exactly two weeks she is dumped by Juan. Angry, she reports him to the police as a suspect drug dealer and he is arrested. In a state of nervous distress, she is admitted to a psychiatric facility. In desperation she calls Mu'min and re-establishes contact with him. Heather now confesses all. She tells Mu'min how she had always slept with others, both men and women, 'but you Mu'min,' she pleads, 'are the only one I ever really loved.' She wishes she could call her mother but her mother is dead. Theirs too, is an ugly story of a daughter abused. Heather is with Mu'min for Thanksgiving and they have a pleasant time. Mu'min's heart has a moment's respite as Heather reveals her feelings: 'Mu'min, I really am not worthy of such a love as this.' Just as the scene ends, Juan is released from gaol having been there only three days.

ACT TWO: Scene 1

As the scene opens, Mu'min is sitting alone in his apartment. Heather who in conflict has mourned her separation from Juan, becomes ill again and goes deeply into stress. On the verge of a nervous breakdown she is readmitted to the psychiatric hospital. She calls Mu'min and he comes to visit her. Standing at her bedside with a heart full of love, he touches her head and asks God to help her and forgive her. He utters these words in a voice so sincere, one could not overhear them without weeping. She asks Mu'min if he would bring some things to her from their apartment, which he leaves to retrieve. He returns to the hospital to find Juan at Heather's bedside. Unable to contain himself, he confronts Juan and tells him that he will beat him to a pulp. Juan not daring to fight, flees the hospital. Heather returns her wedding ring and Mu'min is in shock. The scene closes with Mu'min alone in his apartment again, but now he has taken to drink. In deep, murky waters he enters love's stage of resignation. He isolates himself completely, except for the Shaikh, the only one he speaks to. The phone rings and Mu'min stares at it blankly, not moving to answer.

ACT TWO: Scene 2

The holiday season is approaching and Heather's birthday is near. It is a time full of memories for it was her most important day and Mu'min had always made it special. Now completely obsessed by his love and grief, he cannot forget Heather, no matter how he tries. He cannot say his prayers, he cannot do *zikr*. He cannot eat or sleep. He cannot go forward, nor can he go back. Locked in the cell of love's violent passion, he is a prisoner to himself with no means of escape. In desperation, he calls Heather's psychiatrist to enquire about her state. The psychiatrist, however, aligns with his patient. 'I must tell Heather of this enquiry,' he says, 'I'm sure she'll want to know.' Now Mu'min has to concern himself over the consequences of his rashness, for Heather had asked him never to make such a call. Heather, however, is having troubles of her own. After losing several days at work, she is now having difficulties with the insurance company which gives her a means for financing her schooling. 'Heather's prognosis, from the *dunya* perspective,' the Shaikh informed us, 'is not good. *Dunya* (the world) has no compassion for the sick or the weak.' The scene closes, it is the end of Act Two.

INTERMISSION

Sometime just after Act One had ended the Shaikh was with us in the Tekiya. It was near the time of *Eid ul Adha* and we were deeply involved in the teaching of Heather and Mu'min. The Shaikh had not allowed us to ignore it. Over the weeks he had phoned several of us personally, informing us of some surprising turn of events in the story, or some bizarre behaviour of Heather or Juan and the subsequent pain felt by Mu'min. Repeatedly, some one of us was asking: 'Did you hear the latest about Heather and Mu'min?' This story had a way of penetrating into our lives, our hearts. Each one of us found some identification with some character or event. Everyone, at some time or other, was confronted with some private personal horror, certainly known to themselves, perhaps known to others. It was a seemingly endless ordeal. Most of us simply wanted the story to be over, but the Shaikh was relentless:

'The outcome for *Tasawwuf* (the Path of pure and simple faith in God) is dependent on the outcome of Heather and Mu'min,' he told us. 'I am asking you if Heather will return to Mu'min or is this going to be just another American story coming to an end? I want you to involve yourselves deeply in the analysis of this story. Involve yourself at the human level of *zahir*. Do not attempt to explore it as a mystic, since clearly, that is not where we are.'

During the Shaikh's *muhabbat*, just before *Eid*, there was hardly any mention of Heather and Mu'min, but they were undoubtedly in our minds as we listened to the Shaikh:

'I want to speak to you of love unreturned,' he said. 'People pursue their passions with the idea that the feelings are real love. The one who is really in love doesn't see himself or herself manipulated. Sooner or later one of the two will hurt.'

'There are so many walking the streets, in whose faces we see no life. Their wounds have resulted in so many scars, there is no longer any room for love. It is better perhaps, to lie in solitude.

Each relationship is a little death, physically and spiritually. Thinking to explore each passer-by is a trap . . . hoping. Most will take physical advantage but know that *Jahannam* will be filled with people who hurt others in the name of love.' He then recited a poem:

Oh blessed dawn who is arriving
With a cascade of light in my little cell
You have no power to inflict wounds . . .
Because I am already resting in my grave.
But maybe you will make a fire
From the spark resting under the pile of ashes
For you are already touching with life
The violet in the ground, the lilacs
And the tree . . .

'Love', continued the Shaikh after a moment's silence, 'is everything happening to one who is in love. Everything has more meaning. But for you who wish to make a fire of the spark under the ashes, don't share the spark with everyone or soon it will be extinguished. Those who take advantage and play with the spark will get a big *azab* (punishment). Let us not be hurting others like Mu'min's wife. Love is the most intense feeling in the universe — but let us not use the word too loosely. One cannot, as Heather says, love drugs, alcohol, or food.'

'Next, I must ask you if there is hope? What we are studying is the *Tasawwuf* (spiritual teaching) of life. The person who has no scar of love is either crazy or dead. Yet every true love should have an aspect of submission. Calculation spoils spontaneity and yes, we should be careful, but impose conditions, no. Yet know that when you submit to one who does not care they will walk over you. Here we can blame no one. Our failure is due to our improper assessment. God keep us from being dead and buried.' Then he gave us another poem:

My heart saw April many times,
Never May.

'And how can we keep the heart open? Keep the heart open by keeping balance among *wujud*, *nafs*, and *ruh*, the existence, soul, and spirit. Stay open to beauty. Keep to simplicity. Retain the child. But dead people are too scared to open their hearts.' And again an extemporaneous uttering:

Mother, your son is suffering from
the most beautiful pain.

'But pleasure is beautiful only when anticipated. Don't you see? I am trying to make you a jamat of lovers. *Ashq Muhammad wa ashq Allah* (Love for Muhammad and love for God)! *Dunya* is nothing new to be shaken by a spider. Do not underestimate the power of a spider. Open your heart and I will go into it like a mighty river into a new channel. Shall we not expose ourselves or shall we go from one wound to another? One hundred more experiences, one hundred more scars . . . It is sophisticated surgery, but love born in a scarred heart heals scars.' And still again an uttering:

I still miss something in this little cell without hope
A tiny smile on the beloved's lips,
In the glass of water, a little rose.

'I mean', said the Shaikh, 'that something is missing . . . with all three hundred and fifty nurses (Doctor that I am) I am still in need of love, I have an insatiable thirst . . . but I will not cheat or reject.'

So blessed dawn who is arriving
With a cascade of light in my little cell
You have no power to inflict the death,
But return the love to this suffering Job.

When the day of Eid arrived, the Shaikh delivered the *Khutba*, pressing the themes of human love and desires to greater clarity:

'There was no difference between Ishmael and Isaac. Any differences between them had nothing to do with the point of sacrifice and Prophet Abraham, upon whom be peace. Like him, with his same resolve, you must resolve today to cut the throat of your *nafs* (desirous ego). Know that Hagar was not dumped. As it was for her, so it will be for you, that well springing up when there seems to be no hope. Abraham was one of few. His father and friends were against him, but he was not alone. So it is with us. Know that the desire you put before God — you lose it and God, but also know that there is forgiveness with God. Detachment and ridding oneself of distraction . . . that bubbling well of desires in each of us. This is our urgent work. Mankind is in a state of loss, the society is in loss, our laws are based on injustice. How can we ever fathom this mystery of loss? How can we come upon that road without limitations? Stay open to me and my love will flow into you like the river into a new channel.'

'We must reflect on the aim of life and *fana billah*. Hallaj experienced both human and divine love. But in human love as we know it, usually one is cheated, looking for better options and greener grass. It is as if the ideal of life is to look for and find the ideal life-partner. There are reasons for friends and for marriage, for we find comfort in human interactions. There is too some convenience and comfort in living together. The choice of a celibate life is difficult if you have experience with *dunya* (the world). But the issue of the big romantic love with no serious plan may wind up really needing help. We see the wife with a lover, the husband with the secretary. Is this a happy society? What can make this a truly happy society? God Almighty! The Qur'an speaks of those hardened by sin: *summun, bukmun, 'umyun, fahum la yarji'un*, 'deaf, dumb, and blind they will not return to the path,' and yet in special circumstances, even these can be melted by God's miracle.

'How, I ask you, can any sane human being be oblivious to the signs in the news and media. Is it not apparent that everything in the human sphere is limited? What makes people unhappy is that they want to go on and on without end. This assists those who take advantage. Know that nothing, not even love, is achieved by our effort. In truth, it is only by God's mercy. Tekiyas exist to help us learn to truly love, and to help us to learn to achieve independence from our desires. What stops love from growing is selfishness. Caring for your own need. This is taking advantage. Wanting to extract every possibility. Love, love—how can we love each other with complete love, extending and accepting without expecting anything? Many shaikhs provided the answers, these were the *'ashiqeen*, not those in love with love, but those who knew the love which transcended the human level of relationship. . . . How long does it take to learn about the hardness of the rock, that the rock is harder than your head? If security is more important, why do people repeatedly go in favour of passion, which doesn't bring satisfaction? You drink, but the more you drink, the more thirsty you are. Know this, *haram* (sin) never brings ultimate happiness because the law of nature has to be in harmony with the law of God. If it is not, one is destined to disappointment.' After pausing a moment the Shaikh gave a *Rubaiyat* verse:

A moment's halt — a momentary taste
Of being from the Well amid the Waste —
And Lo! the phantom caravan has reach'd
The Nothing it set out from — Oh make haste!

That Phantom Caravan is telling of the limitations of our life. It is the *qudrat* (power) caravan. Your *qudrat* time has come. Make haste to change your life so it doesn't pass you by. When will you start to live and truly love? It is possible, but only if one is not crude. The issue of crudeness versus refinement must be addressed.' Here the Shaikh gave us a poem on which we were to reflect:

I don't know what it is
Which opens and closes
Yet every fibre of my being
Understands.
The fragrance of your presence
is sweeter than a thousand roses.
Nobody, not even the rain
has such tiny hands.

Later in the day the Shaikh continued his *muhabbat*. He began quoting lines from Shakespeare's Sonnet twenty-nine:

When in disgrace with Fortune and men's eyes
I all alone beweep my outcast state . . .

'Why', he asked us, 'do we weep our outcast state? The only way to keep in the treasure house is to make our love transcendental. When Hazreti Jibreel (Angel Gabriel), upon whom be peace, reached the limits of material existence together with the Prophet, upon whom also be peace, he said 'I cannot go further. If I go beyond this point, I will burn up.'

'I am already on fire,' said the Prophet, 'I cannot stop.' Burning, the Prophet crossed the line of material existence into another world. Can love of *dunya* and love of God be united? Yes. Seek the company of those seeking the love which transcends our human limitations. Diamonds are not found in the mud. I give this advice to those on the Path: Do not seek things where they are not anticipated to be found. But how can we travel above? How can we listen to the growing of the grass?'

After a moment's pause, the Shaikh continued: 'Nowhere is the sky more clear than above that person who opens their heart to God. Lying down I see the sky. What lips I'm kissing! But to whom did I give so many years of my life where I was carried by demonstrations of love? What is the nostalgia of the beings of the street, trying to prove themselves alive? Achieve the state of love by reducing your desires and increasing your gratitude. Here is found the difference between being alive and being dead. It is finding constant love. That other love which incorporates jealousy and lack of freedom, incorporates nails into its coffin. Therefore, following the ancient custom, each spring I free a bird.

The point of today's *muhabbat* is that love is the most intense feeling a human being can experience in existence and includes all that is not crude. When crude, it inflicts wounds, one partner on another. *'Ashq* (love) demands no return. Only giving. Freedom of the Beloved guarantees freedom of the lover and vice versa. I ask the Iranian money-changer how to say to a beautiful girl "I love you." He replies: "There are no such words to say to her." In *'ashq* you walk the streets, your eyes burning like rubies. You understand the wailing of the reed flute. "What is the sign of love?" asks Hazreti Rumi. "It is that unhappy look, the sleepless, yellow, sunken face." Does my own face fit? Yes.' The Shaikh closed his eyes at this point in the *muhabbat* and gave Hazreti Rumi's last verses to Hazreti Shems:

Sometimes I wonder sweetest love,
If you were a mere dream
In a long winter night;
A dream of spring days and of
golden light
Which sheds its rays
Upon a frozen heart;
A dream of wine that fills the
drunken eye.

And so I wonder sweetest love,
If I should drink this ruby wine,
or rather weep: each tear a bezel
with your face engraved,
a rosary to memorize your name . . .
there are so many ways to call you back
Yes, even if you were only a dream.

'But in the *dunya,* the lovers are sleeping. *Dunya* is calling. The lover speaks: "Please look at me before I leave. You are the thirst of my soul, inscribed in my being." But the next day, there are different people. One from last night, the other you. Descend along the road of your burning passion. In the land of illusion you are pushed from one bed to another. Drink, you crazy shadows! When will we realise the limitations of life and human age? We see the people hand in hand, exchanging kisses, behaving as if in love. Their desire not to lose the moment is very apparent. Not keeping the moment in the soul treasure. Not accepting that life's limitations are *yaqin* (certain) and that death is *yaqin*. But know that in the moment of death hope exists for us in the most hopeless and undesirable circumstances. Shaitan is trying to prove that Allah is wrong in giving His trust to man made of clay. But really what does it matter? Clay, fire, and light are all degress below God. Put your trust in God and in each other — but especially, put the work of God above your personal interest. Know that God will not enter your heart with an idol in it. If you can bring what gives you pleasure into line with God's law, OK. If not, turn away from it and finally, remember Omar Khayyam's verse of the Phantom Caravan. The knock inside the wall which signals your time. Make haste!'

ACT THREE: Scene 1

Following Heather's birthday, there is a period of silence. Mu'min is still weak and trying to hold himself together. He returns home one day to find a small box at his door. It is from Heather and contains all of the things he had given her while she had been in the hospital. Among these things is a card, a little stuffed puppy, and a sketchily written note which reads:

Mumin
Please try to understand.
I cannot have you throwing puppy back
to me. I was terrible. You do
deserve better, always have.
Love,
Heather

This incident shatters Mu'min's heart as if it were glass. Cracking up completely, he takes it as the final terminating event. Before he leaves, he is informed by a neighbour, a kindly Russian lady, that Heather had come about eleven that morning, not wearing a coat or carrying a purse. Seeing no one else in the car, the neighbour assumed that Heather was driving. Mu'min barely hears. More deeply devastated than ever, he withdraws into pain and the horrors of his endless heartache. Spinning around in a whirlpool of loss, he reaches out for the hand of his Shaikh. Later, after repeated pleas for help and questions to the Shaikh about what he should do, Mu'min is advised to send Heather roses and an impersonal card which reads as follows: 'You are still a rare friend, regardless of anything.' (End of Scene Two)

Somewhere in the period of silence and separation between Mu'min and Heather near the time of her birthday, the Shaikh called a *hadrah*. In the *muhabbat* of this gathering, now six months into the teaching, the Shaikh made mention of the swords and Mu'min and Heather, for the first time, in the same discussion. He continued to push us into the teaching, and push the teaching into our lives. 'What will happen next?' He asked us, 'Will Heather call? Will she return to Mu'min? What should Mu'min do? Is there any hope?'

Attempting to understand and trying to make sense, many of us took Mu'min and Heather to be analogous to the Shaikh and his disciples. Some took the pair to the absolute and saw metaphors of divine love, although initially, the Shaikh discouraged us from this realm of thinking. But regardless of the metaphor employed, most disciples were not optimistic for the outcome. The Shaikh was displeased, for our pessimism in general showed our lack of faith as well as understanding. As for myself, I did not view Heather and Mu'min's situation as hopeless. I wanted to see the story come to a good end and see love conquer all. I identified with Mu'min's constancy and desire to love. I wanted to believe that no human heart could close itself to love if love was truly presented. I wanted Heather to respond so that my own romantic ideal might be strengthened, and so that I could see love the victor in the end. Somewhere, something shifted and I saw myself more identified with Heather. I thought I knew her, but she disappointed my romantic hopes a thousand times. Somewhere in all of it I saw my own struggle and my own longings and desires. Suddenly, I saw myself as no different from Heather. I wanted love, I felt it near, yet as years of my life in Tariqat raced by, I saw myself, again and again, helpless before myself — wanting to be different, wanting to be better, yet lingering, stuck in suspended animation, marking time, without the will or force of commitment to be the best servant of God I could be. Over the years, I had made so many mistakes, and the Shaikh had clearly told me and others too that there would come a time 'when the doors of the ark would close'.

The discourse of this gathering touched on many issues bringing even greater clarity to things the Shaikh had said before. He opened with the following verses of Suratul Baqara, reciting in Arabic, then in English:

> *When they meet those who believe, they say: 'We believe,' but when they are alone with their evil ones they say: 'We are really with you, we were only jesting.'*

'These are the people', said the Shaikh, 'who with themselves or with their evil friends choose to sleep, to drink, and do drugs. These are those in double-darkness, free willingly rejecting hope. These are those who close their ears with their fingers attempting to be oblivious, attempting not to hear. You must know that the terror for those who are too serious about *dunya* (the world) is death. The wish to avoid this terror is why Americans overdo their senses, searching for all in all in *dunya*, obstructing their senses, attempting to make death less obvious to themselves. If they were to stop and think they would see, but they do not. And even though they stop their ears, they cannot escape. God is always around. Even with those who block and reject faith, there are tiny senses and channels available to God. Here the Shaikh repeated the following lines, then continued in his discourse:

> *I don't know what it is*
> *Which opens and closes . . .*
> *Yet every fibre of my being*

Understands . . .
The fragrance of your presence
is sweeter than a thousand roses.
Nobody, not even the rain
has such tiny hands.

'God has ways of approach, there is no way to avoid Him. Know too, however, that we live in a time of active evil forces and unexplainable *dunya* events, though there is no danger on anyone of you. Hopefully, the states we fall into in times of danger can be dealt with by being more on guard. Beyond prayer, *zikr* (remembrance), and *fikr* (deep meditation) there are words of power. Hopefully, when you are alone you'll be constantly on guard. If you are in the company of Mu'min you will be an inspiration to him and he an inspiration to you, and I will be with you even in my imperfections.' At this point the Shaikh's tone became very serious, very direct and very forceful: 'Each one of you who gave your sword is a *mujahid*, a warrior for Islam. Is there anyone among you who would like to surrender their sword? If you have doubts please surrender it now, for after today there will be no turning back!' Here the Shaikh told a story:

When the king called Abraha was preparing to lay siege on Mecca and storm the city with his magnificent army of elephants, his soldiers took two hundred camels which belonged to Abu Talib, the uncle of the Prophet. When Abu Talib discovered this he was furious and he went directly to the camp of the army. Stopped by soldiers, he told them that he was there to see the king and was eventually presented to him. With no hesitation, but with firmness and *adab*, he spoke directly to the point: 'When your soldiers came to the city, they seized two hundred camels. As they are my own, I have come to claim them. I want them returned, today.'

The king was amazed by the forthright fearlessness of this man. 'I can hardly believe this,' he said to Abu Talib. 'I am about to destroy your entire city and you are here to claim your camels?'

'The city of Ibrahim', said Abu Talib, 'is to Allah. He will take care of it. My camels are to me.'

The king returned the camels, yet none the less, he did attempt to make war on the city. But the city of Ibrahim, alaihi salam, was to Allah and He defeated the army as is told in the Qur'anic chapter entitled 'The Elephant'.

After this story, the Shaikh continued in his *muhabbat*: 'For those who are strongly committed, there is no risk. This teaching is meant for the *jamat* (community) for the purpose of *Tawheed* (unity). The tricks of *Shaitan* (Satan) will not make it fail. Each one of you is to be a *shaheed* (witness) of *Tawheed* in the front *saff* (lines) of *jihad* (struggle). The others who are dead will make their *halka* (circle) around you.'

At this time in the *muhabbat*, the Shaikh made some remarks on how the *dajjal* (Anti-Christ) sparkles at the time of commercial Christmas. 'It is the psychosis of glittering *dunya*,' he warned us. 'Do not be sucked in. Stand up together.' Some disciples asking questions led to a discussion of Jesus, upon whom be peace, his birth as well as the general theme of Christmas. But the Shaikh soon returned to continue his earlier discussion of love, passion, and desire, love of the world and love of God. As he moved away from the discussion of Christmas, he gave a joke about Santa, but after my initial laughter, I reflected for months on the joke and found it increasingly less funny. The joke was an encapsulation of the point of the entire *muhabbat* which followed and the dilemma of one struggling between their longing for God and the longings of their *nafs* or lower self. The more I understood, the more sad I felt. Really, the joke was on me and my fellow seekers struggling between our desires.

Before the Shaikh continued he asked one of his dervishes to review for us the entire story of Heather and Mu'min from its beginning up until the end of Act Three: Scene 1. The dervish did as instructed, reviewing every single heart-breaking detail. The Shaikh then continued in his discourse:

'Can Heather be with Juan without commitment? Do you not know that Allah will not enter a heart which is shared with another? How we disappoint Him and yet He forgives and continues to give us from His *rahmat* (mercy). What happens when Heather is taken to the level of the human race? What is the hope of the dry desert to become fertile and live again? What hope do we have as mankind, as an *ummat* (a nation), constantly going from one *haram* (sin) to another? What is the hope for us, that Allah will not ultimately give up on us? If Mu'min drinks will God's compassion increase or decrease? We instinctively adore God because we see the limitations of human life, and if God is not *yaqin* (certain) for us, we know that death is. What then prevents us from being overwhelmed by Allah? Why does Heather not change? As for Mu'min, how cculd he, a Muslim of Tariqat, be in such difficulties? Could this be a problem of his perception of love? Is his predicament a sign of weakness or strength? But what do we know of the lamentations of the *ney* (reed pipe) and hearts torn of separation? The food for Mu'min's life was his love. Was it only his *nafs* or did he have a rare experience? It is hard for those who are not hungry to identify with the hungry. Are all of the men here above the level of seduction by a woman? Do you know that nations fell for lack of love? Who cannot be attracted by the feeling of love? Let us not judge Mu'min. We only know what we see. This man lost his senses, his job, his everything. . . . Is it his *nafs*? The couple started out with pure love and progressed, but when was that point? It is the same with nations over time. It is the tragedy of the Muslim world today: love for *dunya* and no spiritual life.

We may take Mu'min as the exponent of love of God, Heather as the exponent of love of *dunya*, and Juan as the exponent of *Dajjal* (the Anti-Christ). Know in all of this that Allah is the key, love to Allah, but such love can deteriorate to love of *dunya*. Mu'min's love at some point changed. Heather at some point tested him. We must arrive at that place where nothing replaces Allah. From this stage the seed must grow. Does the blood of martyrs matter? Miserable are the Muslims allowing their *nafs* to lead them to death with no strength to shake the burden from our shoulders . . . from the trampled stem, something will come. From the stone will come the spark. As Muslims we have a responsibility to have faith in that spark of stone, of life coming from dead bones. Open wide the door of your house, the fear is buried in the bottom, down below. Know that your Shaikh is burning in 1983! May *baraka* be upon all pains, all tears, all sweat, all hunger, and all stress. Mercy towards those who did *haram*, let us not destroy hope, even in the hearts of the wrongdoers. Let us harbour nothing in our hearts, the ultimate justice is not with Heather but with God. It is my hope that each of you will become a missionary of *Tawheed* (unity).

In the middle of January I spoke with the Shaikh on the phone. It was not an encouraging conversation. 'More and more of you are showing signs of hopelessness,' he told me in a disturbing tone of voice, mentioning some disciples by name. 'Love is suffocating in front of *haram* (sin), and many are still holding firm to their pessimistic ideas about the outcome of the story.' Referring, I thought, to the spark in the stone he concluded, 'Hope applies only to those who believe — but are we in that category?'

My conversation with the Shaikh nearly put me into shock. Talking with him always generated a great deal of reflection and caused me to explore where I fit into the things which he told me. 'Certainly,' I thought, 'he must have called me with some purpose.' It was hardly two weeks later that the story of Heather and Mu'min was lifted. We were told by the Shaikh that no one really wanted to deal with the teaching. In his next discourse the Shaikh laid everything out. I was not present but one of the disciples who had been there shared with me some of what he'd heard. Later, the Shaikh repeated many of these things and I heard them first-hand:

'It is time to grow up and move to *Haqiqat* (seeing without veils). It is time to realise that there is this possibility within ourselves. It is time to move beyond concern for *halal* or *haram* (right or wrong), but instead to make our only concern stepping out for God. Mu'min and Heather are really to widen our vision. The story is over for us, but not for them. The issues are now out of *zuhurat* (the apparent realm) and have moved to another level. Now is a time of separation, for them and for us.'

In this same discourse, the Shaikh spoke on the art of making swords:

'The ore is first removed from the mountain and heated in the fire. This process of separating out the impurities is known as smelting. This process produces various kinds of steel in mass, varying from hard to soft. These masses are broken into pieces, selected for specific purposes and welded into bars. But if the metal has too many impurities at the outset, it will not be a sword. It is the fire which determines a great deal of the outcome, for if the metal withstands the fire, it can go on to the moulding. So it is that the process of sword-making happens in stages. First, the ore is found and smelted in the furnace, the metal which is produced then goes to the blacksmith, who shapes it into sheets or bars, then these go on to the master craftsman or swordsmith, who shapes the metal into a blade, tempers it, fastens it to its hilt, tests it, and finally produces a combat-ready sword.'

The Shaikh has repeatedly emphasised tempering in his discourses on the sword. More than once I had heard him say words to this effect:

The Master craftsman puts the sword into the fire and heats it until it is red hot. He shapes it by hammering, then cools it by dipping it into the water, but if he cools it too fast it will break.'

Something in this discourse touched me very deeply. Though I had some clues, I was not entirely sure how to apply it to Mu'min and Heather, nor to myself. Thoughts on the sword and the Shaikh's discussion seemed continually on my mind. I decided at last to look a bit further into the process of tempering, to see what I might find. The more I read, the more similarities I saw between the swordsmith and the Shaikh and between swords and *murids*:

> The most essential part of this work [of the swordsmith] is tempering. It was discovered that hot iron could be tempered by dipping it into water. Hammering and tempering the iron afterward, gave durability and flexibility to the blade, but proper tempering was a very difficult job. If the blade was too hard it chipped, if too soft, it notched easily. It was found that the correctly tempered iron blade would take and keep a point suitable for thrusting. Great skill and experience was needed to obtain the right hardness. Tempering became a secret which was often passed from generation to generation in a family. After it reached a certain color in the fire, the glowing iron was repeatedly dipped into water or oil and the blade was tested by beating a stone with the side of it and by using it to pierce a hole through an iron plate. A satisfactory blade could break an opponent's blade in two. (Since a fighting sword should be capable of cutting a man's head off at a single stroke, blades were tried either on corpses or criminals condemned to death.) The hard work therefore, and the secret which went into tempering, made the sword very valuable, and the outcome of a fight depended a great deal on the quality of the armour and weapon.
>
> *('Sword and Masque' by Julius Palffy-Alpar)*

Having done this exploration, I better understood the Shaikh's emphasis on tempering. Apparently, most of my fellow seekers and I had survived the stages of ore and smelting and had come into the hands of the Shaikh, our Swordsmith. We were now being thrust into the fire, our metal being tested, so to speak and its quality made known. The lifting of the teaching of Mu'min and Heather, in many ways seemed a tempering, for our hearts had been in the fire with Mu'min's. We had undergone the hammering of the Swordsmith but we were not yet fit weapons. Not yet ready either, for the combat, we were now in a time of cooling.

Winter, spring, and most of summer passed with no mention of Mu'min or Heather. In late autumn, however, we received some news, in spite of the fact that the story had moved out of the level of *zahir*:

ACT THREE: Scene 2

After months of separation from Mu'min, Heather is seen in a popular bookshop. Alive and well, she is hanging on the arm of a man and wrapped around him as if she were a turban about a cap. The Shaikh, who had known she would be there, sent two disciples to observe her and report back to him. Having seen her, it was obvious to them that Heather had bounced back and was strong as ever. Mu'min, however, knew nothing of her whereabouts as he continued to attempt to recover his senses and get over his grief. (Scene ends. End of Act Three.)

In early autumn, about a month before the time of the fire, another gathering (*hadrah*) was called. There was a great deal of anxiety among us in the circle of disciples, as the Shaikh had mentioned to us that one of our retreat houses (*khanqas*) might possibly be closed. Many of us took this potential action to be connected with the teaching of Heather and Mu'min, together with our general stuckness to our longings and attachments in the realm of the world. In this particular gathering, for me, one particular story stood out from among the many things the Shaikh discussed. It was as follows:

> There was a man who came to a Shaikh asking to receive the *bayat* of initiation. After having waited ten years without gaining acceptance, the man presented himself to the Shaikh again and petitioned for admittance. He was told by the Shaikh, as he had been told before, that he simply was not ready. But the man persisted and still wanted to begin. Finally, the Shaikh consented and said to him: 'OK, you may begin but for your *bayat* you must do the following: Leave your wife and sell your land and belongings. With the money, buy a precious stone and bring the stone to me.' The man did as commanded and came to the Shaikh with a diamond the size of an egg. Taking it, the Shaikh crushed it with a hammer until it was nothing more than a powder which he then threw to the winds.
>
> Later, the Shaikh took the man to the Grand Mosque for a *zikr* which was to be held that night. Around the time of midnight, the police entered the Mosque. As *zikr* was not permitted at that time in

> the mosques, the people began to scatter while the police attempted to gather them up. The Shaikh, who also stood up to run, told the man to follow him and began running around the Mosque. The man ran after the Shaikh and the police ran after them both. On the third time around the Mosque, the Shaikh ran up into the minaret. The murid and the police followed. When the Shaikh reached the balcony at the top of the minaret, he jumped. The *murid* hesitated, if only for a second, but in that hesitation was seized by the police.
>
> When finally, the man was presented before the *Qadi* for the trial of his case, after much questioning by the police, he recognised the *Qadi* as being the same Shaikh who had led the *zikr* in the Mosque. The *Qadi*, likewise, recognised the man and set him free. Before the man left the courtroom, Shaikh returned the diamond to him completely intact. 'Here is your diamond' said the Shaikh. 'Take it. Go back to your wife and buy back your land, I set you free again.'

I did not take it that the Shaikh had told this story with no purpose. I tried to understand what it meant for me. Like the dervish in the story I had been with my Shaikh for nearly ten years, though I didn't think the number of years really mattered. What seemed important is that years were passing and I was remaining unready and running around the world like the dervish running around the mosque. Perhaps my Shaikh too would soon reach the top of the minaret and disappear. Then what would I do?

Over the next year, I had little personal contact with the Shaikh but he was with us as a community at fairly regular intervals. He conducted gatherings and gave discourses in several of our Tekiyas and I attended as many of these as I could. From the time of the Fire an entire year passed with absolute silence on the story of Mu'min and Heather. During the time of *Matem*, the Shaikh was with us in the Tekiya. Interestingly enough, he brought Heather and Mu'min to us again. Mu'min and Heather had come up during the time of *Matem* in the past. The relationship between their story and that of Imam Hussain was still another mystery. As I turned it around in contemplation, I remembered a telephone conversation with the Shaikh just at the end of *Matem*, a year before. The last scene of the first Act was just about to close and I was deeply involved in the drama of Heather and Mu'min. During the days of *Matem* that year I had, for the first time, glimpsed with some understanding, the horror of Kerbala and the trial of Imam Hussain, may Allah be pleased with him. My heart was filled with sorrow and I wept sincerely.

'From this *Matem*', I said to the Shaikh, 'I have taken one thing.'
'And what is that?' he asked.
'Tears for Imam Hussain,' I said.
'Greater than your tears for Imam Hussain', said the Shaikh, 'should be your tears for Mu'min.' Having spoken these words, he gave *salaams* and left me to reflect.

ACT FOUR: Scene 1

After several months of silence and separation, Heather sees Mu'min in a sidewalk cafe. She rushes up and attempts to embrace him. At this gesture Mu'min turns yellow with creeping, quiet horror. Pulling himself away with a controlled jerk his words are few but clear: 'Please be kind, leave me alone.' Masking her surprise, Heather stands waiting speechless for a minute then composes herself and leaves. Later, while alone with the Shaikh, Mu'min reveals that in his dating experiences ten years ago in Switzerland, one girl told him: 'You're going to meet someone who'll break your heart to bits.' (End of Scene 1)

'The story of Heather and Mu'min', the Shaikh later told us, 'is the greatest story of the century. It is a story greater than Layla and Majnun or Romeo and Juliet and it is being written now.' These were the last words uttered by the Shaikh concerning the story during the time of the Sword. One month later another *hadrah* was held. It was a day of powerful lessons and much *muhabbat*. 'We are going to give you heavy words,' said the Shaikh early in his discourse. And heavy words, with heavy meaning is exactly what we got. The Shaikh spoke on many subjects, including the miracle of Qur'an and ontological proofs of Islam, spheres in creation from the earthly realm to beyond the starless heavens, and stations of spiritual progress. It was this latter discussion of stations, however, which stood out for me the most and seemed to connect with my various struggles since the opening of Heather and Mu'min two years before, perhaps even since I had come onto the Path. It was this discussion which later helped me to understand the teaching of the Sword:

'There will come a time when *Ruhul Quddus*, the Holy Spirit will fill you. You will then go out and witness the truth to others. But you must travel through the stations. The first of these is *maqamul nafs*. It is the station of egoism, of domination by the instincts, passions, and desire for success. It is the station of unfulfilled human desires — for food, for money, cars, and satisfaction of our hopes.

'The second of the stations is *maqamul qalb*, the station of the heart. When one reaches that place where things which gave fulfilment before, no longer satisfy, this door begins to open.

'The third of the stations is *maqamul ruh*, the station of the spirit. It is the station where one must be watchful. The stations are not discrete and overlap one another. One must in this station avoid arrogance and self-righteousness.

'*Haqiqat*, the station of reality, follows *maqamul ruh*.'

The Shaikh went on to speak of *maqamul sirr*, the station of the secret and stations beyond. But here I must say, as did the great Shaikh and poet Hafiz, that 'It is better for Muhyiddin if he speaks no more of the secret, but let us remember the possessors of the secret. The possessors are the Prophets and Saints and these, save by God's mercy, are only reached through the door of the Shaikh. In this same *muhabbat*, the Shaikh told us clearly about the exploration of Allah and how one can travel from one station to the next. As anyone who had heard his teachings over the years would guess, the greatest emphasis continued to be on the station of the *nafs*:

'Hazreti Hallaj Mansur whispered to Allah,' the Shaikh told us,' "There is only one veil. It is myself. Please Allah, remove my 'I'." The problems of *maqamul nafs* are depression, unhappy feelings, fear for my family, I, I, I—I want this or I want that. In all of the other *maqams*, "I" is not present. People in *maqamul nafs* (the station of ego) are destined to unhappiness. The more they drink, the more they want. It is the unquenchable thirst, like having a mouth full of sand. They drink all of *dunya* and yet *dunya* in all its seeming vastness, could on the day of *Qiyyamat* (Resurrection) be hidden in a slipper.

'Ninety-five per cent of all mankind is in the station of *nafs* (desire and passion), and this includes Muslims. Neither *salat* (prayer) nor *zakat* (charity) makes them happy. In order to be happy one must have a clean *niyyat* (intention) and do something to help oneself. How can one transcend this station? There are two conditions, one set called open conditions, the other called closed. These must be carried out with no hope for gain, only with hope for Allah.

'Do no delay. Start tonight! Forget about what you want! Who says you have to have it? It may carry your seed of destruction. My happiness should be because I am lost in the mystery of my

Prophet and I am witness to the mystery of God. The millions of Wall Street cannot bring me a moment of the satisfaction I find in *Tahajjud* (the voluntary prayers of night). How to escape to happiness? There are beautiful ways, like cool water in the heat of the desert. Know that standing on the *Sirat* (Narrow Way), the *maqam* (station) of *Muslim* or submission, is in truth the moment of superiority. Coming out of selfishness is the way to the heart.

'The first closed condition is independence from *dunya*. It is the declaration in the name of God to be independent of it, known as *Tajreed*. Know that everything you whisper will be heard in *sama* (the heavens). Ask 'Is it good for me or not?' Put things into God's care. Possess nothing. Remember that upon the Prophet's return to Mecca he ate dry bread with vinegar and water, while the whole city's wealth available to him, he never touched. He only touched the idols, knocking them down, taking them out of the house of God.

'Next, be possessed by nothing. This is *Tafreed*. But be careful, for there is always danger whether you succeed or fail. Do not be like Iblis, who came to his downfall because he closed himself to *Tawheed* (Unity—the avoidance of dualistic thinking). Unable to transcend from himself to God, he found the mystery but could not penetrate inside. Open conditions help to avoid the danger. We must concentrate on ourselves, we must attempt to penetrate our own mystery. But one must keep to *Tawheed* as one makes this exploration, for *Tawheed* is necessary for those who hope to make the leap to ecstasy. Attempt to make your conditions fit with God's conditions. If you have a soul dedicated to God, not permitting yourself to be possessed by any other, if you conquer the *nafs* and achieve your independence possessing nothing, you will go on to *maqamul qalb* (station of heart) and beyond. Keep your service dedicated to God Almighty, want no pay, expect no reward.'

After the discourse of this gathering, I turned the mysteries and advices around for days on end, attempting to see them in truth. Something was near, some understanding was close, but things were not coming to clarity and the last chapter of my own book was not reaching a conclusion. The Shaikh had repeatedly encouraged me to finish the book. For some reason, I could not. After two months of suspended animation, something happened. Returning from a short visit to my parents in the holdiay season, I had a car accident. Falling asleep at the wheel I crashed into a utility pole. Although the car was a total loss, I was not injured in the smallest way. Shortly after the accident, a dervish brought a message from the Shaikh informing me that I had travelled without his permission. This violated my personal commitment to inform the Shaikh of my travels. Just before I had set out, the Shaikh had been in the Tekiya, but I had not seen him. Speaking later to another disciple who wanted to go with me, I was told that the Shaikh had advised him that 'it was not a good time.' I took the decision to travel alone. Later, after the dervish brought the message, I spoke with the Shaikh.

'What got into you?' he enquired.

'I had an indication in the advice which you gave to the other *murid,*' I said, 'but I was careless.'

'Thank God you are alive,' he said. 'But this car incident is interesting. You were almost in the area of the Tekiya. I advise you to think about it as a component of your book.'

To an already long series of mysteries and questions, the Shaikh added another: 'the swords, Mu'min and Heather, Imam Hussain, witnessing for *Tawheed*, escaping the station of *nafs*, and now fathoming the accident and the loss of my car. These certainly seemed a motley chain of events. I searched and reflected and bits and pieces came but still it was not fully clear.

The teaching we were presently involved in had begun more than two years before at the time the Shaikh had called for swords. Those swords were actually the graphic representation of the entire teaching. The sword was the symbol and the embodiment of all we were to learn. The Shaikh gave us two things to begin with. The first was the poem and the second was time. The many months which passed with no discourse should have been utilised by reflecting on why we had been asked to give the gift of a sword. It was a time of tempering and if we had understood the process we would have better understood, perhaps, our own attachments as well as the struggle of Mu'min and Heather. The poem was full of indications but years had passed before I saw how much was contained within it:

I give you my love my dagger made of steel,
My whole and entire love I transfer to you
my sharp, cold friend . . .

The poem opened with the recipient of the gift of a dagger, transferring his complete love. Nothing was held back for he knew the purpose of the dagger and how it had been made. He likely knew the swordsmith as well whose name was engraved on the blade certifying its craftsmanship and reliability as a weapon.

You were made by the blacksmith, and
Cherkez shaped you for the battle.

Beyond the blacksmith and Cherkez, however, there was someone else, some being of love and refinement giving the gift. Realising what an unspeakably precious gift was being bestowed, the recipient could only respond by weeping. We see compassion in a heart which likely belongs to a fighter.

You were given me by a hand as gentle as
a lily, and for the first time,
not blood fell on you,
but a tear — a jewel of my sorrow.

The fighter knew that the gift was given in love with no expectation, not mixed with any secret motive or hope for gain. Yet there was a tear. Why? The fighter realised the paradox as he saw his own tear fall on the blade of this gift given him in such love. At the same time he felt sorrow for he knew that he must if necessary slay with the dagger and blood might fall on its blade again. With this understanding the fighter's commitment was sparked to balance his compassion, and making the dagger the symbol of his standard, he whispers his promise to stand on his *sirat* (way) and keep himself as sharp as the blade:

You were a sign of love, pure and clean
and not a useless gift.
I am going to remain as sharp as you
my friend made of steel.

Near the time of the poem the Shaikh had introduced Mu'min and Heather. In this story there were many indications as well, many levels and many teachings. In the beginning the Shaikh kept our focus on the obvious aspects of the story. The Shaikh forced the experience of exploration, even if vicariously. Through Mu'min and Heather we were given the opportunity to see the beauties and disappointments of human relationships. Clearly there are beauties and comforts to be had, for in spite of Mu'min's pain, he had experienced one or two good years together with Heather before things began to change. How long really does not matter, for it is possible for humans to find joy for a year or two. It may in fact be possible that humans may find joy for a lifetime, but what the Shaikh attempted to help us learn is that such joy is never uninterrupted and flawless, for perfection is only with God. Human relationships have their limitations:

> Is it not apparent that everything in the human sphere is limited? What makes people unhappy is that they want to go on and on without end . . . Know that nothing, not even love, is achieved by our effort. In truth it is only by Allah's mercy.

This desire, this hope for happiness is nowhere better exemplified than in human relationships, in the seeking for companionship, love, and peace of the heart. But it is a desire which often goes beyond bounds, which opens the door to personal interest, selfishness, to greed, to hurting others. So it is that in human love, an arena which is the focus of so many hopes. there is grand-scale infiltration by the phenomenon of *nafs*:

> Tekiyas exist to help us achieve independence from our desires. What stops love from growing is selfishness. Caring for your own need. This is taking advantage. Wanting to extract every possibility. Love, love, how can we love each other with complete love, extending and accepting without expecting anything?

It is a tremendously difficult lesson to learn, for anyone who has truly loved also knows the gripping pain of loss and disappointment. Heather opened another dimension of the story of love. Through her we see the unholy side of human desire. We see her unsuccessful in reclaiming herself and in making her detachment in order to open to Mu'min. The Shaikh had attempted to help us see:

> Detachment and ridding oneself of distraction, that bubbling well of desires in each of us. This is our urgent work.

It was a painful smelting. We were inside the furnace. In every direction there was pain. We had enough pain in our lives already. No one wanted to be involved with Mu'min's pain. What could have been a beautiful love-story was going to nothing but heartache. If Heather would just come back. But there is no avoidance of pain on the path to God. In fact, Shaikh al Akbar advises that 'it is not possible for the traveller to find unimpaired comfort, security or bliss,' which our Shaikh referred to as 'wanting to go on without end'. It was finally our own resistance to facing our personal discomforts, desires, and attachment which led to the lifting of the story. Without facing these things there is no opening. 'The heart', says Shaikh al Akbar, 'cannot acknowledge any lordship other than His [God's]. For you belong to that which exercises authority over you.'

One afternoon just as I finished the prayer at *'Asr*, everything became clear. The Shaikh had all the while been giving us the training and discipline to reach the door of *Tawakkal* (trust). Discipline in *Tariqat* means the refinement of moral character, the endurance of trials and indignities, and the abandonment of heedlessness. The Shaikh's repeated attacks on our hopes for uninterrupted comfort and *dunya* attachments were all a part of this refinement. Such an attack was a strategic act of love. The discourse on stations and *irshad* (guidance) for escaping *maqamul nafs* was a mercy. It gave us the very key. But even earlier the Shaikh had told us just as clearly:

> Resolve today to cut the throat of your *nafs*. Know that Hazreti Hajara was not dumped. As it was for her, so it will be for you . . . that well springing up when there seems to be no hope.

More than ever before, I began to hear my Shaikh. His words this time were engraved in my heart, creeping through my thoughts in the passing days:

> Know that the desire you put before Allah, you lose it, and Allah. Put your trust in God and each other but put the work of God above your personal interest . . . How long does it take to learn about the hardness of the rock? We must reflect on the aim of life and *fana billah*. Hallaj experienced love, both human and divine, complete love . . . The Phantom Caravan has reached the Nothing it set out from . . . How can we ever fathom this mystery of loss? . . . Greater than your tears for Imam Hussain should be your tears for Mu'min . . . Make haste! . . .Your *qudrat* time has come.

My understanding of the lesson of the abandonment of heedlessness came through the loss of my car. After the Shaikh had suggested I think about it, I saw in the newspaper where a man had had a similar accident. He had sustained injuries to his abdomen, however, when he had crashed into a pole and had died soon thereafter. In my case, I had only lost my car, but I could have lost my life. The Shaikh had said it was interesting how near I was to the Tekiya. It was interesting indeed, and in this was a teaching. Namely, that there is a time when 'being near the Tekiya', is not enough. One must in fact, *be* the Tekiya. A moment's separation may bring irretrievable loss. There is a time when a *murid* may be allowed a bit of carelessness, but there comes a time when no carelessness can be allowed. As this one characteristic led to the collapse of entire civilisations, it can lead to the downfall of a not too cautious, unconscious seeker. My personal heedlessness with regard to my Shaikh's indication had cost me my car. But this is a small price to pay to learn the lesson of a Warrior, and how to avoid immeasurable loss in the eternal realm.

The car accident also helped in further opening the story of Mu'min and Heather. The Shaikh had asked us over the months if it was not just another American story. When the story was lifted the Shaikh gave the answer, since he showed us clearly that the teaching was entering another dimension. The story only ended at the level of *zahir* (the apparent). American stories, particularly soap operas, seem endless. That is the characteristic of *dunya* we have so many times been told. It wants to go on without end. At one level Heather and Mu'min is a story of human love, of its joys and disappointments. But it is not just another American story, for the story has implications beyond the human level which touch on the mystery of a loss which no disciple could fathom before the lifting of the story. At the divine level, Heather is flirting with incomprehensible loss. A love of meta-cosmic beauty from dimensions never known to the human heart before, a love of unimaginable scope, depth and powers of transformation, arriving perhaps less frequently than Halleys's comet. The loss may be not just to an American city, but to an entire culture, perhaps to an entire civilisation.

The Shaikh had said to me that my tears for Mu'min should be greater than my tears for Imam Hussain. This advice was a further indication of the scope of potential loss. What Imam Hussain offered to the people of Kufa, namely the opportunity to be warriors in the army of God Almighty and witnesses for the pure ancient faith of submission to God alone, was lost. These people wavered like the dervish behind the Shaikh who jumped from the *minaret*. Dubbed 'the Penitents' by historians, they attempted to make recompense for their cowardice too late, weeping and begging God Most High for mercy at the grave of Imam Hussain, may God bless him, whose call they had not heeded. By the mercy of God, even if after the fact, they were allowed to give their lives against the enemy who still remained.

What is offered to the seeker of today is the same as was before. The same luminous inner light, the same fathomless tranquillity, that same drink which deeply quenches, that explosive, boundless love from the source of Love beyond, that same handhold with hundreds of thousands of Messengers of light, that same blessed transmission being extended from the unfailing generosity and *rahmat* (mercy) of God Most High. The ante remains as it has always been: the surrender of everything entirely, including one's very self. What is at stake, however, is greater than ever before. If you have understood this invitation my fellow seeker, if your heart has heard the calling of a traveller just like you, then take heed now and make haste as the saints have urged. The *Qudrat* (power) time approaches at the speed of light and such an opportunity as this will not knock again.

The Shaikh said to us at the time of his teaching on the art of making swords: 'It is time to grow up and move to *haqiqat*, to realise that there is that possibility within ourselves.' But *haqiqat* can only be reached through *tawakkal* (trust), and *tawakkal* cannot be approached except by one who has achieved that discipline of character refinement, heedfulness, and detachment. After these one comes to trust. 'The person who begins before he has acquired discipline', says Shaikh al Akbar, 'will never become a man, except in a rare case.'

'*Tawakkal*, says Shaikh Suhrawardi, 'signifies that if one trusts one's affairs to God with certainty one will not be left in need. It is the result of true faith in the degree of *Yaqin* (certainty), where the seeker knows that all affairs of destiny are in the hands of God. The seeker's trust is not changed by causes or lack of causes, by whim or the joys or disappointments of life. The seeker sees no existence other than that of the Causer of causes. Such a seeker becomes a *mutawakkil*, a person of true trust who has reached the stage of *Tawheed* or unity. Until one has reached this stage one is in need of amending one's own station (*maqam*) by abandoning causes and in this activity one should be engaged, and continuing to strive and, God willing, one will reach the door of rest.'

The Teaching of the Sword is the lesson of the Warrior's refinement, the development of moral character and the escape from desire and attachments. The polish on the sword is the abandonment of heedlessness which clears the way to *tawakkal*. In the way of the Yaqui Indian Sorcerer, the seeker Carlos is told by his teacher Don Juan that the attributes of warriorship, which is a stage between apprenticeship and becoming a man of knowledge, consists of control, discipline, forbearance, and timing. The activity which consumes the greatest amount of energy is known as self-importance. As this energy *should be* used to face the unknown, one of the first concerns of the Indian warrior is to free the energy and rechannel it. This action of rechannelling energy is called Impeccability. Likewise, in *Tariqat*, the stage in Islam between *Shari'ah* (Law) and *Haqiqat* (Truth), the greatest consumer of energy is that same self-invested *nafs*. Impeccability for the spiritual seeker, the warrior in *tasawwuf*, is the fostering of discipline whereby the seeker escapes the *nafs* and heedlessness to become a son of the moment.

The seeker is himself the sword, shaped by the Swordsmith. The Warrior is nothing less than that sword on the wall. In the beginning stages of training there are wooden swords and room for mistakes. But there comes a time in the life of a warrior when there is only this moment now, and the fight is to the death. The warrior must conquer or die. The final scene, the end of Act Four, is being written now in my life and yours. May God help us to make the choices in our hearts which give the story an ending no one expects, and let us not be among those vanquished by this world. Let us find the reality of an oft-sung dervish song which tells it simply like it is:

Janan gereksen
Vuslet dilersen
Challtatlu nefsen
Seyfi Jalali

If you want to move your soul
along to Union
Take the sharp and swift sword
and cut the *nafs* to pieces

EPILOGUE

The Beginning

Shortly after I had become a *murid*, I was walking along the city street with the Shaikh, late one evening in autumn. As we passed by a cemetery he uttered these words:

> Writing which men carve in stone to last for centuries, is for Allah like writing on the water.

Several years passed before I heard him speak these words again. One year, just at the end of Ramadan, he repeated them again and suddenly their deeper meaning wafted ever so gently across my heart, with all the sweetness of a jasmine-scented breeze. There simply is no peace, there is no security, there is nothing which ultimately endures or possesses that attribute of permanence except God Most High, glorified and exalted is He. Across the centuries human beings have sought to know the secret, to find the key to unlock the treasure, in order to touch and to taste, to experience and fully know the sweet tranquillity of living without doubt and anxiety. The longing hearts of men have always sought what every seeker seeks: that place of lasting inward joy which is unthreatened by uncertainty, despair, or loss. Yet man has often looked in the wrong direction, carving an idea in the stone of his mind, that the material stuff of *dunya* would give him the secret. To this stuff he assigned a reality which belonged to his Lord, thus missing the opportunity to find that which he rather should have sought. Know my fellow seeker that the key to the treasure house is love and nothing else. Said Omar Khayyam in a verse often repeated by the Shaikh:

There was a Door to which I found no key
There was a veil through which I could not see
Some little talk awhile of Me and Thee
There seemed – and then no more of Thee and Me.

'How does one come to love?' remains the seeker's question. This indescribable state has no means of entry save one: the doorway to *tawakkal*, which opens onto the edge of a deep and treacherous cliff. One must close one's eyes, put their hand into the hand of the Prophet, on whom be peace, their heart into the hands of God Most High, then fling oneself over the edge of the abyss. This is the plunge known as abandonment, the beginning place. It is the place of giving all with no doubt or question. Let the seeker know that there is no such thing as giving half.

May God be merciful to all who seek Him and nothing else, and praise be to Him the Lord of the Worlds, the Source of Love, the Friend of Seekers, and Opener of hearts.

Entel Hadi Entel Haqq
Leysel Hadi illa Hu.

Sayings Of The Shaikh

How humble we would be if we knew our true purpose in life.

Your robe of poverty will keep you warmer than all the fur coats in winter.

There is no reason to be without hope . . . ever.

The television is the same as the golden cow.

Fossilized people — living fossils, walking bodies, with no love touching their hearts. Feeling self-sufficient. Everything in this world that is not *fi-sabilillah* is useless.

You cannot come before Allah in the arrogance of your integration and you cannot enter *dunya* in the confusion of your disintegration.

Man claims to the universe that he exists, and the universe answers, 'It puts no claim on me.'

Between God and man the only mediator is deeds. There will be no attorney on *Yaum al-Qiyyamat*.

You recognise *manufiqs* when their comfort is disturbed. It's too cold, too hot — no air-conditioning. Discomfort gives comfort to the spirit but not vice versa.

When you make a *niyyat*, make sure you keep it.

If you are chosen, accept death and you will be chosen in the hereafter. The chosen are those who believe.

A little raindrop makes a hole in the rock by patience and the long journey begins with a single step.

Words are limited, Allah is not.

Adam, peace be upon him, was given as a jewel to the earth.

God can only be known by love.

The path of being a murid is one which is constantly bringing challenges. When to initiate, when to wait. How to listen, how to serve.

Life is a handful of dust in the desert wind.

Science proves religion, there is no discrepancy.

Before you divorce somebody, think twice.

Life without love is empty.

If you find someone in the world who truly cares about you, stay with them.

Godless movements bring crises to nations.

The older we get the faster time goes.

Learn from Star Wars and Star Trek. Behind the Mount of *Qaf* there are creatures different from us.

The heart of a believer is larger than the universe.

The seed of evil never dries out and sprouts more rapidly than good.

I give you the name caution over all your actions.

Dunya is a pass/fail examination. There are no make-ups.

The difficulties we meet in life we cause with ourselves.

Your little trials are to help you to keep your back straight on the Day of Judgement.

If this life is abandoned, then it can be loved.

This life is a gift out of the love of Allah to assist you in the realisation of the better life, and to make us aware of the beauty of Allah.

What is imprinted in the heart is imprinted in the soul.

Be careful of those who have known no suffering: peace comes after long suffering.

The *dunya* is like a dirty window.

The duty of a *mu'min*, which is a person of Faith, is to relieve suffering.

There are nine hundred million Muslims, and yet Muslims are as rare as extinct animals.

Be grateful for all that happens.

Remember at all times that nothing is hidden from God. We can hardly hide from each other.

Those who show reservation about the Prophet, peace be upon him, have doubt in Allah.

Beware of the transient gains of this life.

You cannot call yourself a believer on this Path without doing charity.

Some people say their prayers and then go and worship.

Regarding the establishment: if you are detached and independent you are safe, but if you are dependent they will destroy you.

The establishment lives by self-created superiority. It is like a balloon approaching a pin.

Sufis are Muslims who want more from the mercy of Allah, and we know that Muslims are those who are completely submitted to God.

What is the point of this beautiful life? To go to the mirror and see more wrinkles in one's face and more rotten teeth.

How much we are misled by our passions.

If you spot one tree in the forest, that tree is for itself the centre of the universe.

You can do whatever you want, but not for as long as you want.

Islam is not a sticker put on one's forehead like Triple A or Allstate. It is complete and total surrender to God.

Today our idols are in the television, bank accounts, and the fridge.

Flying to the moon will not guarantee illumination.

Whatever you do in keeping your *sirat*, you will make enemies.

Haram is so attractive that it will even increase your love for God.

Man is man, God is God and what else is there?

Man thinks that he is the centre of the universe around which everything revolves. You (man) are the centre as far as evil is concerned.

Referring to the *dunya*: You kill it or it kills you.

Quoting Shaikh Al Akbar: 'Everyone who sets his foot on the Path of God, he will arrive. If you don't abandon God, He will not abandon you.'

Love leads to salvation and not to knowledge.

Try to keep modesty of life in order to be of those admitted to the Presence of Allah.

Every person carries *Qiyyamat*, the Ultimate End in himself. Do not think the Day of Judgement to be far.

Oh body waiting for the washing, where is your strength, where is your eloquent tongue?

Superstition has no place on the Path of God.

If you are sincerely on the Path, it is promised by Allah that those who are astray cannot be harmful to you.

We spend time alone so that our self becomes apparent to ourself.

Tawakkal is putting your hand into the hand of the Prophet and leaving the rest to Allah.

If you see idols of any kind entering the house of God, take gasoline and burn it and take the head of the Imam first.

Be grateful to Allah without expectation.

Desire grows gradually without you being conscious; Allah leads us step by step to being closer to Himself.

You are only as good as your *ibadat*.

That failure lurking in your life may be a mercy. You are not to judge. Say *Allahu 'Alim*. Recognise that God knows and you do not. The job you didn't get, the success you did not experience. Allah may show you a great blessing two or three months later in what seemed at first, a failure.

Your fasting is suspended between the heavens and the earth until you pay the *zakat* and forgive. Clear your heart of whatever you have held against any Muslim.

Consider the prophets as your grandfathers. They have affection for you. They love us as we love them.

The heart is the means and love is the goal. Man must be known to be loved, Allah must be loved to be known.

Quoting some poet: And goodness only noses the noselessness of men.

The *ruh*, or soul of man, forgets on descent and remembers on ascent.

Love and trust are related.

Do not overdo the pampering of your bodies. Take the reins of the body. The body has its beautiful and its less beautiful qualities.

Allah is relevant. If you submit to Allah, there is no doubt about eternity.

Allah has filled the world with examples of His puzzling *Hikmat*.

Who are you and who am I? We are both nothing and everything.

Open up to those around you. There is not anyone who does not need kindness. All of us share the same destiny and fate without Allah. Knowing this is sufficient grounds for compassion.

Prayer is our phone to Allah. The lover seeks coins, calls on the phone, and waits for the Beloved to answer.

Hizmet cuts away the pieces until there is no you. When you open the channel, Allah fills it.

A *mu'min* should not be depressed. Allah promised the victory. Whatever you desire will be realised.

Jamat-ul Zaman are people of the time: the Muslims who must radiate God by their appearance and be always people of decency, cleanliness and kindness.

Kalima is your safe ground in quicksand.

No false piety! Only Allah is Holy. How much we cannot imagine.

Awareness ends with this material world's end.

All desires should end at the prayer mat.

Everyone has a chance but if you don't want it, you don't get it.

The only way to see is to open your eyes to the universe, to nature, and the creation around you. The signs are there. How can you be happy? Simply open your eyes.

We are no different from people about to go out to do *haram*. Who are resting in their houses until seven o'clock when they'll go out for a night filled with *haram*. Everybody has the same desires, everyone is seeking the same answers.

If you don't realise Allah through your heart, then at least realise Him through your limitations.

Consider the prophets as one family, consider the world as one. Forget divisions of race, of time and space.

Everything in Carl Sagan's book, the Prophets already experienced. There is nothing new.

Until we are rid of our crudeness . . . walking through the earth like elephants, how can we hear?

The highest religion is surrender. There is nothing higher than falling on one's face before Allah.

There is room for everyone in the house of Allah. Make a place for your brother and sister and Allah will make a place for you.

Faith in God, love to everything that lives, even little insects.

Every piece of bread has two halves so share it.

The life of this world is like a shooting star. You know your age. Start living and prepare for the life to come.

Trial is a necessity and was so even for the Prophets.

All of the Prophets are one. The whole of creation is one. God says in the Qur'an that 'Mankind was once a single nation,' and this is a verse to be remembered.

From the moment of death, the *akhirat* or life hereafter comes so very quickly.

Everyone wants to approach God and to know the Unseen, but God requires your whole life.

Kind words are better.

Give what is dearest.

The beginning is *himma,* and do you know what *himma* is? It is your desire for Allah and nothing else. It is this which moves you through *Tariqat*, to *Haqiqat*, to *Ma'rifat* and beyond.

Stay open to me and my love will flow into your heart like the mighty river into a new channel. Open your heart to the Shaikh for the gift of love.

The person who has no scar of love is either crazy or dead.

My heart saw April many times, never May. Tell the fireman to walk more gently over my burning heart.

Jahannum will be filled with people who hurt others in the name of love.

All the murid can do for the Shaikh is to love Allah. After this, love each other.

What makes people unhappy is wanting to go on and on without end. What can make this a happy society? Allah!

Nothing is achieved by effort alone, not even love. Only by Allah's mercy.

Tekiyas are to help us learn to achieve independence from our desires.

Haram never brings ultimate happiness because the law of nature has to be in harmony with the law of God. If it is not, one is destined to disappointment.

Achieve the state of love by reducing your desires and increasing your gratitude.

If you can bring what gives you pleasure into line with Divine Law, OK; if not, turn away from it.

What is close to you is hard to part with.

Don't wonder about progress. Can one distinguish how one's face and body change day by day? Don't be afraid or discouraged, life will take its course.

When you climb the tower, you see more people in smaller sizes.

One who has not reached the realm of faith is not living.

We must tighten up because *dunya* is loose.

All land, like any *murid,* is good for something. How surprised we will be in the *akhirat*.

For some, the love of Allah happens like an avalanche. It starts with only a snowball. Likewise, some people grow while falling.

The path grows wide and some go quickly. The potential to love Allah is in all of us, no matter how miniature or small.

The key to human happiness is remembrance of God.

I give you for your tears the following: The best way to wipe your tears is to jump into the river of tears. These are your jewels on the unsteady string of *dunya*.

The *ruh* in man (which is the spirit) is a sign of the meaning of life.

We have to bring ourselves as close to the example of the Prophet, peace be upon him, and his Companions as possible. The farther from him, the farther from Allah. Imitating the Prophet brings us close to the original message. Accept Prophet Muhammad, and you accept all of the prophets before him.

Keep the doors and windows open for the breeze of the *rahmat* of Allah. The only way to stay awake is to open up the windows.

Praise the ocean but stay close to the coast.

GLOSSARY

Abu Bakr As-Siddiq: The first Khalifa of the holy Prophet Muhammad and the most generous of his companions. Known as *Siddiq* for his peerless sense of truth and personal honesty, he was the friend of the Prophet from childhood and an inheritor of Inner Teachings of Islam directly from the Prophet.

Adab: Spiritual refinement, good manners. In *Tasawwuf*, the way of right action and courtesy of the Path.

Ahlil bait: The spiritual family and house of the Prophet Muhammad. In the broader sense all of those across the ages who have born witness to faith in one God.

Ahmediyya: A type of fez, bound in white turban-like wraps. Awarded in many *madrassas* or Islamic colleges to signify that the bearer has achieved some degree of knowledge of Islamic law, Qur'an and traditions.

Akbar: Greatest or greater.

Akhira (also *akhirat*): The Hereafter.

Alaihi salam: On him be peace.

Alaikum salam: On you be peace (the reply given to the caller of *salaams*).

Alastu bi Rabbikum: Qur'anic phrase: 'Am I not your Lord?' The question addressed to human souls in Eternity before their descent into the wombs while still contained in Adam. To this question they all replied: 'Yes'.

Alhamdulillahir Rabbil 'alameen: All praise belongs to Allah, the Lord of the Worlds.

Ali Ibn Abu Talib: Fourth and last of Righteous Khalifas of the Holy Prophet Muhammad, Shaikh and inheritor of Inner Teachings of Islam also directly from the Prophet.

'Alim: A scholar or person of knowledge.

Allah: God Most High.

Allahu akbar: Allah is Greatest. Greater than everything.

'Amal: action, work, or deed.

Amanat: Something deposited into someone's trust or charge.

Amilus salihat: righteous deeds.

Ammara: The *nafs* in its lowest stage, a mass of blind desire and instinct, prone to evil with no conscience or sense of self-restraint.

Ana: Arabic pronoun 'I'.

Ashadu an la ilaha ill'Allah: I bear witness that there is no god but Allah.

'Ashq: Passionate love, usually attributed to *'ashiqs* who are persons full of love for Allah. (See also *'ishq.*)

Asma: Name.

Asma al husna: The most beautiful names. In the absolute sense, the perfection of God's attributes and qualities.

'Asr: Literally afternoon. Also prayer of midday before sun begins to decline from its apex.

Assalamu alaikum: Peace be upon you (by the caller of the greeting).

Astaghfirullah: I ask forgiveness of Allah.

Attar, Fariddudin: Twelfth-century Shaikh of Persia and noted mystic writer. Author of well-known *Mantiq uttair* or *Conference of the Birds*.

Awliya: The saints and friends of God, plural of *wali*.

Ayat: Literally, a verse, also a sign or indication.

Azab: The wrath and punishment of Allah.

Azan (also *Adhan*): The call to prayer sounded five times daily by the *muezzin*.

Badr: A village near the city of Medina where the Muslim army of 300 defeated 1,000 Qurashite soldiers.

Baklava: A very sweet, nut-filled pastry found in Turkey and Greece.

Baqa billah (see *fana*): The beginning of journeying in Allah after having passed through annihilation.

Baqara: Literally Cow, title of second chapter of the Qur'an.

Baraka (also *Barakat*): Blessing or divine benefit transmitted through holy people, places, or objects.

Barzakh: The interspace between death and the awakening place of resurrection.

Batin: The Inwardly Hidden. Also an attribute of Allah considered in absolute sense. Generally refers to things of unseen spiritual world.

Bayat: A pledge or promise.

Bida': Improper innovation in matters of religion.

Bilal: First *muezzin* of Islam and companion of the Holy Prophet.

Bismillah: In the name of Allah.

Buraq: From the Arabic *barq*, meaning lightning, *buraq* is an energy-form of the angelic spheres. By this energy, which in the night of *Miraj*, appeared as a small, white, horse-like creature, the Prophet was transported from the *Ka'bah* in Mecca, to Jerusalem, then on to the lowest sphere of the heavens.

Dajjal: The Anti-Christ which is to appear at the end of time, dazzling and misguiding those with uncertain hearts.

Dervish: A poor person. Usually the disciple of a Shaikh who has little self-interest and who is inconspicuous to all by virtue of his genuine lack of pride and love of service.

Dolmush: (Turkish) A taxi.

Du'a: Prayer or invocation.

Dunya: The material world of phenomena and experience.

Eid-ul adha: Islamic holiday commemorating the sacrifice of Abraham.

Eid-ul Fitr: Islamic holiday at end of Ramadan, the month of fasting.

Ezel: Place in Eternity where souls gave their response, saying 'Yes' to Allah, that He is their Lord.

Fajr: The dawn. Usually refers to the morning prayer.

Fana Billah: Stage of annihilation where man loses his bad qualities and ends the stage of journeying to God.

Faqir: Literally, a poor person. Usually a person seeking inner wealth.

Fikr: Meditation, contemplation.

Fiqh: Islamic law or jurisprudence.

Fitna: Tests, trials, and difficulties of life.

Fuqara: (Plural of *faqir*) Usually circle of Prophet's companions or Shaikh's disciples. People of poverty.

Ghazali: Twelfth-century Islamic scholar who became a Sufi in his later years. Credited with resolving the split between Sufism and Orthodox Islam by virtue of the brilliance of his writing and discourse.

Grandshaikh: Shaikh over Shaikhs.

Hadith: Traditions of the Prophet.

Hadrah: A gathering.

Hafiz: One who memorises the entire Qur'an and preserves it in the heart.

Hajara: The biblical Hagar, slave wife of Prophet Ibrahim who bore him the son Ismail.

Hajj: Pilgrimage to Mecca.

Halal: That which is permissible by Islamic law.

Halka: A circle of people, usually a Shaikh and murids.

Halveti (also *Khalwati,* secluded dervishes): One of twelve original Tariqats which follow a line of transmission through Shaikh Omar al Khalwati.

Haqq: Truth (also refers to rightful property of another).

Haqiqat: Reality. In *Tasawwuf,* stage after *Tariqat* where seeker sees things as they truly are.

Haram: That which is not permitted by Islamic law.

Hasbi Allah: Allah is sufficient.

Hashr: Gathering. Title of fifty-ninth chapter of the Qur'an.

Hazreti: Title of respect attributed to saintly persons, literally refers to the person's noble presence.

Hikmat: Wisdom.

Himma: Spiritual yearning, drive or ambition.

Hira: Mountain cave a few miles from Mecca to which the Prophet Muhammad retreated for seclusion and meditation. In this place he received the first revelation of Qur'an.

Hizmet (also Khidhmat): Service. In *Tasawwuf* any service done is ony for God's sake.

Hussein: Noble son of Imam Ali Ibn Abu Talib and Hazreti Fatima, daughter of the Prophet. A *wali* of high order and preserver of pure Islam brought by Prophet Muhammad. Martyred with seventy-two persons at Kerbala.

'Ibadat: Spiritual service or worship which includes charity, prayer, work, and *zikr.*

Ibrahim: Prophet Abraham.

Iftar: Food eaten to end day of fasting.

Ilahi: A song praising Allah.

'Ilm: Knowledge or science.

Imam: Religious leader. Most often chosen by the community.

Iman: True faith.

Irshad: Guidance, direction, and instruction for inner development.

Insha'Allah: If Allah wills.

'Isha: Night, usually refers to night prayer.

'Ishq: Violently passionate love. Metaphor for Divine love which travellers on spiritual path seek to find within themselves for God.

Islam: Complete submission and surrender to God and peace with His creation.

Ismail (variant of Ishmael): Son of Abraham by Hazreti Hajar.

Istighfar: Seeking forgiveness of Allah.

Jahannum: Hell.

Jallabiya: In Morocco a commonly worn hooded garment.

Jamat: The community collective. Sometimes a small group of travellers.

Jami': The mosque, usually the largest community mosque.

Jannat: Literally, garden. Usually refers to Paradise.

Jibreel: Biblical Gabriel, the angelic being of power sent by God to bear messages and divine revelation to His servants and Prophets. Hazreti Jibreel bore the Qur'an to the heart of Prophet Muhammad, in stages as God commanded it to be revealed.

Jihad: Struggle, fight, strenuous effort.

Jihad al akbar: Greatest struggle or fight, usually refers to a tradition of the Prophet Muhammad in which he said that the greatest struggle is *Jihad an-nafs*, the struggle with one's own self and one's desires and whims of ego.

Jinn (also *Djinn*): Beings of the spirit world said by the Prophet to have been created from smokeless fire. Usually thought to be evil, they are of species both good and bad.

Jumah: Friday, also the name of the Friday prayer service for which the community of Muslims gather.

Juz: One-thirtieth section of Qur'an.

Ka'bah: The cube-shaped house in Mecca containing the Black Stone and which indicates the direction towards which Muslims pray. The house dedicated to the worship of God alone was originally built by the prophet Adam, then later rebuilt by Prophets Abraham and Muhammad.

Kabir: Great, large.

Kafir: An unbeliever, one who rejects Faith.

Kalima: The Islamic creed, There is no god but Allah, Muhammad is His servant and Messenger.

Khalilullah: Title of Prophet Abraham meaning Friend of Allah.

Khalwat: Retreat into seclusion, usually for prayer and meditation.

Khanqa: A retreat house and gathering place of dervishes, where seekers can find rest, and enjoy the company of others on the Path of God.

Kufiyyeh: An Arabic headdress.

Kulah: A type of hat usually worn by Shaikhs or dervishes.

La ilaha ill'Allah: (Arabic) There is no god but Allah.

Lawamma: Stage of *nafs* where it exhibits conscience, having the ability to see and accuse itself of its wrongdoing.

Maghrib: Literally means west, also indicates time of sunset.

Mahsus: Special, particular, reserved for.

Maqam: A station or stage of spiritual development.

Masjid: Arabic for Mosque.

Ma'rifat: Stage of knowledge and realisation which follows *Haqiqat*.

Marwa: A hill near Mecca connected with the rites of Hajj. Also is one of the hills between which Hazreti Hajara ran in search of water for her son Ismail.

Matem: Literally, mourning. The first ten days of Muharram, first month of the Muslim calendar during which the martyrdom of Imam Hussein is commemorated.

Maut (also *Mawt*): Death.

Mawlana: Title of honour. Our Master or our helper.

Mecca: The capital Arabian city and most sacred of the Islamic world. The birthplace of the Prophet Muhammad, it is the site of the Ka'bah, the sacred cube-shaped house.

Medina: City.

Medina al munawwara: The Illuminated City, celebrated as the burial place of the Prophet Muhammad. Formerly called Yasrib but was distinguished as *al Madina* 'The City' and also *Madinatu'n Nabi* 'The City of the Prophet' after it had become famous by giving shelter to the Prophet upon his flight from Mecca.

Melamiyyat: Those travellers on the Mystic Path whose practice is to take blame upon themselves, accepting the world's attribution of guilt while remaining secretly innocent.

Mevlud (also *Maulid*): A birthday, especially of the Prophet Muhammad, known as *Maulid an-Nabi*, celebrated on the twelfth of Rabi'ul Awwal. This day is observed in some parts of the Muslim world by recitals of *zikr* and *salawat*.

Mihrab: An alcove or prayer niche.

Miraj: Literally, an ascent. Refers to the ascension of the Prophet to the heavens known as *Isra*. From the lowest spheres of the heavens where he was left by *buraq*, the Prophet travelled on with Hazreti Jibreel through the seven heavens. At the limit of the highest heaven, known as *Sidratul Muntaha*, The Place of the Lote Tree, he left Hazreti Jibreel and continued onward, beyond the limits of material existence to a distance of two bows' length from the Circle of Infinity. From the Mystic's perspective, this was the single most important event for mankind. It was the first time ever that a human being travelled beyond the *barzakh* and the starless sphere, and returned back to the planet.

Muezzin (also *Muadhdhan*): The caller to prayer, one who recites the *azan*.

Muhabbat: Discourse or teaching.

Mujahid: A warrior in God's army for the purity of Islam.

Muqaddim: Literally, one who brings forward. Usually a subordinate of the Shaikh who carries out duties in the Tekiya in absence of the Shaikh. *Muqaddim* may be the chief subordinate of the Shaikh or subordinate to a *wakeel*.

Murid: Literally, one with desire. Usually a novice on the spiritual Path.

Musafir: A traveller.

Musalla: Prayer carpet.

Mutakif: A person performing seclusion in the period known as *itikaf* during the last ten days of Ramadan.

Mutawakkil: A person who has reached the stage of *tawakkal,* which is unwavering trust in God.

Mutmainnah: Stage of *nafs* when it is at rest and not a victim to itself.

Nafs: The experiencing self, ego, or aspect of the soul by which the person is primarily influenced by passions and desires.

Naqshbandi (Naqshbandiyya): One of the official Tariqat orders with lines of transmission through Pir Muhammad Naqshbandi.

Niyaz: Supplication or offerings in the name of Allah or His Prophet. Most often refers to Dervish bow or salute to the divine possibility in the other.

Nur: Brilliance, light, or spiritual luminescence.

Pir: Literally, an elder. Usually a Shaikh or Murshid of high order. Often the founder of an order through which lines of Tariqat pass.

Qadi: A judge.

Qari: One skilled in the proper recitation of Qur'an who is acquainted with the science of reading known as *'Ilm-ut-Tajweed*.

Qasida: Poem, chanted song, or mystic story told in verse.

Qudrat: Power, strength. Refers also to moments of power which if not seized are lost.

Qibla: Direction towards which Muslims face for prayer, usually towards the east. Also refers to the heart.

Qiyyamat: The Day of Resurrection.

Qur'an: The Book of 6,666 verses or 114 chapters revealed directly to the Prophet Muhammad over twenty-three years of his life, from the age of 40 when he received the call to Prophethood from Allah.

Qurban: An animal sacrificed to God, and then distributed charitably.

Rabb: Lord. God as the Supreme cherishing and sustaining force in the Universe. (*Rabbi:* my Lord.)

Rahmat: Divine mercy.

Rakat: A unit of ritual prayer which includes standing, bowing, sitting, and prostrating.

Ramadan: The month of fasting in the Islamic year.

Rasul: A messenger.

Rehber: A guide.

Rufai: Tariqat line and order passing through Shaikh Sayyid Ahmed ar-Rufai.

Ruh: The spirit, that aspect of the soul which contains the divine secret and which gives the body life.

Ruhul Quddus: The Holy Spirit.

Sabr: Patience, constancy, endurance.

Sa'ee: The ritual in Hajj where one runs between the two hills of Safa and Marwa.

Safa: Literally, purity. Name of one of the two hills in Mecca, between which Hazreti Hajara ran.

Saff: A line or row, usually refers to prayer or battle.

Sahib: The rightful owner or master.

Sajud (*Sajda*): Prostration. Posture of complete submission, surrender and helplessness.

Saki (also *Saqi*): The wine bearer or pourer of the *saki*, the drink of divine ecstasy.

Salaams: The greeting of peace.

Salat: Prayer

Salawat: The wishing of prayers and blessings of God upon Prophet Muhammad. *Salawat Tabriqieh:* a special *salawat* used in certain Sufi gatherings.

Salih: An honest, righteous person.

Sama': Heaven, the celestial sphere.

Sanan: Shaikh in *Conference of the Birds,* who by his passionate love for a Christian girl, taught his disciples the lessons of loyalty to the Shaikh, attachment and detachment, dominance of the *nafs,* purification, and attainment to true love.

Sanjak: Flag or standard.

Shahada: The process of bearing testimony to the *kalima* and declaring oneself a Muslim.

Shaheed: A martyr. One who witnesses for God by the sacrifice of their own life.

Shaikh: The Master and Superior of an order of dervishes.

Shaitan: The Devil. Chief of Evil Ones.

Shareef: Noble, eminent.

Shari'ah: The way of Islamic law.

Shems: Literally, Sun. Also Damascus. Title of ninety-first chapter of the Qur'an and name of Hazreti Rumi's teacher.

Sherif: Generally one's place, also the sitting place of the Shaikh or representatives of the Prophet.

Shirk: Associating partners with Allah, giving to something or to someone, worship which belongs only to God.

Siddiq: A person who is true.

Sidrah: High Council of Shaikhs. Also *Sidratul Muntaha*: The Lote Tree of the farthest regions in spheres near to the divine presence.

Sikke: A type of tall dervish hat.

Silsila: Chain of succession.

Sirat al Mustaqeem: The Straight Path.

Sirr: Secret, mystery.

Sofra: The table or cloth spread for eating.

Subhana Rabbi al 'ala: Glory to Allah to Most High.

Sunnah: That which was customarily done by the Prophet.

Sura: A chapter of Qur'an.

Tafrid: In *Tasawwuf* it is inward solitude and satisfaction with whatever God gives, not expecting increase of benefit for one's deeds, concealing whatever good God does give, with no self-involvement. In this stage, nothing possesses the seeker.

Tafsir: Literally, explaining. Commentary and learned exposition of the Qur'an.

Tahajjud: Voluntary prayers in the last quarter of the night.

Tajrid: Outwardly it is abandonment of the desires of this world. Inwardly, it is rejecting compensation and expectation of reward in this world or the next. In this stage, the seeker possesses nothing.

Tarawih: Voluntary prayers of Ramadan said after *Salatul 'Isha* usually twenty *rakats*.

Tariqat: The Path in search of inner reality of religious and spiritual life.

Tasawwuf: The Islamic Mystic Path which contains knowledge leading to purification of the human soul. Commonly referred to as *Sufism*.

Tasbih: Literally glorification. A string of beads commonly used to count the names of God, remembrances of Him, His due praises and glorifications.

Taslimiyyet: Submission to God. Literally submission. In *Tasawwuf* deep surrender and total submission to God after long-standing pain, resistance, and struggle with oneself.

Tawheed: The Unity and oneness of God.

Tekiya: Literally a corner. Usually a building established by the Shaikh for instruction and training of murids and dervishes.

Turbe: A tomb.

Uhud: Site near the Mountain Uhud where the Muslims, initially winning, began to suffer severe losses when they failed to carry out the Prophet's instructions and left themselves open to attack on an unguarded flank.

'Umar Ibn al Khattab: Second Khalifah who succeeded Abu Bakr in AH 13 (AD 634) and was assassinated in AH 23 after a prosperous reign and having contributed greatly to the spread of Islam.

Ummat: Community or nation.

'Umra: The lesser Pilgrimage to Mecca, or a visit to the sacred mosque at Mecca. Its ceremonies include circumnambulating around the Ka'bah and running between Safa and Marwa but omit the sacrifice. Although meritorious it is considered to be less meritorious than Hajj. It can be performed at any time except the eighth, ninth, and tenth days of *Dhul Hijjah*, as these are days of Hajj, the Greater Pilgrimage.

Ustedh: Master, teacher, professor.

'Uthman Ibn Affan: Third Khalifa, who succeeded 'Umar. Reigned twelve years before his assassination. Credited with important work in the preservation of Qur'an.

Wakeel: A guardian. Usually chief subordinate of the Shaikh.

Wali: A saint.

Wa rahmatullahi wa barakatuhu: and the mercy of Allah and His blessings

Wujud: An existence, usually of the kinds: *Wajibul Wujud*, a necessary existence, referring to Allah. *Mumkinul Wujud*, a possible existence referring to the manifest creation, and *Mumtainul Wujud*, an impossible existence, referring to an association with God.

Yaqin: Certainty.

Yazid: Son of Mu'awiyah, enemy of pure Islam, who slaughtered Imam Hussein and Shaheeds of Kerbala.

Zahir: The Outwardly Manifest, the Evident. An attribute of Allah in its absolute connotation but is also used generally to denote an external, outer-orientated point of view.

Zainul Abideen: Wali, grandson of Imam Ali, son of Imam Hussein.

Zakat: Literally, purification, but most often refers to portion of property bestowed in alms. Income is included and the *zakat* is obligatory on all those persons with means at the rate of one-fortieth per year.

Zalimeen: Wrongdoers, sometimes those who wrong themselves; people of darkness, oppressors.

Zawiya: Synonymous with *Tekiya*.

Zikr: Remembrance, celebration and invocation of God.

Ziyarat: A visit.

Zuhr: Noon or midday. Also name of prayer at noon.

Zuhurat: Obvious, external, perceptible. (See *Zahir.*)

Zulfikar: Name of celebrated sword given by Prophet Muhammad to Hazreti Ali.